WAGING PEACE ON ISLAM

'This book will excite and perturb the Christian reader. Christine's freshness of approach, borne of years of consistent living amongst Muslims, allows her to move beyond traditional stereotypes and offer another way of "witnessing to Muslims" . . . Christine's unique position of being married to a big-hearted man, from a family that traces its lineage back to Prophet Muhammad, allows her not only to disturb but to suggest faithful ways of living as followers of Jesus in a Muslim culture.'

           – Rev. Dr Bill A. Musk, author of *The Unseen Face of Islam*

'Through a lifetime of living in various Muslim societies Christine Mallouhi is well able to bridge the chasm of misunderstanding, ignorance and fear which separates Muslims and Christians. With gentle sensitivity she challenges Christians to reconsider their stereotypes and see Muslims as normal people just like ourselves in need of a loving Saviour.

'This is a remarkable book, which every person interested in Islam should read. It challenges our attitudes, frees us from prejudice and refreshes the spirit.'

           – Dr Stuart Robinson, Crossway, Melbourne

'She fearlessly grapples with the critical issues for Christians living and working amongst Muslims, provoking us to evaluate the presuppositions of conventional evangelical approaches towards Islam.

'The diagnoses in this provocative and challenging book are accurate, the recommendations are right, and the tone is optimistic. It is a prophetic and practical guide to reframing the way we as Christians relate to Muslims in the twenty-first century. Full of new ideas and new life, this book points us to a journey ahead that will not be easy but will ultimately rescue us from irrelevancy or disaster. A "must-read" for everyone interested.'

– Paul Gordon Chandler, President/CEO, Partners International

'This exceptionally insightful and ennobling enterprise shows the path one can follow to become a beacon of light. Mallouhi's graceful gift of providence does not only make us better, but it might raise the sublime sainthood of the Assisi in every one of us – an unexampled blessing to be cherished again and again.'

– Munir Akash, Editor, *Jusoor*

'In this work Christine Mallouhi undertakes a comprehensive study of Christian-Muslim interaction throughout history and in the modern day. The diverse subjects addressed are bound together by a central focus on St Francis of Assisi, whom Mallouhi considers as "a profound example of how it is possible to relate to Muslims in times of mutual antagonism". Thus whether discussing the Israeli-Palestinian conflict, anti-Muslim stereotyping in the West, or Muslim perceptions of Christians, Mallouhi skilfully encourages the reader to consider adopting the sensitive approach of St Francis, who "did not engage in the battle or the debate". The work benefits greatly by the author's extensive experience in the Muslim world and by her ability to open windows into Muslim minds on a wide range of issues concerned with Christian-Muslim relations today.'

– Dr Peter Riddell, London Bible College

'Christine Mallouhi has "been there and done that", having lived amongst Arab Muslims for 25 years. She and her husband have great empathy, insight and understanding of the struggles of Muslim peoples. Her fascinating insights into St Francis provide us with two books in one!'

– Dr Greg Livingstone, Consultant on Muslim-Christian Relations,
AD 2000 and Beyond

CHRISTINE MALLOUHI

waging peace on islam

InterVarsity Press
Downers Grove, Illinois

InterVarsity Press
P.O. Box 1400, Downers Grove, IL 60515-1426
World Wide Web: www.ivpress.com
E-mail: mail@ivpress.com

InterVarsity Press ® *is the book-publishing division of InterVarsity Christian Fellowship/USA* ®*, a student movement active on campus at hundreds of universities, colleges and schools of nursing in the United States of America, and a member movement of the International Fellowship of Evangelical Students. For information about local and regional activities, write Public Relations Dept., InterVarsity Christian Fellowship/USA, 6400 Schroeder Rd., P.O. Box 7895, Madison, WI 53707-7895.*

Cover photograph: Getty Images

ISBN 0-8308-2304-2

Printed in the United States of America ∞

Library of Congress Cataloging-in-Publication Data has been requested.

P	18	17	16	15	14	13	12	11	10	9	8	7	6	5	4	3	2	1
Y		16	15	14	13	12	11	10	09	08	07	06	05	04	03	02		

To Zainab, the little daughter of Hassan bin Othman in Tunis, who sent me a piece of bread from her house, thereby inviting me to become a member of her family. And to the hundreds of people in the Middle East and North Africa who offered me bread, I dedicate this book in the hope it will be a pinch of salt in the hand of the Living Bread.

CONTENTS

ACKNOWLEDGEMENTS

Great authors can dedicate great books with barely an acknowledgement. This has many. This book is not the fruit of any accredited study programme. Although I have checked the data with various experts whom I now thank, I also offer my apologies if the result is not what they expected. The mistakes are mine. This book is not intended as an academic document, but a plea for grass-root change. I acknowledge it lopsidedly speaks to Christians about our failures with Islam while it does not deal as critically with Islam's failures with us, because we are only responsible for ourselves, not the other. So I include this plea to any Muslim readers not to use our confessions as artillery to escalate the war – Christians fear what will happen if we call off the war and Islam doesn't – but to embark on a similar journey and meet us in a spirit of reciprocity.

I began this story in Morocco and finished it in Melbourne, but the process took a wider journey. As is the way with all books – this one owned its author – it took me on its own wonderful adventure, communicating with Francis' followers from Latin America all the way to the Vatican. His path wove through encounters with Muslims, Catholics and Protestants on every continent who helped in telling the story. My special thanks go to Professor Noreddine Zouitni in Morocco, for his mammoth effort translating French sources. To Sondy Ward and Lorraine Mitchell in Melbourne, for editing the manuscript; to Pat and Maria of the Franciscan Missionaries of Mary in Rabat, Morocco for a supply of source material; to Paul Chandler who insisted I could write this book and helped the birthing process; to Les Editions Franciscaines in Paris for their generosity and trust in allowing unofficial translations and use of their books, and to all the other Muslims and Christians who contributed in many ways of giving, telling or being. And finally to my family who looked after themselves allowing me to discover Francis, and gave me love and patience and help in stressful days, specially Mazhar for untangling Arabic sources and supplying morning coffees in bed. Mum joined in the journey helping track down Early Church Fathers in dim stone theological libraries – we looked unusual students of ancient Latin tomes struggling around with our shopping bags. Our vulnerability caused many to smile and give extra-mile help – and the spirit of Francis lived again!

The symbolism of events in the course of life continues to tantalise me. I knew nothing about Saint Francis when our son was born in Egypt on 24 February 1977. We named him Faris (Knight) – with prayers he would be a true knight for Christ. While writing this book I discovered he was born on the Feast of St Matthew; the day Francis received his call to ministry and understood he was meant to be a true knight of Christ. That call took Francis to Egypt to meet the sultan.

I have honoured the requests of all contributors who requested that their true identities remain concealed.

Chapter One

A BETTER WAY

Islamic terrorist attacks are followed by Western punitive attacks and retaliatory economic sanctions. The West condemns Islam as a religion of the sword and then rattles its sabre with threats of retaliation for hostage taking. The result is new counter-retaliation attacks. Russia fights Muslims in Afghanistan, Chechnya and Daghestan. In Indonesia – the world's largest Muslim country – 107,000 Muslims sign up for a holy war (jihad) against Australia, New Zealand and the United States over the UN intervention in East Timor.[1] Muslims and Christians war in the Balkans and erupt in violent clashes in India and Indonesia.

This sampling of events and the accompanying mutually antagonistic media images leave us with little doubt that relations between Islam and the West are growing more belligerent and polarised. We see a growing general discord between Islam and Christianity. On the personal level, talk of sharing our faith with Muslims makes us feel spiritually inadequate and nervous of meeting a Muslim. These feelings of inadequacy, or even fears, usually kill our best intentions. We don't know how to overcome the current antagonism and when we want to go against the tide we don't know how.

How can a caring Christian approach Islam? Most Christians decide to back away and leave it to those they perceive as the experts. The uninvolved majority of Christians are not uncaring, but they are confused and intimidated. The plethora of books on the market, either warning us about the dangers of Islam or evidently needed for understanding and relating to Muslims, has left us with the impression that Muslims are very alien and possibly dangerous creatures. They seem so unlike ourselves we feel the need to be an expert in Islamics before we invite *one of them* for a cup of tea. And through antipathy or fear the gulf grows wider.

History repeats itself, as the Preacher in Ecclesiastes rightly claims. Islam and Christianity found themselves in the same situation in the Middle Ages. The majority on both sides let the world squeeze them into its mould and mutual ignorance grew into intolerance and aggression, thus sanctioning the Crusades. So the problem is not new and neither is the danger or the solution. What may be new to us is to find that the answer was, and is, found in the life of a Catholic saint, St Francis of Assisi.

However, before we come to the solution we need to recognise the problem. How is this mutual antagonism displayed today and how did we get into a 'them and us' mentality with Islam? Do we feel the same sense of nervousness about Buddhists for example? Whether we view Islam as an enemy to be conquered or a friend to be won, we need to encounter Muslims face to face. We also need to come face to face with ourselves and with the spirit of our age. I believe that when we do this we will know why Francis of Assisi found the solution centuries ago and still has the answer for today.

When the West waged a propaganda campaign recruiting soldiers for Christ in the war against the Islamic block, Francis walked into the Egyptian battlefield to minister Christ's love to individual Muslims. He entered the 'enemy camp' and shared the Gospel with the Sultan, the commander of the Muslim armies, and emerged not only unscathed, but so respected that a new path in Muslim-Christian relations was forged. Church sources even claim that this historic meeting converted the Sultan.

Francis of Assisi leaves us a profound example of how it is possible to relate to Muslims in times of mutual antagonism. Sometimes our faith cannot be shared because we are intolerant of other religious convictions, or at the other end of the pendulum, we are reticent to stand for what we believe in case we sound intolerant in a pluralistic world. I have struggled with this issue since I married into a Muslim family in 1975. For a quarter of a century my husband and I have lived in the midst of Muslim society in a number of Arab countries, and attempted to live our faith while Islamic flags flew over our heads. There were times when we found ourselves in a battle (in the spiritual understanding of the term), and at times also felt embattled. Sometimes, like Francis, we were honoured by Muslim leaders of countries, and at other times arrested by them. We lived in three of the countries Francis attempted to evangelise while his world considered them enemy territory. During the Crusades Christian armies marched through them doing battle to regain the land for Christendom. Once again in this century Christians are on the march in these countries. On one hand, groups of Christians seeking better relations with Muslims follow the Crusade trail in a Reconciliation March apologising to populations for the actions of the Crusaders; while on the other hand, a new group of Christians are storming the same lands in prayer marches and engaging in spiritual warfare to reclaim them for Christ. But have these lands ever been 'lost' to the presence of God and Christ? And is a theology of battle the answer? More importantly: is Islam the enemy?

I am convinced God needs radicals today in the image of Francis who will spurn current aggressive attitudes of suspicion and hostility which stereotype Islam as our enemy. Francis went with the Crusaders to the war in Egypt, but he didn't join their battle. The Crusaders lost their battle. Francis won his.

One of the most successful ways to bring down walls of suspicion is to meet the person on the other side of the wall. So I will take you on a journey, following the steps of Francis, to meet

Muslims face to face. Like Francis, my first meetings with Muslims took place in Egypt. Francis went to Egypt during a war and so will we: Cairo during the Gulf War 1991.

* * *

The telephone woke me from early morning sleep with my mother's voice crackling over the line to Cairo from the Southern Hemisphere: 'Iraqi Scuds hit Israel last night. It's escalating. Are you sure you're safe there? Everyone is so worried about you and the boys. Why don't you leave?' Her last words broke with anxiety and I could picture her fighting back tears. Sitting up I tried to focus my mind on Mum in Melbourne at the other end of my world and take in the implications of this new phase of the war. 'Mum I can't get out. The airport is closed and the one plane leaving each day is booked solid for months ahead. It's very tense but we're safe. And where can we go? The two countries we considered moving into are both at boiling point with anti-Western demonstrations in the streets.' Mum stated the bottom line hope, 'Then why not book to come home!' If only decisions were so simple I thought and replied, 'I need to stay while the school remains open. If the boys pull out they will have to repeat the year. How will they be able to catch up if they move temporarily to an English system? I need to keep life as normal as possible for them. They've had too much upheaval this year. It's better to hang on here.' Mum gave up. 'Where's Mazhar now? He must be worried sick about you.' I told her Mazhar (my husband) was in Washington DC, a guest of President Bush at the National Prayer Breakfast. He was having a terrible time coping with the war delirium and told me he felt like a traitor being there while his people were suffering. Of course he was desperately worried about how we were coping, but could not return to help us. Mazhar had been arrested and deported two months earlier. We could not get out and he could not get in.

'Don't worry Mum, the Embassy advised they will evacuate us if the situation gets dangerous.' But I was worried. I didn't want to be evacuated and dropped somewhere with only hand luggage. Would I be able to return to pack up the house and belongings? And I didn't tell her how insecure the Western contingent felt. Across the Arab world and North Africa many nationals were resentful at their government – dependent on US aid – forcing them to fight the Iraqis, and particularly at their part in enabling the West to strike a blow against the Arab world. One of the popular sentiments viewed the war as Western aggression against a Muslim country and this boiled over into anti-Western demonstrations. People who previously had contempt for Saddam Hussein suddenly sported his picture in their car and home. He alone was striking a blow for Arab-Muslim dignity, a heroic stand against the might of the Western world. The expatriate community worried that there would be a backlash against Western residents in Cairo. American friends teaching at the American University told me of emergency plans to evacuate staff to an oasis where provisions were stockpiled to outlast a siege. My friends insisted they would not leave Cairo while the boys and I remained here. I was grateful but felt responsible for putting their three little girls in jeopardy. My Muslim friends, Mohammed and Isis, were surprised at the Western community's fears and laughed them off adding, 'But if anything happens we will take you home with us and you will be safe.' It was best Mum didn't know all the details. Her experiences of the Middle East were filtered through alarming media images where Muslims were always terrorists or ferocious fanatics and Muslim women were only dark sinister figures living in oppression and degradation. Mum's world was infiltrated by paranoia of Muslims and she didn't know my Muslim friends. I promised her I would not take any risks.

Cairo was quiet during the Gulf War. Too quiet. The Egyptian government pre-empted any popular backlash against fighting Iraq by making a clean sweep in the months prior to the War affecting both Muslim and Christian communities.

The Egyptian government has been involved in an escalating confrontation with the modern Islamic Fundamentalist movement, which has gained widespread support, since 1970. In the 70s the Fundamentalists targeted the university campuses for evangelism with such success that in the latter part of the decade makeshift mosques sprung up and the professors had to bring lectures to a halt to allow the Fundamentalists to pray. The Fundamentalists consider the Egyptian regime bogus and official Islam fake. Muslim militants assassinated President Sadat and made attempts on the life of President Abd al-Nasser and the current leader Hosni Mubarak. A showdown took place in 1989 after the Fundamentalists took control of a Cairo suburb, Ain Shams, intending to encircle the affluent suburbs by infiltrating the predominantly poor areas that surround them. For months the government forces dared not enter Ain Shams. In April 1989, 1,500 Fundamentalists were arrested in the country suburb of Fayoum.[2]

Months later it was not unusual to see paddy wagons convoying prisoners through the heart of Cairo. The noise captured your attention. Men in once-white robes, wearing long black beards and dirty faces, squeezed any part of their bodies possible through the bars of the wagon and chanted anti-government, pro-Islamic slogans while beating on the van. People in the street grew tense with mixed emotions. Many did not support the militants, but numbers of prisoners were claiming that they had been tortured under interrogation. Our Egyptian friend working with a human rights organisation later became so discouraged with the situation he left Cairo and took his family to live in Europe.

In 1990, during the weeks prior to the Gulf War, the government kept an even-handed policy and swept through the Christian communities. The local churches were shocked when an Arab friend running family life programmes in churches was expelled and given ten days to leave. His wife and children stayed behind to sell possessions and close down the Egyptian chapter of their lives. Cairo was their home and they did not know where to go. We joined the farewell gathering at a church hall and wept with their friends. I called to encourage the mother after her husband was gone, never imagining I would be in the same situation a few weeks later.

Mazhar is Syrian, from a Muslim family. As a young adult he found abundant life with God through Christ and has continued to share this treasure with others ever since. It is illegal for Muslims to convert to Christianity and officially impossible: even though Mazhar has been a disciple of Christ for over thirty years, all our papers in Syria still list him as Muslim. As his wife I am also registered as Muslim, as are our children. We are not troubled by this, but it has legal ramifications, for example affecting inheritance rights.

We are both committed to encouraging people on their faith journey and encourage everyone to enter into the knowledge of God's love through Christ. Our lives and our house were open to all. Our life crosses cultural and religious boundaries, so our friends include Muslim Fundamentalist sheikhs, Baptist pastors, Catholic priests and nuns, Copts, Communists, a Jewish rabbi, Bahais and regular Western expatriates with no religious affiliation. This rainbow variety of people flowed through our home like a river. Some came to party. Some came to pray. Some came because friends sent them for help.

In September 1990 four Christians from Muslim families were jailed and two of their friends came to Mazhar for help. We did not know the prisoners personally but Mazhar tried to encourage their friends and went with them to the jail. No one had been able to see the men and their friends hoped to retain a lawyer for them. The officials took all their names and addresses and denied any knowledge of the prisoners. Soon afterwards the prisoners' church took up their case and retained a human rights lawyer. News of their harsh treatment circulated, bringing international pressure on the government. Mazhar was called in to the authorities for questioning.

Martial Law has endured since 1946 and, since the assassination of President Sadat in 1981, Egypt has implemented a State of Emergency rule – which among other things, disallows small meetings for any reason without a permit. If this were applied according to the letter it would forbid families gathering for parties. Houses are searched without warrants and people are arrested and held without charges.

One afternoon a plain-clothes security man forced his way into our home while our ten-year-old son Tarek was alone with his nine-year-old American friend. The invader rifled through our office and phone index while shooting questions at Tarek, 'Is your father Muslim or Christian?' 'Who are his friends who visit you?' Children in the Arab world are taught at an early age to distrust authorities, to know police are usually enemies and never to give any information about the family. Authorities question children and use information given to prosecute parents. Parents have been imprisoned for breaking the Fast of Ramadan in regimes imposing it, or for anti-government comments, on the basis of their children's remarks. Tarek was well trained. He answered every question, 'Mish shuglak' (It's not your business). The boys made many valiant efforts to evict the intruder and hide the telephone and finally in desperation brandished an ornamental curved dagger at him. Undeterred by the dagger, the trespasser eventually departed leaving a summons to appear at his superior's office. When we returned home Mazhar was incensed and called the superior officer demanding an apology to the boys. Interrogating young foreign boys is not part and parcel of Emergency Laws. The boys got the apology and we got more trouble. I wonder if the outcome would have been different if we had been less confrontational.

However, we had also been involved in another incident. We often visited Al Azhar mosque attempting to break through animosity and build bridges by taking Christians, who had not had the opportunity to meet Muslims face to face, to seminars. On a few occasions we organised foreign groups to meet with the sheikh. Muslims and Christians do not understand each other with each side being a closed book to the other. These visits were opportunities for Christians to learn about Islam firsthand – and vice versa. Mazhar enjoys praying and meditating in the quiet reverent atmosphere of the mosque and would sometimes visit the sheikh and then take his Bible and go and sit on the carpeted floor and read and meditate. Al Azhar is one of the most prestigious mosques in the Muslim world. It is a university mosque, famous for the Islamic scholars it has produced, and is the heart of the Islamic missionary movement. One afternoon Mazhar and some Egyptian Christian friends were sitting meditating when someone nearby noticed they were reading from the Bible. They began asking questions and were soon all involved in an interfaith dialogue. Other worshippers within earshot joined in and about thirty people sitting in a close circle took part in an animated friendly discussion. Some time passed and a newcomer entering the mosque saw the Bible there in the midst of people and (as we say in everyday terms) 'went ballistic'. He ran around waving his arms yelling at the top of his voice, 'Blasphemy, blasphemy. The Gospel's in Al Azhar.' At this the precinct security police appeared and told the group they had to split up and Mazhar and his friends had to leave. The Muslim group defended the Christians pointing out the Muslims had instigated the discussion and they were not bothering anyone. They were simply having an amiable talk and they wished to continue. They contended that they 'had the right to find out what Christians believed'. However the police advised them, 'We will tell you what you must believe and you do not need to know any more than that.' This provoked some irate comments so the Christian men withdrew quietly and sat in a nearby coffee shop. Afterwards a number of the men came out to apologise for the incident. We are sure that incident went on our 'secret' file with the Ministry of the Interior and it did not put Mazhar in a good light.

Governments are nervous of anything they do not understand

or control, especially in times of tension, and intimidation continued on the Egyptian Christian house church community. It was difficult to imagine that these normal families were a threat to the government or society in any way, and we wondered what the police were actually looking for. Our home was one of many under surveillance and our phone appeared to be tapped.

We heard of numbers of other foreigners being expelled (mainly from third world countries) and wondered if we would also be told to leave. 'They won't expel me; they know I love them,' Mazhar ruminated as we discussed it. 'But love is the most powerful weapon,' I warned him. 'They can't fight love.' Weeks passed with no change in the situation and I thought the crisis was over. Then Mazhar received a summons to report to the Security headquarters on 13 November, my mother's birthday. He never returned. He telephoned, telling me that he had been arrested and was being deported immediately. This rapid expulsion was so unusual that I thought he was joking. Eventually his exasperation convinced me that it was true and that I needed to gather the things he needed and take them to him: money for a ticket, a packed case to last several months, food and a warm blanket in case he was jailed overnight and had to sleep on the floor – typical treatment for all prisoners.

One of the policemen keeping him under armed guard was sympathetic. He allowed extra time to have our children raced home from school to see their Dad before he left for the airport. Mazhar was held in jail overnight wearing a suit and had no overcoat or blanket – in the confusion I had forgotten them. When the men in the cell (mainly full of Muslim Fundamentalists) asked why he was in jail with them, he told them he didn't know for sure, but it appeared to be because he was discussing his Christian faith with Muslims. On hearing this proclamation, a bearded Fundamentalist sheikh shared his blanket with him and another Fundamentalist Muslim, with a long beard and skull cap, shared his food. The government never pressed any charges and no reason was ever given for his expulsion. He was escorted under armed guard onto the plane and his passport returned – stamped 'overstayed visa'. Our visa date was good for many months. There was no point in contesting the decision. We were guests in their country and they did not want us – no matter how much we loved Egyptians. The officer in the Ministry of Interior told me that their problem was only with Mazhar and that I was free to stay in Egypt. So I took him at his word. I forgot to wish Mum a happy birthday.

The next two months, which happened to be immediately prior to the Gulf War, were chaotic as we rearranged our life across continents. Our boys' needs were our main concern. We had moved to Cairo sixteen months previously and they had adjusted from Arabic schooling to a new French language school and made friends. We decided it was not a good time to move the family anywhere in the Arab world with the possibility of the war destabilising the whole region. I would keep the boys in school another seven months to finish out the year and by then we would know where to move. We were so overwhelmed with the local situation and the struggles to stay in Cairo that the looming Gulf War was only a threatening banshee on the horizon.

It was a shock to wake one morning and find ourselves in the war zone. While we had been struggling to stay in Cairo the foreign community had been totally obsessed with getting out. I was so busy that I had little contact with the expatriate community and was shocked to learn that thousands were gone. Our eldest son Faris took his father's parting words seriously, 'You're the eldest. Look after the family.' Traditionally the eldest son in Arab families takes the load of responsibility when the father is absent. I was unable to convince Faris that he was not responsible for the family, and too often my obvious stress in our situation convinced him that he had best follow Dad's instructions. One afternoon I was not able to reach home before they returned from school. I spent the whole day visiting a myriad of offices wrangling with officialdom – trying to convince them that I should be allowed to pay the car registration, even though it was in my husband's name. I lost that day's battle. When I arrived home two hours late, I found a worried son and with roles reversed he yelled, 'Where have you been all this time. Why didn't you call me and let me know what was happening.' Anything can happen when a parent goes into government offices. He could not face a second disappearing parent. We were stranded, at war, and he was the eldest responsible for our safety. He was twelve.

Cairo's curfew thinned the usual bustling crowds; amusement places and museums were closed. There was no sign of the war here, but there was an undercurrent of anger and fear. Understandably friends at home were worried. The tensions and stresses of daily life were taking a greater toll on me than I cared to admit, but I had to appear in control for the boys' sake. I phoned other parents at the French school. My Egyptian Muslim friend Muna told me, 'There is talk of a bomb threat at the American school, but nothing at ours. Security is doubled at the gate so send them today, but don't allow them to wander in the streets. Call me every morning to be sure it's safe. And don't worry. You're not alone. We're all in this together.'

After talking to Mum and Muna I took a strong cup of coffee onto the balcony and surveyed our area. Below our apartment building the streets were coming to life. Security guards at the various diplomatic residences wandered around carrying automatic machine-guns. Nothing unusual there. However, there were more armed soldiers on the streets than usual and an armoured carrier of troops parked in the shade of a brilliantly blooming flame tree at the corner. Our suburb seemed well guarded in case of trouble. I guessed the bomb threat was just a statement of exasperation as the American diplomatic community was evacuated before the war broke out and the only pupils at the school were mainly non-Westerners. So with the first decision for today accomplished I woke the children and got them off to school.

The next call was from Mahmoud, one of our Muslim friends. 'Fatima and I are going shopping today. We will get everything you need, so you won't need to go out.' I knew they would also refuse payment as they had done since Mazhar left. Jaafar, another of Mazhar's Muslim friends, regularly released me from standing for hours in jostling queues by paying bills for me. He shrugged off my thanks, 'Please don't thank me for my duty. You are our sister and we are responsible for you while you are in our country. It's my pleasure to do this for my brother Mazhar.' Muslim and Christian friends regularly called asking how they could help me with the day's tasks and insisted I delegate something to them. Leila apologised, 'We are very sorry our government has done this to you. We want to help.' Our Muslim landlord enquired about Mazhar and said, 'I am so sorry for you. We are really shocked that our country has come to this point of expelling her friends. Poor Egypt, where are we going?' A well-known Egyptian Muslim author sent Mazhar a message apologising on behalf of his government. In America one of our friends discovered his Muslim university professor was Egyptian and asked him if he knew us. The professor replied that he knew us and had heard what happened and he conveyed a message to us of regret for his government's actions along with his personal encouragement. These Muslims' messages of support and sympathy displayed the difference between regimes and people. Some regimes made life difficult, but Muslim individuals respected and supported us.

After Mahmoud's phone call I answered urgent knocking at the door to find my usually effervescent friend, Yvette, leaning against the wall. She was an amazing French blonde who had once had an Algerian husband, since when she had wandered around the Arab world. She loved the Arab world and Arab men and was considering becoming the second concurrent wife of a well-to-do Egyptian doctor. Although her lifestyle was in conflict with my values, Yvette was a very open-hearted and honest person and I enjoyed her and appreciated her friendship. She was in tears, pale and trembling, 'Oh mon Dieu! It's unbelievable. They are blitzing Baghdad! I can't be alone today.' I sat her in the lounge and we found CNN through the TV snow and watched the computer games of destruction and death. Yvette slumped in the chair sobbing.

Far away in the United States Mazhar shared a plane journey with a European lady married to an Iraqi Jew. She told Mazhar her husband wept over Iraq telling her, 'It's a tragedy. They have destroyed one of the most ancient civilisations in human history.' I thought of our Iraqi friends, Muslims and Christians, and wondered how their families would survive this holocaust. I thought of American and British Christian friends spending sleepless nights worrying about their sons in the Gulf. Images of war razzamatazz flashed like disco images: T-shirts, pens and paraphernalia, rousing speeches and cheering crowds. Believers prayed for God to give their side victory in churches and mosques with both sides disguising war as a moral or holy cause. The two worlds I love were in armed conflict. I was not on either side. I was against the war. I was against this harassment over religion. Waves of anger and frustration pounded over me. There was nothing I could do in the face of this disaster. I was powerless like everyone else caught in the confrontation. I feared that Muslim-Christian relations would be a victim of this war, even though it was not a war of Muslims and Christians against each other. I feared that Christian witness in the Muslim world would be jeopardised and Christ's true gospel would be discredited. How long would this situation last? How long could I last in this situation? There was nothing to do but join Yvette's impotent sobbing.

This was not the first time Christians and Muslims, East and West, had fallen prey to rhetoric disguising war in religious terms. In the Middle Ages people on both sides polarised their worldviews into a 'them against us' mentality and followed their leaders into battle: the Crusades. Both sides declared that their cause was a moral cause and a holy war against unbelievers. But although the Crusades were declared and are remembered as religious wars, they were actually a response to a long, complicated series of acts of aggression and counter-aggression. Religion was exploited as a cloak for politics, power and greed, intolerance and hatred, as is the case in all so called *religious* wars.

In the Middle Ages the Western Christian powers feared Islam as a growing threat to Christianity. It became a scandal that Jerusalem and the Christian Holy Places were in the hands of the Muslim Turks – whom they called Saracen infidels. This Christian territory under Islam's sway had to be reclaimed for Christ. So the love of God and the love of war became confused and Christians dedicated themselves to battle against the enemies of Christianity. The Church's leaders fired believers' passions by inflammatory stereotyping of the enemy,

> [they] went on a tour of the capitals of Christendom . . . preaching a fresh crusade. He held up a representation of the face of the Messiah, adding the figure of an Arab striking it, (saying) 'and they soiled the image of the Messiah with blood . . . Mohammed, the Prophet of the Moslems, is striking it and has already wounded and killed him'.[3]

Thousands of people, who had never been further from home than their farms and never met a Muslim, rushed to join the battle to save Christ from the enemies of the faith.

On the other side, Salahadin, the renowned leader of the Muslim armies (commonly called Saladin), inspired men to battle by declaring a change in the nature of war. War was now a Jihad, a struggle or battle for spiritual truth: 'Saladin demanded every one of his soldiers become a soldier of God. It was not the Christians themselves who were hateful: it was their status as infidels. The Moslems believed they were fighting against a barbarous and backward faith, dissipating the shades of error, and letting the Truth shine forth . . . Motivated entirely by the conviction of the superiority of his faith, and of the inevitable triumph of God over the devil, Saladin may not altogether have understood that the [Christians] might be motivated by exactly the same feelings. He believed that he was setting up the forces of the spirit against the brute force [of the Crusaders].'[4]

Modern Christians look back on this page of history and are astounded that the Church justified warfare. We have trouble understanding those ancients in the Middle Ages so different to ourselves. The Crusades are long past and we all thought modern man was not capable of repeating the tragedy of religious war. But the violence of our century should shock us out of our complacency and warn us that modern man has not progressed so far. The United Nations Hague Appeal for Peace Campaign states that 'We are at the end of the bloodiest most war filled century in history. Nine out of ten victims of armed conflict are civilians and more than half of these are children.' It is estimated that 160 million people were killed last century through wars and armed conflicts. We may have conquered the Moon and Mars but not man's basic bigotry. We still cannot see ourselves as fellow *terrestrials*. We are still consumed by nationalism, intolerance and the *me first* syndrome of our childhood. We have not matured. Jesus teaches that wars are born in the heart. When we fail to see every person as a brother or sister, a little intolerance can grow into a war.

Francis of Assisi understood this need for unity so clearly that he even included nature in his vision of reconciliation – speaking of 'brother sun and sister moon' centuries before anyone voiced concerns for ecology. I find an implicit subliminal symbolism in these symbols. Christianity follows Christ the Son who has been traditionally and symbolically worshipped at sunrise on Easter Sunday and likened to the dawn and the sun in our hymns of praise. The moon summons the call for the month of highest worship in Islam during Ramadan and the Ramadan moon appears on many flags of Islamic countries. Can we reconcile 'brother sun and sister moon'? We should have learned from history that both sides lose in a war. Another point we seem to miss is that God is the first victim of war in his name.

Antagonism is insidiously growing again between Christianity and Islam and is in danger of escalating. It is embarrassing to recognise similar attitudes prevailing today as in the Middle Ages and to note that we are using similar militant language. It's an unpleasant surprise to find that we are not so different from those primitive folk in the Middle Ages after all. We engage in mutual aggressive attitudes (which on occasion erupt into action) and triumphalism. Each religion boasts of trophy converts thereby hoping to prove they are legitimate and the other is not. Each tries to score points in debates drawing worldwide attention. The object is not to build bridges of understanding, or beam light into misunderstanding, but to conquer the opponent thus denigrating his religion. If this is not true why is there so much emotional interest by Muslims and Christians in which side 'won' the debate? In like manner, Eastern and Western media fuel feelings of mistrust, hostility and fear often exploiting stereotypes. (We will look at some of these images in a later chapter.) Both sides wave banners of conquest in mutual competition.

It is true that many Islamic regimes are hostile to Christian witness and minority Christian communities are subjected to various forms of 'second-class citizen' treatment ranging from slight discrimination to direct persecution. Although Christians may become Muslims, Muslims are not permitted to become Christians and may suffer harassment or persecution if they do so. This aversion to Christianity was evidenced during the Gulf War when Western Christian chaplains in Saudi Arabia were forbidden to wear or display crosses. In reaction to this reality some Christians portray Islam as the great anti-Christ, the enemy to be conquered. Their language is filled with militant images of spiritual warfare. Leaders' rhetoric mirrors the Crusades in mobilising the laity to strategically target Muslim countries, engage in power-encounters to pull down Islamic strongholds and reclaim the land in enemy hands for Christ. Of course this is not expressed in overt military terms, but spiritualised in terms of power encounters and spiritual warfare. The battle takes place in prayer.

The battle is seen as a strategic and necessary ingredient for successful witness to take place. Hence, Christians are giving up their holidays to take a prayer march on Muslim lands to conquer the territorial spiritual demonic powers they believe hold Islamic lands captive. Prayers calling to 'demolish the shroud of Islam' and similar sentiments are common in these groups. When we step back from the clash and clamour on the frontline battle scenes, we sense something is wrong. This is the mentality and language of conflict of the Middle Ages built on fear and stereotypes, when neither side felt safe unless the other was totally conquered. Today Christians and Muslims are again lining up on opposite sides with a 'them against us' Middle Ages battle mentality.

These comments are not meant as criticism of those committed to struggling in prayer against evil and darkness to bring light and healing to the world. Christ taught us by word and example to fast and pray. The world and people are changed through prayer and I believe we will ultimately discover that many of the world's greatest heroes are those unknown individuals who agonised in quiet places in prayer. I am concerned about our tendency to take a theological belief and develop it until it reaches an extreme. There are a number of beliefs and practices hiding under the banner of spiritual warfare today that are closer to paganism than the Bible. I am concerned these are being accepted without questioning their validity.

The theology of spiritual warfare has moved from the battle of spiritual forces of evil and God down to our city streets where it is popularly personified in a battle with Islam and impacting Christians' attitudes to Muslims. A high-school student in an Australian city brought his Muslim friend home. The next day his concerned mother called her pastor asking if she needed to cleanse the house from evil spirits. She is not a fire-breathing Muslim hater. She is uninformed and under the influence of current portrayals of Islam. This sad and shameful story should lead us to repent of all attitudes, beliefs and stereotypes that contributed to it.

Recently I was speaking in a church in Australia about my experiences while living in Muslim countries. I mentioned that in over twenty years I never once experienced personal hostility from Muslims over my Christian faith. In fact, because I was a guest in their countries I received preferential treatment. After the meeting a young mother approached me and voiced her surprise. She shocked me with this story: 'Last year God gave me a burden to pray for Muslims so I requested monthly prayer requests from a group compiling news from the Muslim world. But now I don't want to pray for them. I feel afraid of them. The Muslim world seems such a dark sinister place. I don't want anything to do with Islam.' I asked if she had ever had any bad experiences with Muslims. She replied, 'No. I've never met one.' The literature she referred to is a typical portrayal of Islam in certain sectors of the Church: negative images, stories of persecution and harassment, rhetoric and fear bordering on panic. In thirty-one days of information to acquaint the reader with the Muslim world each entry portrayed Islam in an oppressive, monolithic, non-personal way and described some kind of suffering undergone by Christians. There was not one positive description of a Muslim individual to balance the picture. This type of literature portrays Islam as an enemy that must be conquered. It has described Islam as the last anti-Christ to be vanquished before Christ can return and the language is filled with militant rhetoric and banner waving. In this approach prayer becomes a strategic weapon, Islam is vilified and conversion is simply a strategy by which to conquer. The effect of this is the same as the Church's propaganda in the Middle Ages.

This approach has confused us. It blurs our thinking about who the enemy really is and causes us to fight our brothers and sisters instead of the real enemy. The enemy of our souls is Satan, not any particular ideology or religion. If we believe in a spiritual warfare view of history, then we must accept that the entire world order is under the 'prince of this world' and Satan is the force behind every thing opposed to God's purposes. Why should Islam be singled out as being more evil and more under Satan's control than any other belief or ideology, or our own sins of prejudice, greed and arrogance? Why should Muslim countries be particularly besieged by the reigns of territorial spirits? Don't these spirits operate in England, Australia, America and Sweden for example? Are Christians taking as many prayer holidays in these Western post-Christian countries to liberate areas from Satan's domination as they are in Muslim lands? If this is what we believe then we should pray as much in Liverpool as in Libya.

Furthermore we cannot relate to Islam. It is an impersonal theology. We can only relate to, or make war on, people – not ideologies or theologies. How can we declare (spiritual) war on Islam viewing it as an enemy, without feelings of fear and hostility to the Muslim person on the television screen or living in our street? Muslims are not God's enemies. Our New Testament declares they are people God loves and for whom Christ died. This militant approach causes offence to Muslims and does nothing to draw them closer to Christ. The Crusades should have taught us that people do not respond to the Gospel after Christians have waged battle against them. Muslims were sometimes conquered in battle but not converted. The motive for evangelism is Christ's love for every person, not to conquer or convert the world to our religion.

Even if some believe they are justified in this militant view of spiritual warfare with Islam as an enemy, then we are commanded to love our enemies and seek his or her best above our own selves. Is this aggressive manner of expressing spiritual realities in accordance with Christian love and Jesus' example? When Jesus lived in the Middle East his people perceived the Samaritans (ethnically and religiously mixed Jews) as enemies of God. Jesus repudiated the contemporary hostile attitudes towards these people. When the disciples struck up a militant attitude towards an unresponsive village he rebuked them sharply. '[The village] did not receive him. When his disciples saw this they said, "Lord do you want us to command fire to come down from heaven and consume them?" But he turned and rebuked them, "You do not know what spirit you are of. For the

Son of man has not come down from heaven to destroy the lives
of human beings but to save them".'[5] Jesus did not allow his disciples to project the battle in the spiritual realm onto the people
who rejected or opposed him.

The Church has reacted to Islam in a kaleidoscope of ways:
from declaring Islam the last anti-Christ to asserting Muslims
have all the revelation of Christ they need in the Quran and so
do not need the Gospel. It is the age-old problem of balancing
love and truth. If we err on the side of perceived truth we become
defenders and lawyers for God. The Law condemns everyone not
on my side. Fundamentalists in all religions see the *other* as an
enemy to be overcome. Fundamentalism lacks love and often
justifies any means to conquer the enemy. However, if we err on
the side of perceived love we lose the truth, the quintessential
essence for being what we are: Christians. We love because we are
Christians. We love others because Christ first loved us, so we
have a particular quality of love to give to the world. Truth
without love leads to fundamentalism and love without truth
leads to liberalism. This is part of the struggle in our approach
to Islam. How do we react to the person who rejects our message,
that is inseparable from who we are? Do we call down fire from
heaven to annihilate the person or do we remove the offence of
the Gospel in order that the person will not reject us?

Confusion and struggle has continued for 1,400 years and
we are still perplexed about dealing with Islam. Christians are
confused about how to approach Islam and are searching for
strategies to share the Gospel. Yet we have overlooked the successful example of one of the most famous Western Christians
who took the Gospel to Muslims during the Crusades, enjoyed
his time with them, and is still honoured today by East and
West.

Francis of Assisi is not someone who usually springs to mind
in relation to Muslims. He is probably only significant for many
of us as some kind of patron protector for animals. Some
Christians may have deliberately ignored him because the

Catholics claimed him as a saint, thereby introducing another 'them and us' category. I grew up with a 'them versus us' mentality towards the Catholic faith. It was as alien to me as Islam is to many Christians today. I had never been inside a Catholic church, but I passed St Stephen's every day on the way to school. No one had ever told me Catholics were not on our side, but I knew they were not one of us. They were different and since their children would not attend our state school I *knew* they looked down on us. So I took a superior attitude to them to defend myself. Since I had no real contact with them, I was suspicious of them and their dark alien religion. They even wore strange clothes to church similar to Muslims: the ladies wore headscarves and veils and the priests dressed in long robes and often wore beards. Nuns dressed in long dark dresses that covered their whole body except their hands and with flowing veils that totally covered all their hair. It was a strange religion that required all this veiling. Little Catholic girls sometimes went to church in white bride dresses and veils (which I said was stupid but secretly envied).

St Stephen's was a dark red brick church. It looked dark outside and inside and I was sure they practised strange rituals in there. Many cars parked outside during the Mass had bumper stickers proclaiming that 'the Mass never ends', and to prove it an eerie red glow near the altar could be seen through the window at night. When I was in primary school in the sixties, the kids from St Stephen's and our state school had the opportunity to stand on opposite sides of the street and shout offensive rhymes at each other. I yelled loudly 'Catholic dogs stink like frogs' (that would teach them to think they were better than we were).

In 1998 I was sitting in my garden in Rabat, Morocco, with my friend Pat who is a Catholic Franciscan nun, and I recalled this incident. Pat who grew up in Sydney burst out laughing, 'Yeah, I remember and we yelled something about Protestants with no bells and going to hell!' I since discovered that school children in

Brisbane, who had no way of knowing the rhymes in Sydney and Melbourne, shouted exactly the same insulting songs at each other. So these prejudices were probably passed down for generations, coming with our forebears from Great Britain. After all, Australia has never been a religious country and there has been no history of a major Catholic-Protestant struggle, although Catholics were discriminated against in the early settler years. The other side of the street at St Stephen's was an alien world. It was almost thirty-five years before I overcame my prejudice and fears and walked across the street to meet Catholics face to face. I discovered people who love God and who are trying to live a life pleasing to God; people just like me. I also discovered the complete bumper car slogan: 'The Mass (the celebration of our faith) never ends. It must be lived, so let us go forth to love and serve the Lord' and it enriched my faith.

There are other Christians who had a more liberal ecumenical background than I did, but still do not rank St Francis high on their list of examples. Until recently I had cast St Francis in this category and really cannot be blamed. Every picture or statue portrays him as a wispy, wandering human aviary, a tame wimpy monk with an ethereal expression who trips over the hills with chirping birdies on his head, or cuddles furry animals with an impotent glaze in his eye. He was someone my son would call a 'nerd'. Who needs a nerd as an example? So it was a shock to discover the real Francis. He was nothing like a jellyfish, but the wild radical of his times. And he is no tamer or safer for us than Jesus! We have forgotten that Francis of Assisi was an evangelist who brought large numbers of people to renewed faith in God through his preaching. He was the passionate, non-violent alternative to the dominant militant culture of his times. And far from being passive and spineless he set off single-handedly to convert everyone involved in the Crusade wars: Christians and Muslims.

St Francis paved a path for us to follow today in relating to Islam, if we dare, for Francis' way is not the emblazoned battle of power but the lowly path of love and service. It is not the raised fist but an open hand: vulnerable and extended, no matter what the consequences. It is not a declaration of war on God's enemies, but a message of indiscriminate love and salvation for all.

Centuries ago the Western Church was powerful, wealthy and dedicated to conquering Islam. Church leaders offered rewards to all heroes doing battle for Christ and promised powerful encounters where the enemy would be overwhelmed and the oriental lands in darkness rescued by the cross. As a result of this mentality Muslims still harbour a horror of the symbol of Christianity.

Francis understood that God does not need mercenaries, but messengers of mercy. The Gospel cannot go hand in hand with intolerance and aggressive attitudes. When we lay aside all warfare strategies and reach out in peace, we discover in Muslims our fellow human beings, made like us, in God's image. We find open hearts not enemies. And we don't need to be experts in Islam, for neither was St Francis.

Notes

1 'Thousands sign up for Holy War.' *The Sunday Age* 19 September 1999, Melbourne, Australia, p. 5.
2 Jabbour, N. (1993) *The Rumbling Volcano*, Pasadena, CA: Mandate Press, p. 26.
3 Oldenbourg, Z. (1966) *The Crusades*, New York and Toronto: Random House, p. 442; Orion Books, London; Editions Gallimard, Paris.
4 Ibid., p. 438.
5 Luke 9:52–56.

Chapter Two

THE MAD MONK

When we search beyond the images of gentle St Francis traipsing around with birds on his shoulder to find the real Francis Bernadone of Assisi, he comes as a shock. Voltaire called Francis 'a raving lunatic who goes about stark naked, talks to animals, catechises a wolf and makes himself a snow wife'.[1] No one denies these things because they are all recorded in his biography. His own followers tell that he stripped himself in public, talked to a lamb, a hare and the swallows, tamed a wolf and taught it the ways of Christian living, rolled naked in the snow to curb temptations of the flesh and built himself a snow wife and children.

On the other hand he has been glorified as the ideal model for human liberation whose values are essential for survival today. At the beginning of the third millennium we have rediscovered Francis and he is promoted as the panacea for the world's ills. In England alone, a new life of Francis appears every year. Widely divergent groups hail him as their hero: peacemakers, environmentalists, animal lovers, social activists and liberators. Francis is also claimed as the apostle for our post-modern world and, last but not least, many Christians look to him as a faith model in pluralistic societies. The counter-culture hippies of the sixties revived his flower-power image for peace in the American city that his followers named after him – San Francisco. The beginnings of the second largest city in America, Los Angeles, were also founded under the aura of Francis. His favourite church, where he received his call to apostolic ministry, was dedicated to Madre de Los Angelos (Mary Queen of the Angels) who was later named the patron saint of the Franciscan Order.[2] Francis' followers named the city for their patron saint.

There is no disputing he was a radical man who changed the world in his day but he does appear to have been at least a little crazy and was considered by some in his own time as a lunatic. It is often the fate of those who refuse to be carried in the popular currents of their day to be labelled 'mad', not fitted to this world's order. Francis accepted this insult as an honour declaring himself God's fool in the spirit of St Paul's admission that God chooses the weak things of the world in order to show his glory.

The key to understanding Francis is to recognise he was a mystic passionately in love with God and all God's world. Lovers live on the rosy impulse of love and throw caution and reason to the winds. When Francis heard God's voice he responded impulsively in total obedience and with his whole heart in ways that seemed overboard to others. Some of these occasions he came to regret himself.

Francis' desire was to find God and communicate him to others. He was a charismatic preacher, who laid aside the popular sermon aids of the times and preached simply and powerfully, speaking from the heart, avoiding the subtleties of rhetoric and, expressing the inexpressible with a few words and flaming gestures, he rapt his audience. Two records of his sermons remain. The first one was preached before Pope Honorious, 'he was so full of his subject he began to gesticulate and to dance, if not like a tumbler, at the very least like one intoxicated with divine love. No one thought of laughing, on the contrary, all were so moved they could not restrain their tears – in admiration of divine grace in such a man. It was Cardinal Hugolin who suggested he should preach and he was so fearful lest the whole thing should not go off well that he prayed the whole time for God to help his friend. The other sermon was rather like a conversation whose sole object was to extinguish hatred and restore peace. The orator was wretchedly garbed, his appearance frail, his face without beauty; but this did not hinder his words from reconciling the Bolognese nobles who had been slaughtering one another for generations. And so great was the enthusiasm that men and women rushed up to him to tear his garments to shreds and make off with the pieces.'[3]

He is said to have spoken all languages, but this is not to be taken literally – it is symbolic for speaking the language of love that gains an audience and response, even among the fishes and birds. 'The fact is immense crowds assembled to hear him and merchants closed their shops when he preached. He confounded the most learned . . . and had a horror of disputes and attacks against individuals.'[4]

Francis is remembered as the apostle of love, joy and humility. His passionate love for God overflowed in devotion to everything God loves. His love was a scriptural self-giving, serving God's people in their spiritual and material needs. Joy in God is the vibrant aspect of Francis' life and gift to the world. Francis sang through life. Before he knew God, he sang the modern love songs through the streets of his town. When God captured his heart he sang God's love song through the streets of the world. An ever-bubbling song of praise and celebration flowed from him and the darkest moments of his life were never able to overpower this life-light in his spirit. This celebration of life had its springs in gratitude. He even preached to the birds telling them to remember to be grateful for all God's care of them and praise their creator.

He hated the idea of rules and hierarchies and any regimentation that could mitigate against living in the freedom of the Spirit. When he was pressed to write a rule for his order he commanded, 'Let the friars be aware of being sad and gloomy, like hypocrites; but them show themselves joyful in the Lord, gay and pleasant.' When he was pressed to write a last will and testament he only wanted to remind his brothers to love each other.

There is no doubt he was one of the original free spirits, a champion of humanity, and a lover of nature. He was also tolerant and humble but, as with all eccentrics, difficult to live with. Liberation to joy is the keynote of Francis' life that strikes a note for the hungry in our times. Probably more people than ever before are reading the life of St Francis and are drawn to follow his example. There are thousands of entries connected to his name on the Internet. When I began researching his life I was astounded at how many books have been written recently about his life from so many different Christian persuasions. Yet, with so many people reading his message and touched, why are there so few who begin following his advice? We could ask the same question of those who read the New Testament and whose hearts respond to Christ's message, which is the message Francis preached and lived, yet do not follow.

> We are afraid to listen to the reasons of the heart because it embraces our reason and common-sense rationality and leads us beyond our own limits to the totally new and unexpected. Our security is one of self-imposed imprisonment. Isolated in this way we do not know who we are, nor can we recognise the rich depths in ourselves. And ignorance is the best breeding ground for fear. How can we be content and at peace when what is deepest in us, our true selves, is denied the union it is yearning for with the rest of creation. There can be no union unless we go out towards others and that means we have to pull down the barriers we have built around ourselves. Love is the greatest power for good in the universe. Love is vulnerable, it leaves itself open to ridicule and rejection, but it can never be conquered. Francis risked everything for love of Christ. That led him to love and respect the world around him.[5]

Why don't we go beyond the barriers? The frozen river of fear dams us and we fear those outside our self-imposed barriers of faith and culture and we fear ourselves, that we might fail if we try to step out. Maybe meeting Francis will inspire us and his example will encourage us to step beyond the boundaries of our lives and reach a place of new meetings. We are formed in the meetings of our life: meetings with our inner hidden self, meetings with God, meetings with people – for better or worse. When the true meeting with God takes place we are bathed in the pure love of God. God embraces us with his fire of unconditional love burning through our frozen chasms and setting the healing streams free. In the moment of meeting we are made new and we go out from the warmth of his blaze carrying the glowing embers of his love and burning with the desire to bring others to the fire. Francis' life glowed. The warmth and joy of God he shared with others reflected the joy and the fire of his meetings with God.

Who is the real Francis? He born and baptised Giovanni di Pietro di Bernadone in 1181CE in the hills of Umbria, Italy, in the small town Assisi while his father was in France on a business trip. When his father returned home he renamed him Franceso (the Frenchman). His father was a rich cloth-merchant of the new middle class and his mother a gentlewoman. Peter Bernadone had great aspirations for his son. Francis was six years old when the first Crusade against the Muslims in his lifetime commenced. He was one of the middle-class boys of the town enjoying the good things of life. As a young man he roamed the streets with the other lads singing the poetic verses of the troubadours and serenading the girls on their balconies and was reputed to be the leader of all kinds of escapades.[6] He spent the rest of his life in repentance for these years but we do not know if they were in fact riotous and sensual, or whether his overly zealous conscience magnified his youthful exuberance. Being a troubadour he was probably familiar with the dances and music of the Islamic mystics which reached Europe from the Islamic Empire.[7]

In keeping with custom, as soon as he was old enough to go to war he joined a local combat against Perugia, a neighbouring town, in 1202. The pomp and glory of war did not last long. He was promptly captured and cast in a dungeon. The second

Crusade of his lifetime (the Fourth Crusade) was announced while he was imprisoned. This disastrous prison experience depleted his body and drained his spirit. When he was finally ransomed one year later by his father, he returned home shattered and fell into a feverous coma, probably malaria, which lasted one year.

Eventually he recovered health and spirits and in 1204 bounced off to war again. This time he believed he was embarking on a moral and noble war by joining the cause of the Pope against the German princes – one of these was Frederick II who weaves in and out of this story – under the umbrella of Walter of Brienne's cries to join the army of the Fourth Crusade. This was the path for him to become knighted and rise on the social scale to the nobility. He joined Walter's knights and rode off to war. However, the night before he rode into battle he had a dream seeing himself in a vast hall, the walls lined with swords and shields and the trophies of a victorious army. A voice said, 'All these will belong to you.' Francis understood God was on his side and on Christendom's side. God would give them the victory against the infidel enemy. He arrived at the mustering point and that evening, as he lay exhausted in his tent, he heard a voice call his name. He heard God challenge him, 'Francis, why do you follow the servant instead of the Master? Return home. You have misunderstood the vision. It will have a different fulfilment.' Thus began the gradual process of conversion. The next morning Francis left the army and returned home to a derisive and amazed community.

He told no one the reason for his return. This silence about his most precious experiences was a practice he continued for the remainder of his life. He later wrote, 'Blessed is the religious (religious worker or cleric) who treasures up for heaven the favours God has given him and does not want to show them off for what he can get out of them. Blessed the person who keeps God's marvellous doings to himself.'[8] We wonder how he would react to today's Christian mass media programmes fanfaring

God's marvellous doings along with requests for financing and popular acclaim for the evangelist. Even our most conservative ministries are touched by this influence of the modern advertising industry. Francis' silence may not be the answer either, but it has deep ramifications for our church culture today.

Francis slipped back into the social merry-go-round again. One night, after he and his friends had feasted together and were roaming the streets, he was struck motionless in the middle of the street in a spiritual visitation. He fell behind in a mystical experience with God and was given to understand more of the original vision. God's call was to find joy in giving, not in having, to be a servant, not a lord. He would aspire after total poverty and give up all desires except to do the will of God. His friends joked that he was love struck and Francis replied in riddles about being in love with a bride more beautiful and rich than they had ever seen. He was actually talking in the knight's romantic manner about his 'Lady Poverty'.

Francis went off into the woods and caves spending hours in prayer, expecting God would speak to him again and unlock the mystery of his will. He lost interest in all that the world offers and his clothes became torn and his person was unkempt. The town wondered at the change in his behaviour and rumours began that he was mad. Youth ridiculed him and threw stones at him. He endured the ridicule, even welcoming it for it was the way of the new chosen path. But there were no more visions or dreams or directions. Endless dark days and nights passed in waves of despair and inner doubts and turmoil. He obeyed God's voice to fulfil a vision and followed God, but not into victory. He fell into a dark chasm and it was too late to go back. The vision had changed him and he could not return to his former carefree life for it now left him feeling unfulfilled. Feelings of unworthiness to serve God swamped him and he wondered if he had imagined the call. Was he really going crazy in this no-man's-land between visions and reality? Francis found himself adrift in a black tumultuous sea with no sight of the shoreline.

Desperate circumstances give rise to desperate questions that are meant to lead to deeper faith. Therefore God allows desperate circumstances, which often feel like they are overwhelming, to save us from living shallow lives. Our desperate questions and doubts, which others often view with alarm that we are losing the faith, are more often the sign of a growing and deepening faith and trust. They are signs that God is removing our crutches and causing us to depend solely on him, or challenging our smug suppositions about him and forcing us to realise we cannot box God up into our little ideas of him. How do we react when God does not act in the way we believe God should act? Most of us don't do very well. We react like the disciples when in obedience to Jesus' command, they got in a boat to go with him to the other side of the Sea of Galilee. Out in the middle of the sea in the black of night one of the 'furious' endemic storms blew up with waves breaking over the boat, threatening to sink it. The disciples were terrified and called on Jesus accusingly, 'Don't you care if we drown?'[9] The complaint also implied, 'How can you be so uninvolved in our fearful circumstances? Why don't you come to our rescue?' When seasoned sailors are sure they will die we can be sure this was a horrific storm. They were in desperate circumstances and totally out their ability to cope. We may also question with them how this could happen. After all they had followed Jesus' command to set out in the boat and he was in the boat with them. They were in the centre of God's will. Surely the crossing should be trouble free? Instead they are totally pressed beyond their ability to endure and Jesus is not only *not* coming to their rescue, but appears unconcerned. Jesus got them into this mess and he's opted out!

Francis found himself in this same boat. Many of the Christian mystics and those we call saints speak of similar experiences as the 'dark night of the soul' – when God appears to have left them alone. Will they still follow God, cling to him and love him when God is not acting, as he should? How do we react when we find ourselves in the dark cave with no sign of what we believe God should do about it, or not even a sign of God's presence with us? Francis isolated himself in depression; the disciples yelled in fear and anguish.

The disciples sat with Jesus at the Last Supper in a room chosen for its seclusion. It was a sombre meal. Jesus' mission appeared to be failing and his life was in danger. There seemed to be a number of obviously good strategies to counter the opposition. At the very least he could use his powers in a power encounter and prove he was the right one to be followed. Yet instead of rousing his followers to a victory charge against the forces of evil, he did nothing. He even appeared to be succumbing passively to the enemy. This was not how the Messiah should act. The Jews expected him to fulfil their understanding of the prophecies about him: he would lead the Jews in triumphant battle overthrowing the forces of evil and the enemies of God's people in a great war to end all wars proving that Jehovah is God. They continually asked him when would he restore the kingdom, while anxiously looking for the first signs that he was about to give them the power and prestige they believed was promised to them in the Scriptures. Instead of enjoying power and glory they were huddling behind closed doors while their dreams were tumbling around their ears. Why wasn't God acting? Hadn't God promised? Why wasn't he fulfilling the promises for them? The situation was becoming more dangerous every day, yet Jesus was either doing nothing or provoking the authorities. Their bewilderment, fear and frustration erupted into petty squabbles about how the money was being spent and who was going to have the best portfolio in the new kingdom and who would be the most faithful. We are directed to note the darkness they were stumbling around in. Those poignant words, 'It was night', depict how desperate the latest event was – when Judas left to betray him.[10] All light of hope was gone. They subsequently all deserted him in fear and slunk into their dark cave refuges.

But the good news is that God does not leave us forever in the cave, even though the dark time seems endless. The seeds of hope are sown in times of fear and doubt. In order to experience new beginnings and new life we must experience the painful end and death of the old. We must lose our self before we gain back our self in a new way along with something of greater value. Eventually Francis' darkness was penetrated by a touch of peace, the touch of grace. He did not receive the new vision, or the answers, but he experienced God's loving mercy. Now he knew he was totally unable and unworthy to serve God, but he had also felt the empowering touch of God. He left the cavern a different person with an insight into God's character and himself that not only changed him, but also would change the world. Without the hidden dark days there would not have been the new Francis liberated to love and serve God and all humanity.

If we open our self to God, which entails choosing to continue loving and giving, we will be exposed to hurt and pain. We could choose to not be vulnerable and preserve our self, our ego, but then we will not experience the rebirth. For when we open to God and love and the inevitability of pain in the quest, as we experience death to self, we will also find the light on the other side of that death. There we find the face of God and rediscover our true self, that deep spiritual part of us that longs for and will not be satisfied by anything less than reconciliation with our Father. Anyone who has not been tempted to run away from the cross, and the pain and death needed for the rebirth, will not understand the hope and joy in the resurrection. The light is so much brighter after being in darkness.

Francis began serving the poor. In this servitude he found liberation. He sought out the sick to minister to their needs and beggars to give them alms. 'One day as he went through a wood singing hymns in French, robbers rushed out on him and demanded to know who he was. Francis confidently replied, "I am the herald of the Great King. What is that to you?" At this statement of bravado they beat him and cast him in a ditch filled with deep snow saying, "Lie there foolish herald of God!" He lay there until they had gone and then jumped out singing praises to

God.'[11] And we can assume he learnt his first lesson in the importance of humility in delivering God's message to others.

He ministered to all except lepers for he had such a fear and aversion to lepers he would hold his nose when he passed their camp even from a long distance. He wrote, 'When I was in sins it seemed extremely bitter to me to look at lepers, and the Lord himself led me among them and I practised mercy with them.' One day in a rush of experiencing God's love for all men, even lepers, he kissed one and gave him a coin. On another occasion he upbraided a beggar who had asked alms of him and then felt very contrite telling himself it was a great shame to withhold what was asked in the name of so great a King. After these experiences he resolved in his heart never to refuse anyone, if possible, who asked for the love of God.[12] This resolve became the cornerstone of his life. In this incident Francis conquered his fear of *the other* that repulsed him. He did not just serve them but tried to identify with them in every way. On a later visit to Rome he borrowed the rags of a beggar and sat outside St Peter's begging for alms.

After working with the lepers he returned to Assisi and donned a hermit's habit and devoted himself to repairing churches from 1205 to 1208. Again, this was in response to a mystical command from God. He was praying in one of his favourite places, a small abandoned chapel in San Damiano below Assisi. While kneeling in prayer before the crucifix he heard a voice, 'Francis go and rebuild my house which is falling into ruins.' Francis construed this to mean the dilapidated churches in the area and immediately set about repairing them, using his father's money. He loaded his horse with bales of cloth from his father's store and rode to Foligno where he sold everything, including the horse and walked home. The priest correctly prophesied his father's response and refused to take the money for the church; Francis flung it on the windowsill in disgust. He made his resolve to give up all for love of God and ministry and moved in with the aged priest in a windy shelter. His clothes became worn and torn and the townsfolk thought he had gone totally mad. His father did become extremely angry when he returned from a business trip and discovered the state of his son and his coffers. He beat Francis and put him in chains, locking him in the house to bring him to his senses, but his mother secretly took him food and then, after the father left, released him to follow his calling with her blessing. His father retaliated by taking Francis to court intending to break his will or renounce him; thereby cutting him off from all his inheritance. Francis refused to recognise the civil court so his father took the case to the religious court.

This was the background to that famous nudity scene. Francis arrived in his fine clothes and renounced all rights to his father's inheritance, giving his father not only the money claimed but the clothes on his back which his father had provided. Standing stark naked he laid claim to one father only, 'My father in heaven'. His father stomped out and the Bishop covered Francis in his own robe until they found an old patched cloak in a cupboard which Francis gladly accepted. Later in life Francis regretted treating his father so harshly, but it wasn't the last time he stripped off his clothes before an audience!

For two years Francis devoted himself to his calling by raising funds to rebuild churches in what could have been the first faith-promise ministry. He went from door to door begging for stones in exchange for blessings. His church building programme was successful and he managed to rebuild some churches in the region. But whereas today the successful in ministries soon have their own personal ministry kingdom and a flock following in a kind of personality cult, Francis earned heaps of scorn. For although the building programme flourished he followed an almost destitute lifestyle that did not hold out the promise of health, wealth and prosperity. In fact he preached and lived the opposite. He gave away all his family's wealth that passed into his hands, refusing to even touch money or own even a shack and pushed his body so piteously that his health broke and he died a physical wreck aged forty-five. He passionately distrusted prosperity and comfort as a spiritual snare. His impoverished lifestyle was an attempt to imitate Christ who gave up all to become a poor man with us and who had nowhere to lay his head. It is also typical of mystics in every religion who scorn the world in order to find the spiritual path to God.

On the Feast of St Matthew, 24 February 1208, Francis was at Mass in his favourite church, the chapel of the Portiuncola (Little Portion), and heard the priest read the words from Matthew 10:7–10: 'As you go, proclaim that the kingdom of heaven is close at hand. Heal the sick, raise the dead, and cleanse those who have leprosy, drive out demons. You received without charge, give without charge. Do not take along any gold or silver or copper in your belts, take no bag for the journey, nor extra tunic, or sandals or a staff, for the worker is worth his keep.' Francis understood these words of Jesus as a literal commission from God. At the end of the Mass he cried out, 'This is what I want, this is what I seek, this is what I long to do with all my heart.'[13] And in his typical extravagant manner he took off his hermit's habit and sandals and as a barefoot preacher went straight into the market place and started preaching, not in the liturgical Latin of the institutional church, but in the new language of the people – Italian. From now on he devoted his life to proclaiming the gospel of peace, reconciliation, joy and poverty. He embraced his 'Lady Poverty' a further step by begging from door to door for his daily food. He was a regular sight in the streets of Assisi going about in a woollen robe, barefooted, begging for stones and oil for the church and begging for his daily bread 'for the love of God'. This spontaneous, impulsive act of obedience to Scripture typifies his whole life. 'He achieved his ambition by declaring himself the herald of the Great King. He did not suppress his passion, poetry and ambition. Instead he redirected it into the service of his Lord. His literal imitation of the life of Jesus revealed by the Gospels produced the staggeringly unique person that Francis became.'[14]

He continued to love going off alone into the woods and deserted places to pray audibly and weep and lament aloud. It is told the groves echoed with his weeping and sighs. The friars heard him cry aloud, imploring God's mercy for sinners and weeping for the passion of Christ as he saw it before his eyes.[15] From the day the Lord spoke to him from the crucifix in San Damiano chapel, Francis' heart was stricken with love and compassion for the crucified Christ and he contemplated constantly on his suffering. 'I weep for the passion of my Lord Jesus Christ, and I should not be ashamed to go weeping through the whole world for his sake.'[16]

There are some very interesting facets of Francis' journey into his calling. On two occasions he misunderstood God's call. On the first occasion he set off to be a glorious soldier doing battle for God and had to be stopped by a dream before embarking on the battle. The second time he spent years engaged in a church building ministry that was not what God intended. We may well wonder why God allowed him to waste so much time and energy going in the wrong direction, or at least majoring on a minor. But God had another equally important ministry – the growth of his servant into the knowledge of his Master. The dark cave years of self doubt and searching for the guidance that never came and longing for a repeat of the voice that didn't speak were all in God's plan. The faithful years of serving in the wrong ministry were also part of God's programme. While Francis was rebuilding churches for God, God was rebuilding Francis to restore the real Church, that is the people of God.

Many of the Church's great sons and daughters have spoken of the death of a vision in their life only to have it reborn in a new and different way than they expected. But the death pangs and pains were real and the valley had to be travelled in darkness, bewilderment, tears and doubt. These struggles are reminiscent of Francis' Master who agonised over God's will in Gethsemane and cried out with feelings of abandonment and great sorrow as he suffered for obeying God's word. Which one of us has not cried out to God in times of darkness and despair, 'Where are you? Why have you left me?' There is a secret to be grasped in the dark Gethsemane Garden and a secret in the dark cave near Assisi. But it probably won't help us when we have to walk our own dark valley of tears. We have to persevere alone in the dank darkness until the light comes for there is no other way for the gold of faith to be tried and proven.

We cannot live on others' faith or our own past faith-experiences. God will take us out into unfamiliar territory where we are like a fish taken out of the water thrashing around in the bottom of the boat. We want our old familiar waters to swim in, even if they were too shallow and caused us to be dashed under by turbulent waves. We do not want to taken out and released in deeper waters. Maybe there are spectacular depths and a liberating vastness to explore, which we could only guess, but they are too scary because we would be out of our depth. We want security at the cost of being left in the shallows of experiencing God's love.

God acts with a severe love by taking us into new and difficult experiences, or by not miraculously saving us from some of life's most painful experiences. These desperate experiences demand a new relationship with him. We feel wounded and wonder why God allowed this to happen. We struggle with God's sovereignty and the problem of sin and pain in the world and in our own families. What a strange mystery is hidden in the wounds God allows in our faith struggle. We see the wounds in Christ on the cross in his hands and feet. We see them in Jacob's leg as he wrestled with God, with Job, as he is afflicted. We see them in ourselves. Jacob, Francis, you and I are never the same after these struggles. The wound heals but its sign remains with us and we know in our inmost heart that God was present in the wound and will be forever. Yet, we dimly understand that in God's economy these wounds have a very precious value of which we can only sense from this side of eternity. Those awful scars in Christ's body speak to us of the depths of God's enormous love for us. How much does God love us? Enough to suffer those wounds. How we will bless those nail-scarred hands and feet! I believe we will also see the beauty of our own wounds not visible to us now and understand how much God treasures them.

God allowed those desperate years to mature Francis' immature faith. Maybe we also need to mature in order to have a true relationship with God. We may need to unlearn a lot of faulty beliefs about God. Sometimes we cannot meet God because we have someone or something we call God impersonating him and frightening us away from the meeting. Or something we have blamed on God shuts the door to the meeting place. Or maybe we cannot meet God and others because we need to meet and accept our real self. The best place to do this is in the presence of the one who accepts and loves us unconditionally.

We will discover just like Francis that this journey with self and God is lonely because it is intimate. There is no room for bystanders, and those we expect to support us on the way may not understand. When Christians express fears and doubts about God, others in the Church can become very uncomfortable. Christians can act as if we must always be confident of the truth and display a victorious triumphant faith – no questions and no doubts. Our churches give the impression we are clones all having the same experience – all looking and feeling alike. Those who do not use the right words to explain their faith journey are considered to be seriously lacking in their spiritual state. After all, if they don't say they are 'born again' then they probably aren't. A number of people told me they left the Church because they did not have the same experience that 'everyone' described as real faith. This was usually described as a feeling. These strugglers did not know how to get what others said they should have, so they gave up the search. Although some people can have incredible experiences, visions and deep feelings as part of their faith walk, this is not the salvation Jesus promised. He said, 'If you know the truth, it will set you free.' For some, liberation strikes brightly dramatically and quickly, for others it is a snail trail in the shadows only obvious after the sun shines on it. The experience of freedom and liberation will be different for every individual. Why would a God who created diversity and variety have one variety of the new creation? In God's created world there are an amazing number of tree varieties. The biblical writings compare us to trees whose roots go down deep into God's love. Why would God recreate us all looking alike? One of the magnets drawing us to Francis is his abandonment of how he sees God leading and his embrace of others on different paths.

One way we can view faith is as the end of the search – finding the answer to all the questions. Once I have completed the crossword puzzle there is nothing more to be done. I own the book with the right answers and others have either solved the puzzle with the same right answers as me or have failed the test. Or we can view faith as a life-long journey of continuing puzzles. As one puzzle is solved and light dawns, a new puzzle forms needing new understanding. Some questions will not be answered and we write over the blanks 'faith in the goodness of God when nothing proves it' and move on. But what about people who do not have our answers, or have not even completed the first basic puzzle? How do we know they are not on the journey? Christ continually warned not to judge by appearances because only God knows the heart. When we are tempted to think we are the experts in how to know God, we should remember the disciples did not even get the *questions* correct until near the end of their lives.

Too often we are afraid to admit our faith experience is not as watertight as we project. When I shared, in a church of people who knew me well, how in my most desperate days I prayed, 'God if you are there, why don't you help?' the speaker after me said, 'Of course we never really doubt God is there.' Why are we so afraid of being truthful, or allowing others to be truthful? Who has never doubted God? – doubted that God's acts are always good? Wouldn't it be better if the sick person was healed, the mother didn't die in childbirth and the gunman was apprehended before the carnage? Did God allow these acts or are they simply things that happen in life? And if this is so then how is

God sovereignly in control of all events and history and still loving? When will God bring justice to the oppressed and food to the hungry? Every evening on the news broadcasts we see oppression and people starving and wandering around the world in search of a place to call home. Some of these people are Christians trusting God to supply their needs. Why are they dying of starvation? Why are these questions too big to ask? Are we afraid that if we do not find the answers our faith will shrivel or God will die? Faith comes into play when we choose to have faith in spite of the circumstances and in spite of, and along with, doubts.

Since accepting that faith includes questions and doubts, I now have a greater measure of peace. I am now strong enough to have faith without all the answers. When I saw God as my fairy godfather granting my every wish to make me triumphant, and God's character and ways of working were all neatly classified and filed like an index card system to refer to in times of need, my faith was resting on a shaky foundation. When I was not victorious or an event did not correspond with God's index card entry, God and faith went into crisis.

The victorious and triumphant Christian life does not conjure up pictures of suffering and death and feelings of abandonment. But this was all part of God's victory in Christ. If this was the path the Master trod why should it be any different for the servants? Jesus cried out 'why?' and 'where are you?' to God when circumstances were crushing him. God is always greater than our understanding of him and there will always be mystery about him that causes us to fall down in awe and worship. This mystery, which we want to tidily categorise, keeps causing struggles in our life. Every time we get God tidied up like a ball of rubber bands, another end bursts out and the struggle begins over again, until we learn to live in faith with untidy ends. If everything is clear then faith is irrelevant. We are not called to solve the mystery, but enter it.

While meditating on these questions raised by Francis' life, I discovered why he was devoted to Mary the mother of Christ. Mary's life and her faith struggle in the difficulties of keeping her 'yes' to God is a wonderful example. Since that day I recognised that we have a great affinity with her. Mary treasured in her heart God's promises for her son. She knew his life was secure with God as his protector. True, his birth had caused her some difficulties that were hard to align with the promises, but now his path to glory would be smoothed by God, just as God smoothed the initial trouble with Joseph when she conceived.

However, when she promised, 'Let it happen as it may', she wasn't expecting these type of hardships. Firstly, political circumstances had forced her to travel on an uncomfortable journey when she should have been caring for her advanced pregnancy. Then she gave birth far from home and without the help of her family women, without even a proper private roof over her head. It was incongruous that the son of promise, the 'King of Israel', should be born in a borrowed manger situated either in a stable or on the lower floor of a home. It seemed God could have given them better help than that. She missed out on all the traditional joyful birth celebrations in her village. But again God didn't forget her and showed he knew her longings. Wasn't she amazed when the shepherds reported God sent his own orchestra to celebrate the special birth in Bethlehem? In the place of one midwife announcing the birth to the waiting village, the whole sky filled with angelic beings announcing the birth of her son to the world. How she needed this special caring touch of God in those difficult days. Then when life was settling into an all too normal routine, although still a little difficult, the visit of the magi reaffirmed those early promises. Then just when she was expecting to return home, there was the sudden terror and panic of a coming massacre followed by their long flight to Egypt. In those years as refugees from violence in the Holy Land she wondered if they would ever be able to return to their home. She would have questioned the promises in those unsettled years and mourned for the infants who perished in her son's place. Jesus' road to glory wasn't going quite as she imagined, but yes, there certainly was evidence that God was with them in a special way. He would bring his Christ into public glory in his good time, then they would be liberated from their enemies and evil would be overcome. God would fulfil his word and be triumphant. She decided to still her heart and be patient. Just once she needed to give God a push when the wine ran out during the wedding in Cana. That surely was a foretaste of the coming glory for her son.

She left God to work his way and found herself with other Galilean women clinging close to Christ as he carried his cross through the streets of Jerusalem under Roman guard. Mary's grief was far deeper than any others. This was not only her first-born son, but also the embodiment of all God's promises. The security of her son was shattered by violence and he was treated unjustly and brutally. She saw him imprisoned and tortured and then done to death as a powerless common criminal. She watched her hopes of his future and the nation's glory bleed into the dirt of Jerusalem's garbage dump. Mary entered the dark cave of living in the questions between God's promises and the current reality. Had she reared Jesus through all the difficulties for this terrible end? Had she failed God? Had God failed her? How could God allow this suffering? Why was he silent? Where was God's mercy now? Where was God's promise now in this God-forsaken end and death?

Mary is strangely absent from events after the crucifixion. She is not mentioned among the women who went to the tomb to complete the burial procedures. As Simeon prophesied, her very soul was pierced with a knife. Her whole understanding of God was buried in the beaten body of her son. She lost her son, her God, her theology, her hope for the future. Her God was buried in darkness and the nation was not liberated. Her 'magnificat' of joy and praise ended in despair and ashes. Was it better never to have hoped? We easily see why she was not able to join the other women at the tomb. She was buried deep in her own tomb, her own dark cave. Mary stayed with her son all through the exhausting hours of his suffering in crucifixion. It was a short time in comparison to other types of long drawn out deaths like terminal illnesses, but crucifixion is one of the most horrific forms of torture. Mary saw and felt every pain and every laboured breath. Unable to help him and not bearing to watch, but experiencing in her own body his every muscle spasm, she was unable to leave him. She had to be there giving him support by her presence whatever it cost her.

Most of us have known or heard of families suffering with their terminally ill member, nursing their loved one until the last dying breath. We stand in awe at their strength and commitment while their own needs are ignored, sometimes for years, in order to comfort their loved one. Then when the vigil is over and they have released their loved one to death they collapse. Finally the body and emotions make their voice heard telling them they ran out of ability to cope a long way back on the road. They were living on borrowed strength and their bodies needed to be replenished. Faith in God's love and goodness has also been stretched to its testing point. It's no surprise that people at the end of this endurance test deflate, withdraw behind protective walls or become ill, or the painful questions renew and threaten to overwhelm their faith. Like Mary they have been to death and back and need time to be healed. We note there is no comment on why Mary is not present with the women to administer the burial oils. We are not told that she is prostrate with grief, or that she is in frozen shock and emotionally exhausted. I suspect she was all of these things. I picture her immobilised staring at the wall with pain too great to express thoughts that were too terrible to think. The writers of Scripture allowed Mary the privacy of her pain. They knew Mary had given all she had and they gave her the respect she deserved. If she was out of action, numb with grief, with no feelings of faith, or if she was furiously angry and bitterly disappointed – we are not told. She was allowed to have the time she needed. Mary disappearing from the scene did not traumatise God. There is no hint of condemnation for her silence and lack of excitement about what God was doing at that stage in life. Her silence and absence did not mean that she had lost faith. God did not ask Mary to respond to him with another resounding 'yes' for the record in these circumstances. God simply blessed her sleep and waited for the moment when she was able to receive him again to refresh her. God's loving hands are always in the dark and painful silence. They may not be recognised or felt, but they are ever present and embracing his suffering children.

We hear nothing about Mary until after the resurrection, when her name appears among those believers gathered in the upper room. After passing through desperate dark days, Mary is again one of the faithful followers of God. We don't know how God ministered to her. Maybe nothing happened for some days until Jesus met her after being raised. But we do know that just as Mary was raised up, so God will come to us and bring us out of the cave into a new beginning. Once again we see Mary praying and praising and waiting expectantly for God's next promised act, still saying, 'yes'. For although Mary's soul was pierced she never withdrew her original 'yes' to God. She encourages us to trust through every dark circumstance of death, doubt and despair. Sometimes circumstances are so overwhelming that we cannot respond in faith to God – we feel lost. However, we are not lost. The Father who helplessly suffered watching his son Jesus Christ die a victim's death knows what pain can do. He knows how much we can take and he allows the body and mind to withdraw and take the time it needs to heal a wound. Faith takes similar journeys and can sometimes diminish to nothing but a painful question. God waits until we are able to respond again and then we will hear his voice. This is the wonderful message of the resurrection: there is a resurrection of new faith and strength promised for us in every tomorrow, so hope always comes anew with every sunrise.

It is so encouraging to discover the dark days of our faith

heroes. It demythologises them, making them people just like us. In the end we all stand before our Father, just like Francis – all on the same journey. There is nothing God requires from us, nothing we can bring him or do for him or even take pride in knowing the truth about him or in having special visions from him. We simply need to trust him, even when we don't know what on earth he is doing in our lives. This is the exercising of real faith. The prophet Isaiah was given an inkling of the strange ways of God in the great passage, 'Lead out those who have eyes but are blind. "You are my witnesses," says the Lord, "and my servant whom I have chosen."' We get excited about the call and expect the end of the passage to read 'to bring the lost to know and believe in God', but it concludes with a shock – 'that *you* may know and believe me.'[17] Surely God's chosen witnesses know him and believe him? What's God's point in relying on fragile unsure people to be his ambassadors?

One reason is that God is the one who works in a person's heart. This means we do not have the job of convincing people. We do not have to worry about finding just the right words or the right method to be successful witnesses. If a person responds to the light of God reflected through our words and deeds then the glory is God's. We cannot claim success. In fact we should question whether we should ever aspire to this type of success. At Peter's confession that Jesus was the Christ, Jesus said 'You are blessed Peter, for you did not get that answer out of books or from teachers, God himself let you in on the secret.'[18] People are blessed when they make their own discovery of Christ. We can take this blessing away when we stop being God's witnesses and become his lawyers. How impoverished people are to answer Jesus' question, 'I believe because someone successfully convinced me with the steps of salvation.' Did the Father reveal anything to them? Do they know the Christ revealed personally by the Father, or have they accepted a bunch of theological statements? God wants to reveal himself to every individual in a personal way.

Another important reason that God chooses us to be his representatives is because God is just as interested in working in us as through us. By allowing us to go through the ups and downs of the life of faith we will eventually realise how we limit God by our dogmas and experiences and be stripped of them all in order to come to know God – just God as God is. The journey of faith is crucially important to God. However, we want to rush through the journey in order to get to the end, believing the end is what counts. Jesus reminded us that what counts is today and how I am trusting in God on the journey. But trusting and having faith does not mean everything is OK. It can mean in spite of shouting at God about my painful doubts and fears and agonising questions I am still hanging on to God until the shaft of light penetrates my cave.

Francis' spiritual experience birthed a new kind of religious order. Up to the thirteenth century in the West there were predominately two forms of religious life: the Monastic, established on the Rule of Benedicts, and the Canonical, based on the Rule of Augustine. These orders were based on stability and the important place given to liturgical worship. This marked them off from the mendicant order of Francis. Francis saw his call in terms of an apostolic ministry that requires mobility to go where the needs are most pressing and therefore giving up certain forms of liturgical worship. Francis' commitment to apostolic works and his beliefs on brotherhood versus hierarchy curtailed him and his eleven followers from joining the existing Orders. So in 1209 Francis went to Rome to Pope Innocent III and gained approval for his Order. It was the first Order to include in its rule a chapter dealing with foreign missions. As a form of protest at the contemporary practices of the Church, Francis never accepted ordination but remained a deacon all his life. In spite of this the Pope authorised Francis to preach in the Church, along with authorising the Order's apostolic manner of life, poverty and preaching of penance. 'Without a word of criticism of the Church or state of which he was a part, Francis opted out of the

medieval rat-race and cut right across the system of feudal privilege creating in its place a brotherhood, founded on simplicity
and poverty, where individuals could be themselves in their
dignity and uniqueness and at the same time belong to something greater than themselves which guarded their dignity and
fostered their uniqueness. There is never a word of criticism from
him of the medieval Church, never a word of condemnation of
its officials. Nevertheless everything he stood for from the
moment of his conversion was in open contradiction to the scan-
dalous worldliness of the medieval Church.'[19]

Francis remained totally loyal to the Catholic Church through
many struggles over his life. His relationship with the Church's
leaders typified his relationship with every other human being.
He looked for what is good in man, found it and emphasised it.
The heart of his vision was living out the Gospel in a literal
manner with a message of love, compassion, forgiveness and reconciliation. These are still the hallmarks of his followers, where-
ever they are found: Franciscans, Catholics, Protestants or
others. As he preached in churches his order grew, not with followers, but as Francis called them 'Brothers'. In contrast to the
medieval Church he steadfastly resisted any hierarchy within the
order, eschewed riches and power in preference for living with the
poor and welcomed women as equal workers with equal responsibility for ministering the Gospel.

Two news-making events happened in 1212. On Palm Sunday
18 March, Francis received Clare Favarone (one of the nobility)
into the Order. This dramatic event has all the makings of a soap
opera or a legend similar to Maid Marion and Robin Hood's
exploits. Clare's family was fiercely opposed to the plan and she
ran away in the night and joined Francis and his Brothers in the
forest. Francis cut off her hair, covered her with a nun's veil and
gave her a simple habit in exchange for her fine clothes. He
lodged her under the protection of the Bishop. Clare's younger
sister tried the same exploit but this time the family attempted to
forcibly drag her back home by a literal tug of war with the

maiden's body. They didn't succeed. Clare's mother later joined them (which raises very interesting speculation about what home was like), along with a number of other women, and they were given their own chapel to reside in. But the Pope won this round of events and would not break tradition and allow the women to share the life of the mendicant order. So the women spent their lives in a monastery and their days in prayer. Hence Francis' attempt to liberate women and give them equality in the Church was frustrated and women are still waiting for another Francis in the Catholic Church. Clare is the foundress of the Order of Poor Clares who live a completely cloistered life. In one of the incongruities of life, in 1958 Pope Pius XII declared Clare the universal patroness of television. That may be a warning for us to not allow the TV set to cloister us from real life!

But there is a more intriguing twist to the story of Clare and Francis. It appears they loved each other, but gave up their love for a higher cause and ideal: to serve their Master and literally follow his steps of celibacy. The records show Francis was very tempted by the eremite lifestyle and struggled with his calling wondering if he should become a hermit or a preacher. He asked Clare and his brothers to pray that God would reveal to them his calling. Clare and the brothers all brought back the same answer so he resumed his mission to the world. Although Francis practised a severe asceticism he did not show any signs of fleeing life like a hermit. In the same way he did not deny love for Clare, but this human experience that mirrors God's love for us enriched him. He did not sublimate love for Clare, but redirected its energy to include every person. The depth of their relationship is well attested to and their enjoyment of each other's company caused gossip, so Francis (in true radical form) decreed that they must not be seen together henceforth. After this they only met infrequently and with a chaperone. We can only speculate if they shared a romantic love, or the deep attraction of similar spirits. The same sort of magnetism and bond existed between St John of the Cross and St Theresa of Avila. But these vibrant male/female relationships should not surprise us. Although they all were committed to the celibate life they lived deeply in the Spirit and their lives reflected the nature of God. We are made in God's image, that is, male and female. It takes both men and women together to reflect the nature of God. So, as Francis and Clare shared their spiritual journey, the one brought the opposite dimension, and enriched and completed the other.

The other newsworthy event in 1212 was the disastrous Children's Crusade. The grisly toll of the Crusade wars continued as the stage-set for the events in Francis' life. God was forming his servant and the day was coming when Francis would know what God wanted him to do about the Crusades.

Between 1209 and 1220 the brotherhood increased rapidly. As Francis preached many responded to his vision and wanted to live the gospel life without joining holy orders. So Francis set down for these people 'in the world' a way of life which is now called the Secular Franciscans. He directed they live simply in food and dress in order to share what they save with the poor. They were not to commit any sinful action for the sake of profit over other people. And they were to work for the peace of Christ by refusing to bear arms or take the oath of fealty. In this manner Francis helped bring down the feudal system. Many thousands refused to take up the sword and lords were having a difficult time raising armies for their petty feuds.[20]

An incident in 1213 demonstrates Francis' commitment to serving the world in love and how his actions changed those he served. A group of robbers who had fallen on bad times came to the monastery begging for food. The monks turned them away. It is noteworthy that one of the monks was a former Crusader who hung up his sword in response to Francis' preaching. Francis was very upset when he returned to the monastery and discovered that his rule to never turn anyone away had been broken. He had decreed that all people be treated equally and welcomed at their door, and even specified thieves and robbers. Francis commanded the monk to go searching for the robbers and bring them back and serve them an excellent meal. And 'Then, and not until then, ask them not to kill anybody anymore. And I do not doubt that the Lord in his mercy will inspire them with better sentiments.' The robbers were found, fed, and duly converted. They promised to live by honest means and daily brought firewood for the monks. They eventually joined the Order. Francis' indiscriminate love won them to Christ.

Although local wars were decreasing the Crusades were still staggering on and the cruelty and savagery of the Fifth Crusade is well documented by Muslims and Christian chroniclers. Francis decided to try and stop the war. He 'wanted to challenge the rampart dividing the two communities each accusing each other of being the dominion of Satan. The misunderstanding between them was the size of the sea dividing them.'[21]

He sent his Brothers out into the wider world to preach the message of mercy and peace, in an age of war and retaliation. Brother Giles left for Tunisia and Elias for Syria and the first Brothers to gain the crown of martyrdom left for Morocco. We will take up their story of how they were killed in Marrakech in another chapter. Francis made two unsuccessful attempts to take his message to Muslim lands. In 1211 he tried to reach the Holy Land by sea, but ill winds turned him back. Then in 1213 he tried to reach Morocco via Spain, but illness prevented him and again he turned back. The Christian world continued waging its war against Islam, attacking its strongholds and reclaiming Muslim lands for Christ. So Francis sailed a third time – with the Crusaders in 1219. But in contrast to the Crusader knights, and the spirit of his age, he went armed only with the Gospel. He preached to the armies, both Muslims and Crusaders, in Dalmatia, Spain, France and Egypt. It is not known for certain whether he made a later trip and reached the Holy Land.

Francis' method of evangelism with Muslims was radically different from his approach in Europe. He boldly preached the Gospel everywhere he ministered in Europe. But he instructed his brothers going to Muslim lands to not preach, but simply live the Christian life in such a way as to be a positive influence. In an age when aggressive strategies and harsh Christian criticisms blocked Muslims from seeing Christ, Francis sought to direct Muslims to Christ by loving service, with few words. He instructed his Little Brothers not to preach until they had demonstrated the Gospel of love and peace and reconciliation for a lengthy period; 'Wherever you go share the Gospel, sometimes with words.' He said, 'A man is a good preacher just in as much, as he knows how to do good works faithfully and humbly.'[22] While the Crusaders marched with wieldy swords fashioned in the sign of the cross, Francis went singing hymns and speaking of Christ and peace.

The true Christian approach of his method must not be lost on us today when we live with similar antagonistic attitudes to non-Christians at large in the world. The Christian world in Francis' day regarded Muslims as our modern world regards terrorists. A Muslim contemporary with Francis who was generous and kind was described in terms of wonder that 'The savage heart of a barbarian' could be moved by the Franciscans' manner of life.[23] In both ages Muslims have been painted as the archenemy of Christianity. A Canadian concerned that Muslims are invading his country exclaimed, 'We must do all we can to stop them and convert them before the year 2000.'

There is no record that Francis held these attitudes. Francis saw people created in the image of God. His profound respect for God's presence in everything God created allowed him to treat every person with courtesy and love and he respected and honoured all people. While the Crusaders hated Muslims and tried to annihilate them, Francis attempted to love them into the special relationship he shared with Christ. The most famous event was when he went into the Muslim camp in Egypt in the autumn of 1219 to talk to the great Sultan Al Kamil about Jesus Christ. Both Arabic and English sources tell us he won the Sultan's heart. This meeting radically changed both men forever. Moreover, it appears that Francis never got over the savagery and suffering which he witnessed during the Crusade at Damiettia. The Church he belonged to and represented betrayed Christ and the Gospel. This had irreversible effects not only on Francis' preaching and relationship with Muslims, but right down to present days – in our living with them and sharing our faith with them. He returned to Europe with a wounded heart and an eye disease that plagued him for the rest of his life. The actual illnesses he suffered can also be the psychological suffering caused by things he wished he had never seen and the heartache it caused. More trials were awaiting him.

On his return he faced what was the greatest and most bitter disappointment of his whole life. Twelve years earlier his Order had been a small group of twelve. Now there were more than 5,000 and few of these had personally met Francis. The essence of the Order was changing and new friars were not committed to the ideals of Francis, of being wandering poor disciples. The Pope had always been uneasy about the Franciscan's vulnerable lifestyle. He now insisted that the brotherhood needed more organisation and control in order to survive. Rules and hierarchy were anathema to Francis and his whole vision of living out the Gospel and he angrily fought against it. The episode is recorded as a 'terrible spiritual temptation'. Did he eventually see the wisdom in the Pope's counsel or did he realise he was fighting a losing battle? It appears it was the latter. The oldest account states: 'He felt greatly disturbed, both interiorly and exteriorly, in spirit and in body, to the point of avoiding contact with the other brothers, because of his not being able, owing to the temptation, to show his usual smile. He mortified himself by not eating and not speaking. He took refuge in the forest near the church of the Portiuncula in order to pray; there he could express his pain and shed many tears before the Lord, so that the Lord, for whom all is possible, might send from heaven some relief for this malady. For more than two years, day and night, he was tormented by this temptation.'[24]

Thus he appears to have suffered a major depression. The

cardinals worked on convincing Francis to see that his evangelism and simplicity was not adequate for the new age. Francis angrily responded that the Lord wanted a humble life and the path of simplicity. Francis reiterated that he was God's 'new fool in the world'. He complained that friars were opposed to him when he was finally doing the will of God for the good of the Order. It was a battle of reason and common sense against the foolishness of living in the Spirit. He gave in to temptation and wrote a rule for the Order. His companion Brother Leo wrote: 'because he was an enemy of all scandal, he condescended, much to his regret, to the wishes of the brothers'.[25]

In those years of 1221–23 the Franciscan Order was a different order from the simple egalitarian community Francis had established. By 1220 the Order had taken its new direction; many new friars supported the new organisation and laws and Francis resigned as head of the Order. His spiritual leaders betrayed all that he believed in, worked for and built. This was the most devastating episode of his life. Only those who have had similar experiences can know how Francis felt, others can imagine the pain and frustration of defeat and betrayal. The new generation in the movement took over and institutionalised it in ways which he not only disagreed with, but also saw as a betrayal of Gospel living.

One of the most painful experiences in life is to be betrayed by those closest to us. I wonder if Francis took comfort by reminding himself Christ was betrayed by Judas and then deserted by all the disciples. 'I was wounded in the house of my beloved' poignantly scrapes our hearts like a sharp knife. Francis retreated to his old cave. He was confused, anguished, wounded and abandoned. What happened to the vision God gave him in his youth? How could God abandon him now and let his vision and Order be twisted and ruined? What would he do now at the end of his life? Maybe he was mad and misleading others? This was truly the death of his dream and vision. How could he forgive those who betrayed him? He was in the remaining years of his life when energy is sapped and blows are heavier. Would he be able to overcome this deathly blow?

What did Francis do? After such a great blow near the end of his life Francis found new strength in God. He told his closest friends (was he still too vulnerable to share his heart with others?), 'Let us begin again. For up till now we have done nothing.' Yeah Francis! How magnificent! What an example of Gospel living. I had to take time out while writing this section to complete a seventy-times seven exercise of forgiveness. To once again shed remaining old hurts of betrayal, from lost visions and frustration at past good works destroyed, from family suffering caused by others' foolishness, and last but not least forgiving self for the wrong things done and good intentions undone. I thought of others going through similar trials in their vocations: not recognised for years of faithful service, passed over for a new young executive, made redundant just before long-service benefits. This is one of the many types of suffering that is the narrow door stopping many from entering the kingdom or remaining on the kingdom road. How easy it is to remain hurt and angry and grow bitter and be lost. How difficult it is to forgive. We may find enough grace to forgive. But what about a new beginning? It takes the work of the Holy Spirit to begin again, not with gritted teeth, but with a baptism of joy and new hope. It only takes a word to ask for it. 'How gladly will your Father give the Holy Spirit to those who ask.'[26]

Francis never returned as head of the Order, but he returned to his original calling of serving lepers and living with them. He continued his attempts to bring the living Christ back to Europe in an original form. On Christmas 1223 at Greccio in the Rietti valley he built the most famous crib ever made. He ordered a wooden crib brought and hay and oxen and ass to literally recreate the manger scene. Francis preached and sang about the birth of the poor king. 'In Jesus he saw the childhood of God, which revealed to him the divine poverty. God cannot appear to us as God. [He needed to make himself] known as less than He is himself. It was not only the grown man and the Transfigured One who manifested God in the world, but also the helpless little child. Never before had God been at the mercy and the carelessness and forgetfulness of men. Francis' tender love of the Child Jesus came from his deeply maternal soul. Francis wrote in his Letter to All the Faithful: "We are mothers to him, when we enthrone him in our hearts and souls by love with a pure and sincere conscience, and give birth to him by doing good." This child brings to birth in us a tender love for the eternal God, and this love in its turn generates in us a love for everyone and everything. During the Mass one of the worshippers saw a vision of a child lying lifeless in the manger and he saw Francis rouse the child from a deep sleep. The message of the vision is that Francis made Christ live again on earth.'[27]

Francis evidenced a strong artistic feminine side.[28] This is shown in his great concern for reconciliation and harmony in relationships and in the world. He was very influenced by his mother. It was his mother who encouraged him in his spiritual calling while his father opposed him. Devotion and love to his mother was easily mirrored in loving devotion to Mary, the mother of his beloved Christ. It is significant to note that his favourite place to pray was a simple small chapel (fitting about twenty persons) dedicated to Mary. In the years after Francis' death Mary Queen of the Angels was declared the patron saint of the Franciscans. Francis allowed for Franciscan hermitage communities where no more than four persons could live a life of seclusion for prayer and where they could be joined occasionally for a short stay by others. Francis made a rule that in these communities two of these should act as 'mothers'. In the mother role this person is to be alert to the emotional needs of the members of the community, to notice when someone is ill or emotionally and spiritually suffering and bring him or her the help they need and to keep harmony among the community members. The mothers were modelled on the role of Mary of Magdalen's contemplative life and the children's role modelled on Martha's active life. They could exchange roles when they saw fit. It is no accident that many of Francis' prayers centre on ministering to personal needs, harmony and peace. One of his favourite blessings was:

> The Lord bless thee and keep thee,
> The Lord show his face to thee and have mercy on thee
> The Lord turn his countenance to thee and give thee peace.
> The Lord bless thee.[29]

Francis prayed this blessing over everybody and particularly his companion Brother Leo who was assailed with temptations. Today among Catholics this blessing is written on wallet size paper with the following exhortation:

> The faithful are advised to wear this holy blessing of saint Francis because experience teaches that it is a most efficacious remedy against all the devil's temptations, lightning, contagious diseases, heart ailments, danger at sea, snares of the enemies, storms, fire, throes of childbirth, fever, sudden death and countless other evils. It has special grace to keep in the power of God those who wear it.

It is interesting that Francis is identified with childbirth rather than a female saint. The flip side of the paper says, 'Holy name of Jesus save us'. Franciscans display this side above the doorway of their home. Friends who are sisters in the Order told me when they enter or leave they are reminded to place their trust in Jesus for salvation as they glance at the paper during the busy day of coming and going.

Francis continued to love poetry and music all through his life. He wrote the Canticle to Creation in Italian (the people's heart language and mother tongue). He had it put to music and it was always sung but the music has been lost. It was the first Christian music in the vernacular Italian in the Roman Church. When there was lack of harmony or strife in the Church Francis sent his Brothers to sing the Canticle to usher in a restoration of peace. On one occasion when Francis was feeling low he asked the Brother called 'the King of the poets' to play the sitar to cheer him. This Brother, who had been renowned for his golden verse, refused to sing answering 'I have left the world'. Legends state that during the night two angels came and played for Francis and released his spirit from the depression. The implication is that God uses the world's music to bring his blessings.

Francis was not the first person to try and radically live out the Gospel. This idea was common to many groups in the twelfth and thirteenth centuries. What was different about Francis is that he wanted to literally reproduce the life of Christ and this is what led him to such a literal understanding of the Gospel and literal re-enactments of the life of Christ. He attempted to literally model his life on Christ's. This life of identification with Christ and a particular passion to complete in his body the sufferings of Jesus led to the remarkable events in September 1224 when in Tuscany the marks of the crucifixion – the stigmata – appeared on Francis. Ever since his conversion he had desired to follow Christ and the Gospel according to the letter. Thus he re-enacted the birth at Bethlehem, Christ's forty days of fasting on an island in Lake Trasimene and on three occasions he re-enacted exactly the account of the Last Supper. In literal interpretation of the Gospel he embraced a life of total poverty. After a life spent in deep meditation on the cross and sufferings of Christ, it is not surprising that the marks of the crucifixion appeared in his body. Some biographers see this as a psychological enactment of how deeply wounded he was by the Church. He identified with Christ's betrayal and crucifixion at the hands of the religious leaders.

The stigmata is understood as the fulfilment of his first vision on the eve of going into battle and seeing the room full of knights' armour.

O valiant knight of Christ! You are armed with the weapons of your invulnerable Leader. They will mark you out and enable you to overcome all your enemies. It is for you to bear aloft the standard of the

High King, at the sight of which the rank and file of God's army take heart. And you bear nonetheless, the seal of the supreme High priest, so that everyone must regard your wounds and example as genuine. You bear the scars of the Lord Jesus in your body so that no one should dare oppose you. The very first vision you saw has now been fulfilled; it was revealed to you that you would be a captain in Christ's army and that you should bear arms which were emblazoned with the sign of the cross. At the beginning of your religious life the sight of the Crucified pierced your soul with a sword of compassionate sorrow. At the end of your life the seraph marked your body so that your bear the seal of the living God. At the outset of your religious life Christ's cross was put before you and you took it up and carried it always by living blamelessly, giving others an example to follow.[30]

Prior to receiving the stigmata Francis received an extraordinary sense of the presence of God. According to Celano he desired that 'the will of the Father in heaven might be mercifully fulfilled in him'. At significant moments of his life he always consulted the gospels three times. On this occasion each time his eye fell on the passion of Christ and he knew that he would 'enter the kingdom of God with many tribulations and with many trials and struggles'. Francis is understood as the perfect imitator of Christ. At the end of his Letter to a General Chapter he writes that through the enlightenment of the Holy Spirit 'we may be able to follow in the footsteps of Jesus Christ to the Father'.

Francis was a mystic who was deeply in love unconditionally. He paraphrased the Lord's prayer:

Thy will be done on earth as it is in heaven: that we may love thee with our whole heart by thinking of thee always, with our whole souls by longing for thee always, with our whole mind by directing all our intentions to thee and by seeking thy glory in everything and with all our strength by spending all our energies and affections of soul and body in the service of thy love alone. As we forgive those who trespass against us, And if we do not forgive perfectly, Lord, make us forgive perfectly, so that we may really love our enemies for love of you, and pray fervently to you for them, returning no one evil for evil, anxious only to serve everybody in you.[31]

Francis was now a legend and when the crowds saw him coming they knelt by the roadside and touched his sandal or habit hoping to be blessed. In vain Francis tried to dissuade them from these things, but news of the stigmata had already raised him to the platform of a saint. People heard about the stigmata and in an attempt to stop them seeing it, he kept his hands covered in his sleeves and wore sandals. Others observed the stigmata but Francis never spoke of it. In fact he never spoke about any of the most profound experiences of his life. Everyone knew Francis was close to God and they hoped his touch would bring them closer too. It is easy to imagine the reputation and honour Francis had over the world of his day when we think of a similar Franciscan spirit today – Mother Theresa. Both Francis and Mother Theresa eschewed personal glory and lived out their calling as simply and faithfully as they could. We never cease to wonder how that little nun had such a great influence by such a simple life. She simply served the poorest of the poor, just like Francis. In trying to become the least they both became one of the greatest. Our spirits recognise true spiritual greatness and so both found people flocking to join them in living out the Gospel.

Francis had treated his body so harshly that his health was broken with malaria, he was almost blind from glaucoma contracted in the Middle East, and suffered stomach, liver and spleen problems and dropsy. He was in constant and prolonged pain in all parts of his body, which left him in a state where no flesh was left and the skin clung to his body. He was so weak he could no longer walk and needed to ride a donkey while he preached. We note immediately that he chose the humble beast ridden by Christ.

In 1225 during a visit to Clare in San Damiano he was taken gravely ill for about six weeks with the painful eye disease which now left him almost totally blind. This was the last time he spent with Clare and it was a special gift of time together as she ministered to him while he lay prostrated by his illness in a shelter in the garden next to the Poor Clares' Convent. Not only was he blind, but light was so painful to his eyes that he laid all day in a darkened cell with no light penetrating – unable to tell night from day.

Although his physical suffering was severe, his greatest sufferings were spiritual. He wandered once again in his dark cave of mental agonies and believed himself damned. But eventually God broke through the darkness and after a mystical experience in which it was revealed he would be given eternal life he composed his most famous song (mentioned above) – The Canticle of Creation. This hymn of praise to the unity and beauty of creation which resounds with high notes of joy is all the more amazing when put in the context of when he wrote it. He had just been in another period of deep darkness and he was too weak from the effects of the stigmata and disease to sing it himself. He had it sung by a Brother. He wrote about things he could no longer see, but only remember. His joy was tempered by the thought of how men were greatly offending their Creator by misusing the creature world God had given them. 'For his praise, I want to compose a new hymn about the Lord's creatures, of which we make daily use, without which we cannot live, and with which the human race greatly offends its creator.'[32] Some weeks later he added the few lines on forgiveness in connection with a quarrel between the civil and church authorities which according to reports occasioned reconciliation between them.

However, between the glowing accounts, there are aspects of Francis' character which make us uncomfortable. We may not go as far as Voltaire and think him a lunatic, but he certainly was a bit crazy. He regretted not adequately caring for his body at the end of his life and apologised to it. However this act does not redeem his actions committed against it. How can you wreck your body and yet have such a high view of being created in God's image? He was strict to a fault. He would not let his

Brothers own or even touch money. On one occasion he ordered a friar who innocently touched money to place it in ass's dung with his mouth. Once he commanded the hood of a friar to be burnt because the friar visited him without his superior's permission. Another time he ordered a Brother to preach in his underwear as penance, but Francis quickly regretted his harsh instructions and went to the church, removed his outer clothes down to his underwear and joined the Brother in the pulpit. They preached on the humility and shame Christ willingly endured on earth for love of us. The story is told that the crowd who had been mocking the Brother gradually became repentant and many turned to God. So Francis both inspires us and repels us. He is both a model and an enigma; a success and a failure. But in him we see a simple human struggling with the life of obedient faith and a personality with great highs and great lows. In this we find a soul mate as well as an example.

He endured two further treatments on his eyes by having his temples and ears cauterised. Before the red hot irons seared him, in days without anaesthetic, he spoke to 'sister fire' asking her to be merciful to him. She was merciful but the treatments were unsuccessful. By late 1226 he was deathly ill and vomiting blood. All knew the end was near and Francis asked to be taken back to Assisi where he dictated his testament. When he felt sister death at the door he asked to be taken to his favourite church, the Portiuncola, and had himself lain out naked upon the naked earth. He did not want to die in a better condition than Christ. He added to the Canticle a verse on sister death. Clare was also deathly ill and was inconsolable because she thought she would not see Francis before she died. He was unable to go and could only send her a letter. 'I poor Brother Francis desire to follow until the end the poverty of our Lord Jesus Christ and of his most holy mother: I beg you, my sister, that you will never stray from this path, although in the future they will suggest something else to you.' He told the messenger 'Go and tell Lady Clare to banish all sorrow and sadness she experiences at the thought of never seeing me again. Let her know in truth that before she dies she and all her sisters will see me again and have great consolation in this.'[33]

In his last moments Francis told the Brothers, 'I have done what was mine to do. May Christ teach you to complete yours.' He laid hands on them in blessing and in true spirit of the younger radical Francis reminded them, 'The holy Gospel is more important than all the rules.'[34] The rules contingent may have had their way with his Order, but Francis had the last word and in typical fashion did it powerfully and without a word of criticism. With other notes sent and all farewells over he welcomed death as the doorway to life on 3 October 1226. The accounts picture him 'feeling so close to God that I cannot help singing'. The Brothers knelt around him in the light of a candle, singing Psalm 141 with him. It is reported that Voltaire died screaming. The lunatic Francis died singing. The Brothers took his body to San Damiano and held it up to the window of the Chapel for the cloistered Sisters of Clare to see him and the stigmata wounds. According to the accounts they were consoled in this way, although they wept bitterly and felt great pain at his loss.

Francis left his mark on the world. It seems everybody has heard of him – even if they don't know why he is famous. What is primary is his humanity and his total commitment to Jesus and the implications of this to serve the world. Francis believed that all creatures belong to God because he alone is Creator. Francis' belief in creation shaped his appreciation for the uniqueness of every person and thing and his ability to celebrate our differences. He loved and respected God in every person, whether that person was peasant, pope or pagan. As God loved the *other* as the *other* so we ought to do the same, while proclaiming Christ in our life.

Francis was filled with the love of God and totally in love with God. Therefore he had no fear of the *other*, for as the disciple whom Jesus loved most claims, 'There is no fear in love for perfect love drives out fear.'[35]

We cannot escape the hovering question: is it love or fear that drives us in our relationships with others? Is fear playing a part in our attitude to Muslims? We return to the quote at the beginning of this chapter: 'Ignorance is the breeding ground for fear.' The way to overcome fear is to defeat ignorance by acquiring knowledge either through information or better still, through a relationship by meeting the other, whether it is God or Muslims.

Notes

1 *Oeuvres Completes de Voltaire*, Tome XXXVI: Philosophie Tome 1, Paris 1829 cited in Doyle, E. (1980) *St Francis and the Song of Brotherhood*, New York: Seabury Press.

2 Francis received his call to ministry in the chapel called La Portinucula which was dedicated to Santa Maria de los Angeles. His followers gave this name to the infant city which was to become the second largest city in the USA.

3 Engelbert, O. (1965) *St Francis of Assisi*, Quincy, Illinois: Franciscan Press, p. 212.

4 Ibid., p. 215.

5 Doyle, op. cit., p. 6.

6 The troubadours were inventors of poems or rhymes, singing of knightly love and exploits. The jongleurs were not inventors but sang the songs of the troubadors. They sang of Charlemagne, the Holy Grail, Queen Guinevere and Merlin. They were the popular storytellers. *Omnibus of Sources for the Life of St Francis*, p. 17.

7 Noonan, H. & Gasnick, R. (1987) *Francis of Assisi: The Song Goes On*, Los Angeles: Franciscan Communications, p. 3.

8 The Admonitions of Francis XXVIII. Virtue should be concealed or it will be lost.

9 Mark 4:35ff.

10 John 13:30.

11 Celano's *First Life of Francis*, *Omnibus*, p. 242.

12 Ibid.

13 Ibid., p. 247.
14 Doyle, op. cit., p. 15.
15 Bonaventure's Major Life of Francis, *Omnibus*, p. 707.
16 Legend of the Three Companions, *Omnibus*, p. 904.
17 Isaiah 43:8,10.
18 Matthew 16:16.
19 Doyle, op. cit., p. 17.
20 Noonan & Gasnick, op. cit., p. 29.
21 Jeusset, G. (1996) *Recontre Sur L'Autre Rive: Francois d'Assise et les Musulmans*, Paris: Les Editions Franciscaines, chapter 2.
22 A New Fioretti 14, *Omnibus*, p. 1841.
23 Bonaventure's Major Life of Francis, *Omnibus*, Chapter IV.
24 Boff, L. (1984) *St Francis: A Model for Human Liberation*, Quezon City, Brazil, Claretian Publications, p. 140.
25 Ibid., p. 144.
26 Luke 11:13.
27 *Omnibus*, p. 96 cited in Doyle, p. 25.
28 Doyle, op. cit. p. 211.
29 Numbers 6:24–26.
30 Bonaventure's Major Life of Francis, *Omnibus*, Chapter XIII, p. 736.
31 *Omnibus*, p. 160.
32 Quote Speculum Perfectionis 100, *Omnibus*, p. 128.
33 *Omnibus*, p. 1084.
34 Celano's Second Life of Francis, *Omnibus*, p. 216.
35 1 John 4:18.

Chapter Three

TROUBLED ENCOUNTERS

You conquerors of Jerusalem, put away your swords.
The Cross was made of wood – not metal.

Ahmed Shawqi: Egyptian poet

In order to grasp the depth of the problems between the Muslim and Christian communities today, it should be helpful to review some of the encounters which influenced their relations. This is not intended to be a comprehensive survey. In a book of this size and my limitations as an historian this review will be somewhat selective and staccato, brushing over large periods of history without comment while highlighting certain events that I feel are interesting or significant. This overview is not about history so much as about broadening our view of that history.

The Rise of Islam

Islam, from its beginning, was a problem for Christian Europe. Those who believed in it were considered the barbaric enemy on the frontier.[1] The Muslim prophet Muhammed began his ministry during the decline of the Byzantine empire in the West and the Sassanid-Persian in the East. These two powers had been fighting each other for 300 years. Although the Byzantine empire was Greek in culture and Christian in religion with its base in Constantinople, it oppressed the Christian sects of the fifth

77

century flourishing in Syria and Egypt. The Syrian Assyrians and Egyptian Copts were treated as minority communities and paid a high tax, hence they had grievances. There was widespread dissension in the Christian community which was divided over theology and had lost the vitality of the faith.

A similar situation existed in the East. The state religion was Zoroastrianism and sects and its branches were fighting each other. Under the state's military dictatorship people were paying a high tax to support their leaders' affluent lifestyles. So the people of both East and West were looking for a saviour from their oppression. The time was ripe for Islam which spread like wildfire in the early years.[2]

There was no spiritual vacuum in Arabia when Muhammed began preaching. There were thousands, and even entire tribes, of Christians and Jews. Muhammed respected them and discussed their beliefs with them, both in his hometown Mecca and along the caravan routes. He was also known to have long talks with the Christian cousin of his wife Khadija.[3]

In the seventh century CE, Islam spread through the Middle East gaining ascendancy over predominantly Christian lands. The new wave of Muslim armies, then known as Saracens, invaded a large part of the Orient, that is, Syria, Jerusalem, and Egypt, and then spread into Asia Minor. The idea of the sword of Islam scything over unwilling Christian populations is not correct. Some Christians initially welcomed the Muslim armies as liberators. A Christian tribe in the Jordan sent the following message to the Muslim army as it approached:

> O Muslims, we prefer you to the Byzantines, though they are of our own faith, because you keep better faith than us and are more merciful to us and refrain from doing us an injustice and your rule over us is better than theirs, for they have robbed us of our goods and homes.[4]

On the next wave, the Muslims embarked on their conquest of the Christian lands of North Africa and Europe, beginning with

Spain. The intrepid soldier Tarek Ibn Zayyad landed at Gibraltar with 7,000 men in 711CE and burnt his boats behind his army, yelling 'The sea is behind you and the enemy is before you. There is no way ahead except the battle.' Gibraltar still bears the anglicised version of his name: Mountain of Tarek (Jebal Tarek).

Next, Sicily fell under Muslim rule and became a dependency of Tunisia. In 831CE the Muslims occupied Palermo and used it as a base to attack the mainland. They threatened Naples, Rome and Northern Italy and forced one of the popes to pay tribute for two years. The colonisation of Sicily was so successful that the tenth-century traveller Ibn Hawqal found 300 mosques in Palermo alone. There are many easily discernible Arab place names surviving today, particularly fountains. Between the eleventh and thirteenth centuries the Christians counter-attacked. The Normans, under Roger I, invaded and recaptured Messina and most of Sicily in 1061 but the Muslims remained in the outposts.[5]

The Arab advance was spectacular and covered much of the land once ruled by Rome, which included about half the Christian world. In the earliest years of Islamic rule Christians were recognised as strange bed-fellows with Muslims as they followed the earlier Scriptures and therefore were on the rightly-guided path. The Arab Christians were not required to convert to Islam, as the pagans, but treated as a subject group and paid the subject-peoples' tax. When Christians converted to Islam this deprived the Arab rulers of the discriminatory tax. However there were no rushed en masse conversions as Christians were fairly well integrated in society in the Middle East, taking an active part in all areas of life. This is evidenced by Al Akhtal, a famous Iraqi poet to the Caliph's court in Damascus during the Umayyad dynasty in the first century of Islam. He wore a large cross to his court appearances. 'At the outset the non-Catholic Christians were better off than they had been under the Byzantine rulers, for the latter had attempted to force their faith upon them. So too in the former Persian realms Christians, notably the Nestorians who were the most numerous, were better off than they were under the Zoroastrian princes.'[6] The Islamic Fathers Baghdawi, Ibn Al Arabi and Ghazzali were tolerant toward Christianity, which was considered one of the 'peoples of the book', that is, the three monotheistic religions following the revealed Scriptures: Judaism, Christianity and Islam.

However, although Christians were not subjected to outright persecution, life under Muslim rule was not easy. Their communities were not encouraged to expand and they were forbidden to build new churches. It was unusual for them to rise to prestigious positions in the community and they were forbidden from high ranking military positions. Eventually Christianity dwindled in Muslim realms. Christians in North Africa fled the Arab invasion to Italy, Spain, Greece and even Germany. This large exodus weakened the remaining national church. 'There were extensive defections to Islam. Occasionally, but only infrequently, these were accomplished by force. Some were from the conviction that Islam had a later higher revelation than Christianity. This conviction was reinforced by the military victories, they appeared to prove that Islam was under the peculiar favour of God. Many moved over from quite mundane reasons: from the worldly standpoint it was better to be identified with the ruling class.'[7]

As Christians struggled to come to grips with Islam a number of views emerged which have remained until today. The following are three views within the framework of which most views fell. The first was St John of Damascus' view which explained Islam as a punishment on Christianity for not living up to its beliefs. St John (675–749CE) was the first Christian theologian to seriously look at Islam. He served in the administration of the Umayyad Caliph in Damascus and knew Arabic. He believed Islam was a Christian heresy because it took certain truths, but denied others. Because of these denials he asserted that even the truths Islam accepts are voided and he would not consider Islam a religion in its own right. A second view was that Islam was an evil religion, a tool of Satan and an anti-Christ, with no truth or light. In the middle of these views there were those who recognised a kind of spiritual relationship.

> Occasionally the kinship was acknowledged. Pope Gregory VII wrote to the chieftain Al Nasir in Algeria (or Morocco) in 1076 saying, 'there is a charity which we owe to each other more than to other peoples, because we recognise and confess one sole God, although in different ways, and we praise and worship Him every day as creator and ruler of the world.' There may have been political reasons behind the letter as the pope did not write favourably about Islam on other occasions.[8]

The Crusades

Relations were not amicable from the Muslim side either. The Church of the Holy Sepulchre (built on the site where Jesus was believed to have been crucified) was destroyed in 1009 and reports of Muslim ill-treatment of Eastern Christians filtered back to Rome. The Eastern Byzantine Christian Empire requested help to fight the Muslim Turks. Only twenty years after Pope Gregory's hopes for a mutually charitable relationship based on recognition of mutual worship of the same God, Pope Urban II called for the First Crusade at Clermont in France on 26 November 1095. He urged the kings and leaders of Europe to 'bring back the Holy Land from the Turks who serve the evil power' and promised them 'whoever carries this holy cross to the land of milk and honey to serve the Lord in battle with infidels can consider it as a pilgrimage'. The Church also assured her flock that those who died while undertaking the enterprise were assured of heaven. With the Church proffering such wonderful hope in the midst of a bleak economic situation that offered little hope, the whole of Europe responded.[9]

Jerusalem was a central issue, with both Muslims and Christians claiming it as their holy place to be freed from foreign domination and oppression of their peoples. One of the rallying points of the Pope's call was to come to the aid of the Eastern

Christians suffering under infidels. But Jerusalem held another more important key for Christians. 'The struggle to reclaim Jerusalem from the forces of Islam was seen as part of a great eschatological plan, since Jerusalem was to be the scene of the last days.'[10] Christians could give God a helping hand by hastening the battle of Armageddon, or the return of Christ, through their activities in Jerusalem. What happens in Jerusalem today at the beginning of the third millennium still continues to inflame passions in the three monotheistic religious communities and Christians are still trying to help God work out what they believe are his plans for Jerusalem.

In June 1099 the Crusaders arrived at Jerusalem's walls and an incident occurred which was the precursor for one of the worst crimes in history. The common Christians believed that angels were fighting on their side and the poor and just would win the battle and reign peacefully over a Jerusalem flowing with riches of all kinds which had been purified forever. Thus the end justified the means. They set siege to the city for forty days during fierce summer heat intensified by a water shortage due to the water supply being poisoned.

A state of exultation overtook the Crusaders as they came close to capturing the city of their visions. The physical exhaustion, thirst and religious passion gave rise to visions, mass hysteria and a longing for purification. Both armies consisted of many simple ignorant peasants and soldiers of fortune. The Muslim soldiers on the city walls ridiculed and insulted the Crusaders' veneration for the cross and thus provided the Christians with 'proof' that Muslims were the enemies of God.

Five days later, on 15 July, the Crusader army broke through the walls and got revenge for Christ. The leaders were powerless to enforce their orders to protect citizens as the rabble (made fanatical by the preaching of a holy war) rampaged through the alleys breaking down doors of houses and mosques and killing all who fell in their path – soldiers and then men, women, children and old people. A wild two-day massacre followed in which the Crusaders, numbering about 10,000, exterminated most of the population of the city, killing nearly 40,000 people. The great majority were unarmed civilians. The Jewish community took refuge in the Synagogue but the Crusaders set it on fire and the entire Jewish community perished in the flames.

The leading knights took over the refined homes, washed themselves and went to Holy Communion served by the priests who had hidden in the churches. While the knights felt they had 'entered into paradise', two hundred yards outside men were still murdering each other blindly and savagely and wading in blood and trampling on corpses of thousands upon thousands belonging to people whose skins were somewhat darker than their own and who did not dress like Christians.

The massacre of the population of Jerusalem filled the Muslim world with horror. Islam had little idea of the real reasons for the Crusade and their chroniclers blamed it on Roger of Sicily. Pope Urban II had a clearer idea what it was all was about and in his sermon he claimed Christendom was being ruined with impious wars and the warriors had a duty to atone for their crimes by turning their weapons against God's enemies.[11]

Both Muslim and Christian armies viewed themselves as the true believers defending God's truth and the other faith as the *infidel*. Christians called for holy wars and Muslims called for Jihad. In both religions they believed they were obeying God's command and the battle was necessary to a victorious faith. Both believed it was an honour and sacred privilege to die for the defence of the faith and that martyrs would be rewarded in heaven. Urban II who was largely responsible for igniting the Crusade died before the letter announcing the news of the massacre could reach him.[12]

Eastern Christians

The Eastern Christians, whom the Crusaders ostensibly went to save, fell into the gulf between the opposing sides. The Muslims treated them with suspicion – during the siege of Jerusalem they were put out of the city. During the early Crusades, a number of Christians identified with Muslims as fellow Arabs and joined them fighting the foreign Crusader invaders. This was no doubt a knee jerk survival response. The first Crusaders, who arrived in the holy land and looked for the pagan enemy, slaughtered the national Christians whom they saw wearing Eastern dress – assuming them to be Muslim infidels.

Armed men, travelling with Peter the Hermit in Asia Minor, 'stormed a fortified village of Greek peasants and mistaking the Christian villagers for Saracens, they butchered them all with unheard of cruelty – according to Anna Commena children were spitted and roasted alive'.[13] The brutality of accounts such as this one have to be understood in the light of an event in the pre-ceeding campaigns and first contacts between Franks and Turks. The Franks found themselves struggling at war in a hostile and strange country and resorted to terror to enhance their campaign. In order to strike dread into the hearts of the enemy, a Norman commander in Tyre had a number of prisoners killed and their heads roasted on spits – encouraging the rumour that the Frankish barons fed on human flesh. This impressed the local population. However, the Archbishop of Tyre, who showed open amusement at the stratagem, seemed 'to have forgotten that a reputation of cannibalism might be considered undesirable by men claiming to be soldiers of Christ'.[14]

Meanwhile the battle for the Holy Land escalated and Salahadin retaliated, launching a holy war against the Crusaders, and recaptured Jerusalem in 1187. His campaign was far more humane and civilised than the Crusader campaigns (and a number of Eastern Christians fought alongside him), but this time he destroyed all the Christian places of worship.

'Christendom lived in a real dread of seeing the Saracens overrun Europe. The North African chieftain Nasir – [Muhammed al-Nasir Caliph of Morocco, 1199–1213CE] – who already was master of part of Spain, boasted that he would push onto Rome and "purify the church in a blood bath".[15] Pope Innocent III ordered universal prayers and called on all Christendom to take up arms. But Christendom was too busy warring within itself to respond – only the Spaniards went to war. However, they won such a decisive battle – against essentially Moroccan armies at Las Navas de Tolosa – that Europe stirred with new enthusiasm to get on with the wars and finish with the Muslim armies forever.

Richard the Lionhearted led the Third Crusade against Salahadin. Meanwhile, in the East, the Crusaders had been excommunicated by the Pope in an attempt to bring them to order for occupying themselves with commerce and the petty kingdoms they founded for their own profit.[16] In one way or another the knights sent to win back the Holy Land had proven a disappointment. Some had not found the Muslims to be the barbarians they expected. They discovered in fact that the Arabs evidenced a superior level of culture and refinement and some happily integrated into the Muslim community, much to the scandal of their contemporaries. These knights made another discovery that was forgotten over the centuries – Muslims are simply ordinary men and women. Wars raged on and after a savage battle at Acre in 1192 King Richard and Malik Al Adil – Salahadin's brother – negotiated a peace. Under these agreements Christians were allowed to visit Jerusalem as unarmed pilgrims. Salahadin died the next year aged fifty-five.

The Crusades continued taking their toll and the Fourth Crusade was a disaster for relations between the Christian East and West when the Pope sanctioned the Crusaders to sack Constantinople (the Eastern capital of Christendom) in order to pay their debts. The next incredible Crusade offensive was by children. In 1212 50,000 children responded to the call to 'go to the Cross' in what is known as 'The Children's Crusade'. All died en route, or fell into the hands of slave merchants, before ever reaching the 'Promised Land'. At approximately this stage of history, when the Christian West and Muslim East had been warring with each other for two hundred years, Francis made two aborted attempts to take the Gospel to the Muslim world. He lacked the finances for the trip, but was so desperate to reach Muslim lands that he 'trusted in God and stowed away on the ship'.

Salahadin's successor Al Adil built a fortress on Mount Tabor and a new wind of fervour arose in Europe to return to the original cause of winning back the holy places. The Pope called for a new Crusade in 1215 to be fought against Egypt. This Fifth Crusade, in kind of pathetic irony, would start at the foot of the Mount of the Transfiguration and move to Damiettia, Egypt, for the main battle. Once again Francis set out on his mission and boarded a Crusader vessel for the war front to join the battle at Damiettia. His third attempt was successful.

In 1236 Al Nasir's boast was undone and the Christians retook Spain and evicted the Muslims. In the next stage of conflict the Ottomans launched an offensive against the Balkans in the fifteenth century defeating the Serbs in Kosovo. This is another battleground which has returned to haunt us in this century. In this recent conflict in 1995, 8,000 Muslims were massacred by Bosnian Serbs in Srebrenica.

The impact of the Crusades in Europe was enormous. 'They were a movement which included nine Crusades between 1096 and 1291 and directly affected the life of almost every single person in Western Europe in one way or another for a period of around 400 years. Those who didn't go on Crusade were making enormous sacrifices to enable others to go, looking after entire families and property of those who went, paying higher taxes to support the movement, listening to stirring sermons or hearing news of successes or disasters.'[17]

There is a fascinating mural on the walls of the Wartburg Castle in Germany demonstrating the profound effects of both the Crusades and Francis' preaching in Europe. If Wartburg sounds familiar it is due to Martin Luther. He took refuge in its walls in 1521 when declared an outlaw for nailing his Ninety-five

Theses to the church door of Wittenberg. For one year he hid in Wartburg from the Pope, protected by a pseudonym and plagued by depression. During this time Luther translated the New Testament into German. Wartburg's small study is the scene of his famous inkwell story. A tour guide today will explain that Luther's remark about 'fighting Satan with ink' does not refer to throwing the inkwell at Satan, but to his translation of the Gospel and putting it into the hands of the people. But this was still to cross history's pages in Francis' day when the Wartburg was influential for other reasons. It was the seat of one of the most influential German families in the Holy Roman Empire of Frederick II (who weaves in and out of Francis' story) and the home of one princess who followed Francis and became a saint.

The walls tell the story of the Hungarian princess Elisabeth given in marriage at age four to a German prince. At fourteen she was married and living in Wartburg, devoting her life to the sick and poor and building a number of hospitals. The Crusades and Francis forged her life. The murals paint her story: Elisabeth farewells her husband on a Crusader ship that carries him to his death. She gives up the crown as a gesture of Christian humility. She leads her children out of the castle to espouse a 'life of poverty as preached by Francis of Assisi'. She ends her life serving in her own hospital. Elisabeth died aged twenty-four (five years after Francis died) and she was declared a saint four years later in 1235.

Mutual Cultural Impact

We would be focusing only on the negative aspects if we thought all the interactions between the two religious communities were violent. Woven between the battles was a mutual cultural impact and amazing vignettes of interfaith dialogue and close personal friendships, especially between the commanders of the forces. During the Middle Ages there was little information on the Arabs in the West. It was generally believed that they were few in number, concentrated in the Arabian Gulf and were ignorant marauding tribes. So when the Muslim armies conquered Spain and appeared in Europe evidencing a high civilisation, Europe was totally unprepared and shocked into a great fear. This galvanised Europe into a rush to catch up – causing a Christian leader of Cordoba in 854 to complain, 'Many of my co-religionists read the poetry and tales of the Arabs, study the writings of Muhammeden theologians and philosophers, not in order to refute them, but to learn how to express themselves in Arabic with greater correctness and elegance. Among thousands of us there is hardly one who can write a passable Latin letter to a friend, but innumerable are those who can express themselves in Arabic and compose poetry in that language with greater art than the Arabs themselves.'[18]

At about the same time the Archbishop of Seville deemed it necessary to translate and annotate the Bible in Arabic, not for missionary purposes but for his own community.[19] At the end of the tenth century some scholars in the West were interested in the Arab sciences and Pope Herbert Al Catalooni (999–1003CE) translated many writings of the Arab thinkers into Latin. When Spain was retaken by Christians in 1085, Toledo was the stage for an integration of Muslim and Western cultures. 'Toledo became the first great city for the transmission of Muslim ideas to the West. Christians from many countries came to study with the native Spaniards under Arabic speaking Muslim and Jewish teachers and translated many books from Arabic into Latin. A great part of the legacy of Ancient Greece became known to the West in the Arabic translations found in Spain. Thus Spain and Sicily became the channel for Islamic culture and opened the way for the renaissance to Western theologians in the 13th century.'[20] During this time many scholars were translated into both Latin and Arabic and thus Arab intellectuals and philosophers, such as Ibn Sina (Avicenne), Al Razzi, Kendi, Firaabi, Ibn Rushd (Known as Averroes), were translated into Latin.

Sicily is a striking example of this period. The Christian

Normans in Sicily adapted themselves to Arab culture. They looked and dressed like Muslims and spoke Arabic. The ruler Roger II (1130–1154CE) was known as 'the Pagan' because he favoured Muslims. He used Arab troops and engineers in his campaigns and Arab architects for his buildings. His coronation crown bears an Arabic inscription. He also maintained the Arabic tradition of a court poet as eulogist. A later Muslim anthologist has preserved fragments of Arabic poems to this king and condemns writers for demeaning themselves by eulogising 'infidels'. At Roger's court, Idrisi, the greatest Arab geographer, wrote his compendium of geography and dedicated it to the Norman king. It is known as 'The Book of Roger'. Latin gradually replaced Arabic but Arabic culture 'survived and flourished under Frederick II (1215–1250CE) strengthened by his extensive dealings with the Muslim Orient'. Frederick established a Sicilian colony on the mainland and in 1266 signs of Arab influence were still evident: the Christians prayed five times a day following the Muslim tradition for times of prayer. This practice is also said to have its roots in the Eastern Church's tradition of praying seven times a day.[21]

The West's View of Islam

In general the Western Christians' attitude to Islam was intolerant and their usual purpose in studying Islam was to gain knowledge to overcome it. The West was influenced by the philosophy of Ibn Rushd and nicknamed him 'The Great Explainer'. 'Rushd asserted the thinker's right to submit everything, except supernaturalism, to the force of reason.'[22] 'It is acknowledged that the intellectual movement initiated by Ibn Rushd continued to be a living factor in European thought until the birth of modern experimental science.'[23] Raymon Lull was Bishop of Toledo in 1026, the year Ibn Rushd was born. Lull was also a Christian missionary to Islam. He founded an institute to translate Arabic sources into English, ran the first school for preaching to the

Arabs and instituted the study of the Arabic language in Europe. We should note that all this happened under Muslim occupation before 1085 (when the Christians recaptured Toledo). However, there were many Christian thinkers against Rushd and some years later there was a reaction among the Christian intellectuals, including Raymon Lull, and finally Thomas Aquinas. Rushd ended up being named 'The Cursed Arab'.

During the twelfth century, Western thinking continued to be influenced by Augustine – intertwined with the influence of the Arab Muslim philosophers. Four schools of theology were established which were influenced by Greek and Arab philosophy, some with more interest in Islam than others. The foremost was Franciscan-Augustinian: a combination of Augustine and Ibn Rushd. The second school was Dominican-Aristotelian. The leader of this movement was the Dominican, Thomas Aquinas. Aristotle was translated through the intermediary of Arab-Jewish philosophy, (particularly Ibn Rushd of Spain) and became the most popular philosopher despite Church bans on reading him. Through Aristotle there was a tremendous expansion of knowledge for European scholars in the fields of the natural sciences, medicine, anthropology and metaphysics. Thomas Aquinas was concerned with reconciling the Christian faith with Aristotle and was a prolific writer. Aquinas was involved in the challenge of Islam and 'always had the works of the great Muslim philosophers on his desk. However, he did not know any Muslims personally nor engage in personal dialogue with any of them. He did not know Islam from the Quran itself, which had been translated by the Abbot of Cluny into Latin. Aquinas had a rudimentary knowledge of Islam and had no access to the self-understanding of Muslims. The Franciscans attempted to influence the Muslims by simple preaching and practical example, whereas at a very early stage the Dominicans engaged in intellectual argument with them.'[24] The third school combined Ibn Rushd and the Latin, Al Brabant, who was also condemned by the Church. The fourth was the Oxford school espoused by Roger Bacon who studied Arab scientists, particularly natural sciences, and philosophy and meditation. Bacon becomes more interesting, and somewhat enigmatic, when we look later at his interest in the Muslim mystics and their influence on him. So there were two stages in the Middle Ages' attitude to Islam. The first was to learn from Islam because it was strong and the second was to fight it as an enemy ideology. These two attitudes are evidenced in the change of attitude to Ibn Rushd.[25] Between the sixteenth and eighteenth centuries awareness of Islam increased in Europe as a new type of political relationship appeared with European states growing closer to the Muslim world through consuls in the Ottoman empire. The development of European science and medicine made what was written in Arabic less important to the West. But still the same spectrum of attitudes existed.

'At one end there was a total rejection of Islam as a religion. Pascal entitled the seventeenth of his Pensées (*Thoughts*) "against Muhammed". Christ is everything, he asserted, which Muhammed is not . . . "any man could do what Muhammed has done none could do what Jesus Christ has done". Muhammed took the path of human success. Christ died for humanity.'[26] As time went on there was less denigration of Muhammed as a man and a greater recognition of his extraordinary achievements, but not as a prophet.

These were the centuries of Western imperialism in the Muslim world and all kinds of strategies were used to spread Western domination. One of the most amazing is Napoleon's effort to convince the Egyptians that he was not their enemy and did not plan to abolish their religion. In his speech he claimed that the 'French are true Muslims . . . and I more than the Mamlukes serve God – may He be praised and exalted – and revere His prophet Muhammed and the glorious Quran.' He further pushed his claim by telling them 'in confirmation of this [the French] invaded Rome and destroyed there the Papal See, which was always exhorting the Christians to make war with

Islam. And then they went to the island of Malta, from where they expelled the knights, who claimed that God, the Exalted, required them to fight the Muslims.' This proclamation written in Quranic Arabic began, 'In the Name of God the Merciful, the Compassionate. There is no god but God. He has no son, nor has he an associate in His dominion.'[27]

His strategy worked and the population quickly lost its distrust of the colonisers, but the more astute chronicler was not impressed. He writes that as to Napoleon's serving God more than the Muslim Mamluke rulers, 'This is a derangement of his mind . . . [And the rest of the statement] is a lie. As for his statement that he destroyed the Papal See, by this deed they have gone against the Christians. So these people are opposed to both Christians and Muslims, and do not hold fast to any religion. You see they are materialists, who deny all God's attributes, the Hereafter and the Resurrection and who reject prophethood and Messengership. They believe the world was not created . . . and that nations appear and states decline according to the nature of the conjunctions and the aspects of the moon.'[28]

Muslim View of the West

Over on the other side the Muslims relied on the Quran and Sunna (traditions of Muhammed) and did not seriously consider other religions or make serious attempts to understand them. Christians have charged Muslims over the centuries with not understanding anything about Christianity, because Muslim theologians have tended to take their knowledge of Christianity from the Quran. This is still happening today and more than one sheikh has admitted to us that he is teaching Christianity from the Quran and has never read the New Testament.

Muslims believe Christianity left the truth and follows a false Gospel and they are certain they understand Christianity better than the Christians, as Muhammed brought new revelation to the teaching of Christ. A verse in the Quran stating that

Christians changed the meaning of the Scriptures has gained popular acceptance that it means Christians have falsified their written Scriptures. However, some Muslim theologians posit that it really referred to the incidents when Christians and Jews deliberately misled Muhammed in order to limit his power, and does not state that our Scriptures are falsified. This version of the problem suggests Muhammed's relationships with the Christians and Jews began amicably as long as he appeared to be a searcher who would join them. When this did not happen, the Christians and Jews tried to limit his influence by deliberately concealing the truths of the Scriptures. The Scriptures were foreign languages to Muhammed and he was not able to read them for himself, so when he asked what their books taught they changed the meaning in their verbal explanations.

In the Middle Ages there were some Muslim theologians who wrote about comparative religions and different schools of Islam: Abu Al Hassan Al Ashari, Ibn Hazem Al Andalouci, Abu Mansour Al Bagdadi. However, Muslim theology became increasingly anti-Christian during the years of conflict. Muslims were not innocent bystanders in the carnage of the Crusade wars. In the mosques the call to prayer and worship, 'In the Name of God the compassionate and merciful', was replaced with passionate calls to forget mercy and obliterate the Christian infidels. In one incident the motley band known as the 'People's Crusade', mainly peasants with a few experienced knights among them, refused to listen to the knights and set out to recapture Nicea. The Sultan Arslan had been warned and 'they fell on the group of pilgrims, only a quarter of whom, if not less, were men able to fight. The result was a fearful massacre. Out of the thirty or forty thousand only about two thousand survived. On this occasion the Turks did not sort out able bodied men and women for slaves. All the historians describe it as a straightforward massacre.'[29]

In spite of Napoleon's astounding claim, Christianity did not usually deal with Islam in a sensitive way. Muslims are chagrined that the West did not recognise the Arabs' past great civilisation.

It was only recognised in relation to providing the West with the teachings of the Greek philosophers, not for its own sake. The Muslims encountered the Christian West as a hostile enemy. The bloody images of the Crusades and a militant Christianity continued to be presented in Muslim countries through the Western colonisation of Islamic lands over the last centuries. When France took Algeria in 1838, the Bishop of Paris said it was a 'victory of Christianity over Islam'.[30] During Algeria's war of liberation from France (1954-62) the Bishop of Algiers, De Valleint, thought it necessary to condemn those who were claiming it was a religious war.[31] The Muslim world sees the Church today as the same group that fought the Crusades, so Muslims scrutinise Christianity's attempts to evangelise the Arab region for any signs of the old Crusade mentality of hostility or antagonism.

I have found that Muslims who are genuinely perplexed by Christianity's antagonism toward Islam often lack appreciation for how deeply their repudiation of the heart of our faith strikes. When someone tells me that my own side falsified my Scriptures and that Christ did not die, that person has attacked the very core of my religious experience and what I believe to be eternal truth. Although I try to discuss this on an academic level, I do feel attacked and become defensive. Muslims are no different in the way they experience perceived attacks on their beliefs. They often describe Christianity in terms of our acceptance, or lack of acceptance, of their religious experience.

The following descriptions of renowned Christians and their relationships with Islam is taken from a moderate Arab Muslim publication.

Martin Luther: When Luther saw the Turks take Vienna in 1529 he declared it was a punishment from God on Christians for not living a holy Christian life. He spoke of the Turks, the Pope and Satan as the three enemies of God. It seems Luther had pre-conceived ideas about Islam and judged according to them. On the other hand he encouraged the printing of the Quran in Latin saying, 'I would love to read the Quran'. Calvin followed Luther but was less favourable to Islam. Henry Martin, the missionary to Persia, put all his efforts into defeating Islam. The first significant change in attitude in the Protestant Church came with William Temple Gairdener (an Anglican) who believed Islam prepared the path for the Gospel especially in the Sufi tradition. Samuel Zwemer, the founder of the magazine *The Muslim World*, left aside the controversy but continued to maintain that the Christian faith is superior to Islam. (However) he admitted Muhammed's genius. In the 19th century Muhammed and Islam became interesting to Europe and scholars such as Johann Goethe of Germany, Richard Forster (an Anglican minister), Alfonse Lemartine of France and Thomas Carlyle of Scotland, brought more positive approaches. Montgomery Watt, a Scottish Bishop and lecturer of the University of Edinburgh, was a specialist and undertook a serious study of the life of Muhammed and the progression of Islamic thought. He remained neutral and did not enter into the theological controversies. He had a positive influence on Christians in their relationships with Muslims.

Vladimir Solovyov (Russian Christian philosopher) influenced the West in the latter half of the 19th century and was interested in Muslim Christian dialogue. He saw that in the historical battle between the two religions one basic problem was the East's special tradition relating to the eternal valley between God and man: Muslims could not accept the idea that God became a human. He believed that Muhammed completed God's promise to Ishmael in Genesis 21:17. He considered Muhammed's teaching not complete, but not deceiving either.

Louis Massignon stirred the old pre-suppositions of the Catholic Church towards Islam. Massignon was a friend of the orientalist Charles de Foucald (1858–1916). Foucald, a French soldier, visited parts of the Arab world and subsequently became a monk living in the Algerian desert among the Tuareg. Massignon was also friends with the philosopher Jacques Maritain and the mystic poet-diplomat Paul Claudel. These people from various walks of life had one common experience in their spiritual life (mysticism) and all greatly influenced Massignon. He visited Algeria in 1904 and caught a life-long interest in the Arab world. On a later visit to Iraq he became interested in Al Hallaj which challenged his whole spiritual walk. He wrote, 'All my life I want to follow his example' and dedicated his life to studying him and writing two volumes, *The Passion of al Hallaj*. Massignon's studies prepared the road for the Catholic church to change its thinking about Islam. Muhammed Talibi (Tunisian writer) notes Massignon is very dedicated in his Christian belief, but also had compassion for Islam saying he is different from all the western writers against Islam. He takes the other side in trying to bring both religions together in understanding. Massignon was afraid the two civilisations of Islam and Christianity would eventually meet in a violent clash if they continued on the same path of ignorance and fear of the other. He believed Europe was responsible for destroying much in Muslim culture and needed to engage to raise it up again. He did not see Islam as a Christian sect (an idea popularised among Protestants at the time) but as an independent religion in its own right and blessed by God.

Kenneth Cragg is to Protestants what Massignon is to Catholics. He is accepting of different views. In his book *The Call of the Minaret* he explains the value of the Islamic experience of God. He has a positive attitude to Muslims and tells Christians to remove their shoes when they enter a mosque in order to hear God. So Protestants played a major role in knowledge of Islam in the West.[32]

Although Luther was not sympathetic to Islam there are similarities between his mission and Muhammed's mission – they fought for the same renewal of faith. They both believed the practising Church had left the original purity of faith and allowed idolatry and worship of Mary and intermediaries to come between God and man and they preached reform. Luther saw a Church without the Holy Scripture in her mother tongue and struggled for it.[33] Muhammed saw a people group who lacked a Holy Scripture in their tongue. The Jews had their Hebrew Scriptures and the Christians had their Scriptures in their languages. When Muhammed gave the Quran to the people he proclaimed, 'At last we have an Arabic scripture.' The Quran included the Jewish and Christian teachings he received through oral transmission from both communities, including those views on the nature of Christ which were not accepted by the Western Church. So Muhammed appears to believe the message was in the same tradition as the

Jewish and Christian Scriptures. The Quranic passage referring
to this includes interpretations in parenthesis, 'Truly, it is the revelation of the Lord of all being, brought down by the Faithful
Spirit upon thy heart (Muhammed), that thou may be one of the
warners (title of messengers/prophets of God's message), in a
clear Arabic tongue. Truly it (Quran) is in the Scriptures (The
Bible) of the ancients. Was it not a sign for them, that is known
to the learned of the children of Israel? (knew it was true). If We
(God) had revealed it to any of the non-Arabs and he had recited
it to them, they would not have believed in it (for lack of understanding its language).'[34]

The Arabs could now hold their heads high. They were just as
esteemed by God as other groups with God's message in their
mother tongue. Fouad Accad, a Lebanese minister and scholar
who knew ancient Hebrew, Greek, Syriac, Aramaic, Armenian
and Arabic, and who spent his entire life ministering to Muslims,
wrote the foregoing comments on the Quranic text and writes,
'As I've studied the Quran for thirty years, I've found it overwhelmingly pro-Christ, pro-Christian, and pro-Bible.'[35]

For most of the Middle Ages and during the early part of the
renaissance in Europe, Islam was believed to be a demonic religion of apostasy and blasphemy. Alongside this view, 'for hundreds of years great Islamic armies and navies threatened
Europe, destroyed its outposts, colonised its domains. Even
when the world of Islam entered a period of decline and Europe
ascendancy, fear of "mohamadenism" persisted. The great civilisations of the East – India and China among them – could be
thought of as defeated and hence not a constant worry. Only
Islam seemed never to have submitted completely to the West.'[36]

Our ideas of Islam today are probably shaped more than we
realise by a heritage from the Middle Ages when Muslims were
seen as fearsome barbarian infidels. However, there was one discovery some of the crusading Christians made which is being
obscured today – the discovery of good, and God, in the enemy's
heart.

Notes

1 Hourani, A. (1992) *Islam in European Thought*, New York and Melbourne: Cambridge University Press, p. 7.
2 Attiyah, E. (1972) *Al Arab*, Beirut.
3 Accad, F. (1997) *Building Bridges*, Colorado: NavPress Publishing, p. 39.
4 Chapman, C. (1998) *Islam and the West*, Cumbria, UK: Paternoster Press, p. 41.
5 Lewis, B. (1966) *The Arabs in History*, New York: Harper & Row, p. 118.
6 Latourette, K. S. (1975) *A History of Christianity*, Volume 1, New York: Harper & Row, p. 289.
7 Ibid.
8 Migne, J. P. (ed.) (1853) *Patrologia Latina* Volume CXLVII, Paris, cited in Hourani, pp. 450–452.
9 Attiyah, E., op. cit. p. 35.
10 Chapman, C. (1998) *The Faith to Faith Newsletter*, 1 November 1998. Trinity College, Bristol.
11 Oldenbourg, Z. (1966) *The Crusades*, New York and Toronto: Random House, p. 112, 122–41, 583; Orion Books, London; Editions Gallimard, Paris.
12 Ibid., p. 142.
13 Ibid., p. 85.
14 Ibid., p. 113.
15 Engelbert, O. (1965) *St Francis of Assisi*, Quincy, Illinois: Franciscan Press, p. 125. Used with permission.
16 Ibid.
17 Chapman, op. cit.
18 Lewis, op. cit., p. 123.
19 Ibid., p. 124.
20 Jourevski, op. cit., p. 51.
21 Lewis, op. cit., p. 120.
22 Shah, I. (1964) *The Sufis*, New York: Doubleday, p. 267.

23 Hitti, P. (1974) *History of the Arabs*, New York: St Martin's Press, p. 584.
24 Küng, H. (1994) *Great Christian Thinkers*, London: SCM Press, p. 123.
25 Jourevski, op. cit., p. 58.
26 Hourani, op. cit., p. 11.
27 *Al Jabarti's Chronicle: Napoleon in Egypt*, Weiner, M. (1993), Princeton University Press.
28 Ibid., p. 32.
29 Oldenbourg, op. cit., p. 85.
30 Jourevski, op. cit., p. 37.
31 Ibid.
32 Passait, Jean *Al Ijtihaad* Issue 31–32 (1996), Beirut: Al Falah Publishers, pp. 54–8, The Protestant View of Islam.
33 Hamra, V. (1997) Einsichten Und Erfahrungen Zum Thema, 'Islam', *Studien-Ergebnisse*, September-November 1997, Berlin. Unpublished paper used with permission.
34 Sura 26:192–199 Interpretation by Accad, F. (1997) *Building Bridges*. Colorado: NavPress Publishing, p. 10. (Used by permission. All rights reserved.)
35 Accad, op. cit., p. 10.
36 Said, E. W. (1981) *Covering Islam*, New York: Vintage Books, p. 9. Reprinted by permission of Pantheon Books, a division of Random House Inc.

Chapter Four

THE PROBLEM OF PALESTINE

'We'd love to join you in prayer for Palestine. But why in a church? Western Christians don't love Palestinians. You are against them.' We realised how badly tarnished Christianity's reputation was when a number of Muslims made this comment. Just as Palestine was the heart of the matter during the Crusades, it is a central issue today for the Arab and Muslim world. The way the modern state of Israel was established with the help of the Western powers and supported by branches of the Western Church is perceived to be a continuation of the old Crusade against the Muslim world.

We were living in Tunis and had invited the Tunisian and expatriate community to join us in prayer at St George's Anglican Church which was hosting the Women's World Day of Prayer for Palestine on 27 March 1994. The PLO was still in Tunis operating as a government in exile, so I invited Mrs Arafat to represent Palestinian Christians and liaised with Muslim and Christian Palestinian women to present a cultural display. This was one opportunity where we could show some rare public Christian support for a comprehensive peace that included the Palestinian people. The night was a wonderful success and a unique experience. The church was filled leaving standing room only, even though it was in Ramadan soon after the evening meal, which breaks the fast. Every continent was represented and many faiths and ideologies – Protestant and Catholic and Orthodox Christians, Muslims, Marxists, atheists.

Mrs Arafat arrived with her entourage, including a press agent from Paris and a journalist writing an article on her for the New Yorker magazine who was under the wrong impression that I had organised the service. Our prayer night took on political significance earlier that week when the Jewish settler Baruch Goldstein massacred twenty-nine Muslim men and boys at prayer in the Hebron mosque and Muslim extremists retaliated by killing Christians at prayer in a church in Lebanon. The incidents demonstrated the popular Muslim belief that Christians and Jews are in the same camp against Muslims – killing Christians was the same as getting revenge on a militant Jewish settler. President Arafat's office called to ensure that we included all sides in our prayers and we assured them that that was planned from the very conception of the night. We decorated the church with paintings by a Muslim artist of the Muslim and Christian Holy Places in Jerusalem – which he painted from memory because Israel would not allow him to enter his hometown. When worshippers entered the church they came face to face with the painting of the Dome of the Rock above the baptistry.

It became apparent that Mrs Arafat's entourage expected me to host her, so I found myself sitting next to her in the front row. She was visibly affected during the service and thanked me a number of times. But it was when we were singing an Arabic praise song and she was warmly grasping my hand in hers that it suddenly struck me. I had maligned God. I heard what God was telling me during this event: 'So you think I didn't hear or care about your prayers for Palestine. Who is thanking you now?'

Ten years before I thought God did not hear my prayers (or anyone else's) for the Palestinian people. It was hopeless to cry to God for justice and their situation was so discouraging that it was too heavy a burden to keep carrying. Added to this, our hopes to adopt a Palestinian baby girl also came to nothing and added weight to my conclusion. Prayers for Palestinians seemed to disappear between earth and heaven like incense dispersing into the air. When the streets of the Sabra and Shattilla[1] refugee camps ran with Palestinians' blood, including many babies, I stopped bothering God. Over the years we found ways to help by writing and speaking in churches, supporting children and aid organisations, but it seemed so little. It also seemed this was my project, because God didn't care.

In the prayer night in 1994 I suddenly realised that while I was stonily ignoring God, God was engineering the events of my life leading to this and subsequent similar events. I am a very ordinary person. Why else would I find myself with Suha Arafat hand in hand calling on God's mercy, and she thanking me for caring? God was showing me he hears prayers even if we do not see the answer, or understand it when it comes. Incredible as it seems, my disappointment in God was important enough for God to give me friendships with the Palestinian secular and religious leadership in order to set the record straight. This was one of the reasons God needed me in Tunis, not Cairo. On another occasion at a dinner in their home, President Arafat also thanked me. And a Palestinian Christian leader, Elias Chacour, helped us understand how I unfairly closed the door on God explaining, 'It's not that we are more compassionate than God and try to interest God in our burdens. God shares his pain for the world with his people so that they can take it up and carry it. Burdens like this are a gift. It's the fellowship of Christ's sufferings. Your prayers and others' prayers are ministered to us by the Holy Spirit. We receive strength to go on because people we may never meet pray for us.'

It didn't answer why God would single me out for a special answer and not help millions of suffering Palestinians, or rescue millions of Jews from past persecution, or other people in terrible suffering, but it was a turning point in my life that allowed me to turn back to God with my questions, anger and pain and not walk away. God was not answering the enormous question of why he does not act to eradicate injustice and suffering now in this life, but reassuring me that he not only hears prayers and mends broken hearts when given the chance, but is compassion. God actually addressed that question in the death of Christ on the cross. God cared enough about our pain to enter human life and suffer and die with us. The Scripture tells us, 'He did not deal with the problem as something remote and unimportant. In his Son, he personally took on the human condition, entered the disordered mess of struggling humanity in order to set it right once and for all.'[2] Our problem is living in the interim between the cross and the final deliverance day – living in the gap between the promise and the daily reality. 'Is that grounds for complaining that God is unfair? God told Moses, "I am in charge of mercy. I'm in charge of compassion". Compassion does not originate in our bleeding hearts or moral sweat, but in God's mercy. God has the first word initiating the action.'[3] King David understood this when centuries ago he said to God, 'You have kept track of each tear and each ache.'[4] God embraced my anger with his grace and this called for my gratitude. How could I refuse God's overtures for our reconciliation because I didn't understand what he was doing in someone else's life?

I first met Suha Arafat when we were arranging Elias Chacour's visa to Tunisia under the auspices of the PLO. It wasn't until we were being greeted by three women in her office that I realised I had no idea what she looked like and had not thought to find out! Finally we were left alone with one woman who by process of elimination must have been the President's wife. Suha Arafat's genuine warmth is disarming. She refused to be waited on and served us Arabic coffee herself. She refused to answer the continually ringing telephone in the old Arab tradition of honouring the person in your presence. We discussed the problems facing the Palestinian Christian community and she suggested Mazhar form a committee. She had not seen Mazhar's one piece of artwork in his office which states 'For God so loved the world he did not send a committee.' The committee idea was scratched.

The prayer night occurred before Chacour's visit and, in the interim, I met Mrs Arafat on a number of other social occasions. She threw her total support behind us for the Chacour tour and attended many of his public functions. It was a very hectic week with the PLO offices telephoning routinely after midnight for business. It was common knowledge their staff turned night into day for security measures and Mr Arafat often didn't sleep. They used a number of different houses and sometimes Suha didn't know where she would be whisked to meet her husband. During that week the Old Testament story of Esther kept coming to mind and her close parallel with Mrs Arafat. God's people were threatened with annihilation by a hostile foreign state. God brought one of his servants from the minority faith into the political arena of power 'for such a time as this'. She married the ruler and was in place to help her people and she was called to act in courage. One of the reasons Esther succeeded is that she had in her uncle a wise counsellor with no political or other motives. He did not want to exploit her for a private political agenda and she could trust his advice. Secondly, God's people prayed and fasted for her. The Arafats were preparing to return to Palestine and I decided to hold a private dinner where we could give Mrs Arafat time to talk about these things with Father Chacour. Mrs Arafat insisted on sending food also. I wondered if she thought I couldn't cook, but one friend told me she always sends food because her entourage follows her and unexpected guests could turn up and she does not want the hostess to be embarrassed by lack of food. That was just what I didn't want – unexpected guests making quiet talk impossible! The day of the dinner her security staff checked out our house and delivered enough food dishes to last us for a week – unless a great number of uninvited guests arrived. I prayed God would protect the aims of the dinner.

On the evening of the dinner her office called advising she would be late since a Bulgarian film crew were still conducting an interview with her. Another call – they requested to bring the crew and finish filming in our house. That sounded ominously like they had forgotten this dinner was not a party like the one for diplomats I had given earlier in the week. At 10 pm we answered the door to Mrs Arafat and her secretary in a flood of light from the Bulgarian delegation filming her arrival. Mazhar, Elias Chacour and I tried to look like a large crowd at the door. They finished the filming with all five of us trying to look like a busy party. Naturally we had to invite the film crew to stay for dinner and I was seeing the end of my plans for a tête-à-tête. Fortunately, they declined and left. We did have an unexpected guest join us during the evening when one of Mrs Arafat's friends tracked her down and arrived unannounced at 1am, just in time for dessert at 2 am. In spite of the erratic nature of the night it was an intimate dinner.

At one stage I was sharing how I met Mazhar and offhandedly said, 'I prayed for an Arab husband and . . .' Mrs Arafat gasped, laid her hand on mine and with wide eyes said, 'You did that!' It was such a normal part of my life I had lost contact with how unusual it must sound. Her warm and sincere personality had drawn me out and I was rambling on about my life's joys and trials and our struggle to make our home in the Arab world. Being a refugee is an experience she could empathise with. I shared with her how God was bringing the example of Esther to me and her parallel situation and she wanted to take home a Bible to read up on the story. I promised her I would mobilise Christians to support her in prayer wherever I urged Christians to pray for justice and peace for the Palestinians.

Elias Chacour mentioned we were in the process of leaving Tunisia. Hadn't she noticed the sparse furnishings and the camping chair she was sitting on? In her typical manner she exclaimed, 'Oh no, don't move far away. Come and live near us. I will provide you with a house.' I wondered if she really meant it or was just being polite. During the evening, she presented me with a parting gift of appreciation, a beautiful Palestinian hand-embroidered jacket. I wish I had kept the box. It hopefully declared it was from 'The State of Palestine'. Eighteen months later when she heard of our experience in Syria, she sent word again offering us a home in Gaza. However Suha Arafat ends her life's story, I will always remember her as a minister to me of God's comfort and encouragement.

Some months after the dinner when we were living in the USA I dreamt she was pregnant and had a baby girl. Some weeks later Mr Arafat's office announced she was pregnant. I believed God gave me that dream and I prayed through her pregnancy for her unborn baby which I believed was a daughter. I remained in contact with her personal secretary who put in an order: 'Dream a baby for me!' Unfortunately I couldn't dream them into existence at will, or I would have one myself! One morning I entered the office and colleagues called out, 'You got your girl. Mrs Arafat had a daughter.' So there was a sense in which God answered my prayers for a Palestinian baby girl.

During Chacour's visit to Tunis, Mrs Arafat invited us and the minister of St George's to dine with the President. We presented the Arafats with a pair of white doves as a parting gift for their imminent return to the homeland. Tarek, aged thirteen, was chosen for the presentation and turned out to be a great asset. He began his rehearsed Arabic speech, but as he later related with relief, 'I didn't have to finish it because Mr Arafat hugged and kissed me.'

President Arafat is known for his simple lifestyle and apologised for his modest home as we sat down to dinner around the dining table. It was situated in the stairwell on the second floor next to a refrigerator. The furniture was years out of date and well worn. I realised why Mrs Arafat did not notice our home was sparsely furnished. She pointed in one direction and laughingly commented, 'Those two rooms are ours. We share our home with the PLO offices.' I noticed some of the things she objected to in this scheme. One machine gun lay beside the President's desk and I knew others were stashed around for security. The PLO offices are filled with pictures of their former leadership, mostly assassinated by the Mossad. Mr Arafat wore his pistol on his hip. The meal was a typical feast of true Arab hospitality, with the Arafats personally serving the guests and staff. Suha Arafat proudly commented that she cooked the chicken dishes, which brought a snort from her husband, declaring (with a wink to Tarek) that she 'couldn't cook anything and never goes near the kitchen'. Some more of the same banter passed between them. I recalled Mrs Arafat's declaration to an interviewer that their relationship was a love match. When we later reached home, Tarek announced, 'They must be in love or they wouldn't tease each other like that.'

The peace doves seemed a brilliant initiative until in a meeting earlier that morning, Father Chacour (unaware of the gift-wrapped cage) likened Palestinians to birds in a cage needing freedom. It was our misfortune that Mrs Arafat not only applauded the remark, but wiped tears from her eyes. The presentation of imprisoned birds now seemed criminal and callous and the ceremony was carried out with furtive glances. The President was probably the only person who looked into the cage and saw two beautiful white doves symbolising peace and hope for Palestinians as they returned home. We saw the victimised Palestinian people whom we had incarcerated. Suha Arafat didn't show any sign of remembering the comment but, as we expected, she was unable to bear the birds in a cage and decreed their release from oppression. However, liberation wasn't so simple. The birds panicked and almost came to a violent end, causing their liberator to shriek, 'Oh poor things, don't hurt them any more!' When someone prophesied that freedom would probably result in them being massacred by militant birds she looked strained. (Why didn't we have forethought that white was the colour of martyrs?) With our gift already such a splendid encouragement, the President now pronounced they couldn't guarantee the birds' safety in Jericho because they 'could die there'. The ice age descended on the assembly while we pictured the different catastrophes that could befall the party about to return to Jericho. It was common knowledge that because of potential danger Mrs Arafat was not to accompany her husband during the first homecoming week. Glancing at our frozen faces, he hastily added with a reassuring smile, 'The weather is hot there.' Recalling Jericho's atrocious weather had a remarkably restoring effect on his wife. Wreathed in a beautiful smile, she apologetically assured us that the weather was very hot and she would hate them to die. Ready to declare the climes of Jericho absolutely hostile to every form of birdlife, we accepted them back as a gift to the church. I silently vowed to abstain from political gestures forevermore.

After dinner, as we drank coffee in the President's office (doubling as a sitting room) the relaxed atmosphere bore no resemblance to earlier meetings held there when the Palestinian National Authority (PNA) had thrashed out the Peace Signature details. Mr Arafat seated Tarek in his presidential chair behind his desk. While Tarek sat in the seat of power, the President enjoyed the moment chatting with him, and in echoes of Goldilocks, Suha exclaimed, 'Nobody ever dares to sit in that chair!' After more embraces, men to men and women to women, and some photographs we left. As we descended the stairs the President noticed a piece of bread on the floor, fallen from the table above. Bending down he picked it up and asked an aide to return it to the table. I have observed this custom of honouring bread as symbolic of the grace of God among all Arabs. The sight of the dishonoured bread caused him to stoop down without thinking, although he was suffering severe back pain and had been carefully sitting in straight-backed chairs all afternoon. I have also observed less important people who asked a servant to retrieve bread. The Arafats walked us to the gate to farewell us and we left – carrying the birds. Two weeks later Mr Arafat was hospitalised for exhaustion.

Later, we noted the Arafats did not settle in encircled Jericho, but the doves did come back to haunt us. Two years later we were invited to dine with them at their new home in Gaza, but were prevented from keeping the appointment. An Israeli soldier was kidnapped by fanatics and in retaliation the Israelis sealed off the

Gaza strip and positioned tanks around the town. Mrs Arafat's office told us by phone it was not safe for us to go there. Unknown to us, the other PLO office in Gaza sent a car to the checkpoint to wait for us. While they waited we drove back to Jordan. As we passed the road to Gaza the taxi driver lamented, 'They are shut up like birds in a cage.'

Just being Palestinian can be a problem for Palestinians no matter where they live. On the campus of an American school in an Arab country I asked a woman wearing a scarf, 'Where are you from?' Her moments of hesitation as she weighed my possible reactions to the truth told me she was Palestinian. My query put her in the same quandary all Palestinians face when confronted with such a difficult and loaded question. How could she claim to be from a country which does not exist to most Westerners and admit belonging to a people whom I probably think of as undesirables at best or terrorists at worst. We stood frozen in the interminable minute while she decided if she had enough emotional energy to answer this question which tapped into her own family's problems and a whole nation's catastrophe. I wondered if she would take the easy way out and tell me she was a national of the country that gave her a passport – like the Palestinian teens in that year's graduating class. None declared their ethnicity, all choosing to be known by their passport identity. She risked all and with the smile that all Palestinians smile when they speak of their story said, 'Well . . . I am from Palestine.' Her answer came across as a request for understanding rather than a statement. Whenever I meet Palestinians I want them to know they have one more friend than they realised. I embraced her and kissed her forehead telling her I was honoured to meet her and sorry for her history and prayed that one day God would help her people to go home. The Palestinian smile that inevitably is part of their telling their story used to perplex me. At the end of a litany of personal tragedy and family separation for generations the storyteller's lips would form that half smile and a gesture of resignation with their hand or shoulders.

Then I heard a proverb that explained it: 'Some things are so sad that you can only smile.'

She told me her name was Basima and introduced me to a group of Palestinian women who included me in their small circle and who met regularly at Suad's for afternoon tea. They were all upper class devout Muslims. They wore fashionable clothes and covered their heads with large silk scarves when outdoors. I looked forward to our afternoons together, even though I struggled to understand their accent. They were true to my general impression of Arab Muslim women – kind and considerate. For example, one day when we were discussing food I mentioned a favourite dish my in-laws made in Syria. It is excessively time-consuming. The first step is to sun-dry hot red peppers by deseeding them, cutting them into strips and stringing them up for days to dry. The second step is to boil kilos of eggplants, drain them for a day, hollow them out and stuff them with the peppers and walnuts and then pack them into jars of olive oil. To this day I've never attempted to make it. The next time our group met for afternoon tea the hostess had prepared this dish and insisted I took a giant plate home to enjoy at my leisure.

Suad, a grandmother, was among the Palestinian families expelled from Kuwait after the Gulf War. This was the third country she'd lived in as a refugee since her family lost their home and land in Palestine in 1948. One afternoon, one of the women related how the British offered her grandfather immigration to England just after the partition of Palestine, but he rejected it as he was still stung from Britain's betrayal of the Palestinians. Though the family understood how his pride and patriotism prevented him, they half wished for their children's sake that he had accepted. For three generations the family was split around the world and, struggling to find a country for a home, providing education was a constant problem. They looked to their children's education as the means to a better future for the family and made great financial sacrifices to achieve this, often enrolling them in expensive foreign French and English schools.

Basima sent her daughter to the American school. However, when her daughter was accepted to a university in Canada it raised insurmountable problems. They did not want her to be alone in a Western country where there was no family close to her. They struggled through many plans and in the end gave up the opportunity to study in Canada. Basima and all the children moved to Lebanon where her daughter attended the University of Beirut, thus allowing them to stay close to the father who remained in North Africa for his employment.

The Palestinian problem began with their exodus from their homeland in 1948, when the State of Israel was declared. The Jewish people needed a homeland after suffering years of persecution and ethnic cleansing under the Nazis, and the world leaders offered them half of Palestine. The problem was that Palestine was already populated with Palestinians. The world was understandably sympathetic to the Jews who had suffered, but it ignored the rights and plight of the Palestinian people. Fighting between the two freedom fighter groups on both sides of the conflict drove 650,000 Muslim and 55,000 Christian Palestinians from their homes. The new Zionist government in Israel destroyed over 400 Palestinian villages with the land either designated as security zones, with no building permits reissued ever, or rebuilt for Jewish immigrants. The homes that were not destroyed were commandeered by the Jewish immigrants who were given the right to purchase them from the National Land Trust that only sells houses to Jews, not Arabs.

Ellen Siegel is a Jewish American and founding member of the Jewish Committee for Israeli-Palestinian Peace. She worked as a nurse in Beirut during the massacre in the Sabra and Shatilla Camps in 1982 and testified before the Kahan Commission of Inquiry in Jerusalem. Ellen tells the story that some don't want to hear.

A year before I was born, the last phase of the Nazi attempt to find a 'final solution to the Jewish problem' began. By the time of my birth, millions of European Jews had been exterminated. It was against this backdrop that I, as a second generation American Jew, grew up. In November 1947, I remember sitting with other children in my synagogue. Through a loudspeaker, we listened to the broadcast of the UN General Assembly proceedings on a resolution to partition Palestine and thereby establish a Jewish State. After each 'yes' vote we clapped and cheered. Six months later, in May 1948, friends and neighbours marched joyously through our streets, most waving small Israeli flags and singing 'Hatikvah'. The word means 'the hope'; the song is the Israeli national anthem. We had survived, the State of Israel was proclaimed independent. The voice that had come so close to being extinguished was once again heard.

I became aware of both the existence and the suffering of the Palestinian people in the late sixties. By this time, I had graduated from a Jewish school of nursing and was practicing what I had been trained to do: alleviate suffering, commit myself to those in my care, and perform my profession faithfully. The aftermath of the 1967 Arab-Israeli war brought stories of thousands of Palestinian refugees living in tents under an Israeli military occupation in the West Bank and Gaza Strip. Information was difficult to come by; the issue was too controversial, even for anti-Vietnam War activists. Nothing, ever again, was going to threaten the existence of the Jewish people.

The desire to find out more about this issue took me to Beirut in 1972. I wanted to see and hear first-hand who the Palestinians were and what were their grievances. It was there that I met my first Palestinian. I learned the history of a people that I never knew had existed as a people. I visited their homes in squalid refugee camps, met with their leaders, read books and poems which eloquently expressed their despair and anguish. I listened to stories of a journey that took them from their orange groves and olive orchards in Haifa and Jaffa to overcrowded, tin-roofed dwellings with open sewers threading the narrow streets. I knew that Jews had been a people without a land; I learned that Palestine had been a land *with* a people.

From Lebanon, I travelled to Israel. I visited Jerusalem, kibbutzim and I learned what it meant to live in a Jewish nation. No longer were Jews at the mercy of others – they controlled their own destiny. Jews lived together freely, without fear of anti-Semitism. But I was disturbed by the militarism. Repression and denial of rights of the very people who had been born on the country's soil were evident. I wondered at whose expense had we made 'the desert bloom'? At the same time, I found some Israelis desired to live in peace with their Arab neighbours.

I left Israel knowing I would devote myself to doing what I could as a Jew, as an American, and as a nurse – to bring about a peaceful resolution of this conflict – to try and right a wrong. I arrived in Beirut on 2 September 1982. The ashes were still smoldering. The Israeli invasion was over, the PLO fighters and administration had been evacuated, the Israeli forces had pulled back from the city. The invasion horrified me. American weapons were being used to maim and kill helpless Palestinian and Lebanese civilians and refugees. Israeli soldiers were preventing food, water, and much-needed medical supplies from entering West Beirut. The hurt and suffering of those in pain was unattended to; no dignity was even given to the dead.

I was assigned to a hospital called *Gaza* in Sabra camp. The Sabra and Shatila camps of the UN Relief and Works Agency (UNRWA) lie side by side in West Beirut. They are two of the twelve camps established in Lebanon since 1948 by UNRWA to shelter Palestinians exiled from their homes because of the creation of Israel. Before the 1982 invasion about 90,000 people lived there, a fourth of them poor Lebanese. The houses were mainly one-storey concrete dwellings with corrugated iron roofs. Camp buildings and homes were tightly packed together, separated by numerous narrow alleyways. The camp inhabitants lived and worked together. A welfare and educational system, municipal councils, and trade unions existed. Committees organised vocational training in such areas as embroidery and carpentry and operated kindergartens. By the time I arrived in Beirut, the camps' population had shrunk to about 10,000.

The Israeli army had left behind the effects of the US implements of war. Shrapnel, ammunition, rocket casings, and other such armaments, many of them 'made in USA', were everywhere. Because of them, the hospitals were filled with victims of chemical burns, with dehydrated babies, with recovering amputees. Supplies were limited, conditions poor.

On 14 September the newly elected president of Lebanon, Bashir

Gemayel of the Phalange Party, was assassinated. The next day Israeli war planes flew over West Beirut. Machine gun fire increased as the day went on. On 16 September Israeli planes again flew over the camps; light artillery fire continued, but it was now accompanied by heavy artillery. Thousands of refugees sought security in and around the hospital. They were panic-stricken; they screamed, 'Israel! Phalange!' and made a slashing motion across their throats. That evening, I watched from the tenth floor of the hospital as flares were shot into the air, lighting up neighbourhoods of the camp. Sounds of machine gun fire followed each illumination. The high explosives were coming so close that we had to move the remaining patients to the lower floors. Smoke poured in the windows, windows cracked, doors slammed, equipment reverberated. Everything was shaking. By evening, we heard only the sounds of machine gun fire. Tending to the very ill was more difficult than usual; to some, the bombardment made the difference between life and death.

Early the next morning, all the health care workers were told that the 'Lebanese Army' was downstairs and that we must assemble at the hospital entrance. The armed militia we found below were in fact not the Lebanese Army but Phalangists. These were the military wing of the Phalange Party, a nationalist Christian party founded in the 1930s on the model of European fascist groups. They marched us down the main street of Sabra and Shatilla, past dead bodies and hundreds of camp residents guarded by armed militiamen. One woman tried to pass her baby to one of the physicians, but the militiamen stopped her. Sporadic machine gun fire could still be heard as we marched. Bulldozers, at least one marked with a Hebrew letter, were busy: homes that had stood at the edge of the camp were now rubble. As we walked along, our captors called us names: 'dirty people', 'un-Christian' (because we were treating 'terrorists who kill Christians'), 'Communists', 'Socialists'. The militiamen lined us up against a bullet-riddled wall just outside the camp. Rifles ready and aimed towards us, they paused, then filed back into the camp.

Other militiamen came and took us to a courtyard on the road to what had been a United Nations building. The courtyard was littered with Israeli products and newspapers. There they questioned us about why we had come and who had sent us. Afterwards, they marched us over to a building occupied by the Israeli Defence Force

(IDF). From its roof, Israeli soldiers with binoculars were looking down on both Sabra and Shatilla. Here the Phalange turned us over to the Israelis. Israeli soldiers drove us into West Beirut and dropped us off near the American Embassy. I went in and reported to an embassy official that 'something wrong was going on in those camps'. He said the man in charge was out: 'Come back later.'

Later Ellen met Nabil Ahmed who is one the survivors. He comes from a line of survivors. Ellen tells his story.

Nabil's grandparents were born in a village near Acre in northern Palestine. They were farmers and they sold the oil they pressed from their olive orchards. Nabil's father was born in 1938, his mother in 1943. And so they lived peacefully until May of 1948.

After the U.N. partition vote, violence erupted in Palestine. Palestinian Arabs objected to the creation of a Jewish state in what they considered their country. Jewish militants – some belonging to the semi-official Jewish defense force (Haganah), some to the dissident underground groups (the Stern Gang and Irgun) – responded to this opposition by terrifying the Arab population in order to encourage a mass exodus. These Jewish forces dynamited homes, destroyed villages, and in April of 1948 massacred several hundred unarmed civilians in a small, peaceful village on the outskirts of Jerusalem called Deir Yassin. Word spread quickly; panic ensued.

In May Nabil's father's village was bombed. The family fled to the mountains and found refuge in a cave, thinking that they would soon be able to return to their homes. Nabil's mother tried to reach her house to get some blankets and clean clothes, but was turned back by sporadic shooting – Israeli soldiers had surrounded the village. Fearing another massacre, Nabil's grandparents and their families escaped to the north, dodging intermittent Israeli bombings. One of his father's brothers was wounded and had to be carried to the Lebanese border. The families made their way on foot to the Baalbek area in northeast Lebanon. Goro castle became home to them and to thousands of others who soon became known as 'Palestinian refugees.' Its huge rooms were divided up, each accommodating many families.

When he was 17, Nabil's father found work as a mason in Tal

Zaatar, located in the eastern outskirts of Beirut. In the mid-1950s, UNRWA rented this land and established it as a camp for refugees from the northern coast of Palestine. The region around the camp was an industrial center which attracted Lebanese and Palestinian workers to the area. The camp kept expanding. Nabil's father and grandfather built a home there and in 1960 Nabil's parents married and settled down in the family house. About this time all Nabil's grandparents moved from Goro to Rashidieh, an area in South Lebanon which was being transformed into a camp.

Nabil and a number of siblings were born in Tal Zaatar. Factional fighting in and around Beirut began in 1973. It had little effect on Nabil's life. His father worked as a carpenter and Nabil attended an UNRWA school. By that time about 30,000 Palestinians and Lebanese were living in overcrowded, tin-roofed rooms in the central part of the camp. Animosity grew between the Christians of East Beirut and the poor Palestinians and Lebanese Muslims in Tal Zaatar. A series of atrocities on both sides gathered momentum. In April 1975, a bus carrying thirty Palestinians back from a demonstration in West Beirut to their homes in the camp was riddled with hundreds of bullets fired by militiamen of the Lebanese (Christian) Phalange. For the next year, the Phalangists tried, and failed, to overrun the camp. Bombings were frequent and casualties high. Nabil's older brother was killed in October 1975. Finally, in June 1976, Tal Zaatar came under siege by Christian militiamen and their Syrian allies, who continually fired shells and rockets into the camp. The following month, Nabil's father was killed.

After a two months' siege, the militiamen overran the camp. Two thousand Palestinian and Lebanese refugees were slaughtered. Nabil, his mother, and his seven surviving brothers and sisters made their way out of the camp. Phalange militiamen put them in pick-up trucks and took them to their headquarters. There, they separated all men aged 14 and older from the women and children. They took the women and children almost to the 'Green Line' between East and West Beirut and dropped them off, telling them to keep walking without looking back. When they crossed the border, trucks furnished by Palestinians and sympathetic Lebanese took them to the center of West Beirut. There relatives found them and took them to Rashidieh camp. The men were never heard from again.

For the next two years, Nabil's family lived in Rashidieh with one of his mother's brothers. Israel was waging an escalating war on the Palestinian camps – shelling and bombing. It became an increasingly dangerous place to live. In 1978 the family moved to Shatilla camp in West Beirut. For four months they stayed there, in a rented room with no kitchen, and in the end they returned to Rashidieh to continue school. In 1979, the daily shelling from Israel forced them to move to Sidon, a city between Beirut and Rashidieh. For three months their home was a garage, shared with five other families. But the Israelis were bombing Sidon. The family moved to Ein el-Hilweh, another camp close to Sidon. There they lived in one room with another family for three months. They also lived for short periods in other camps which also came under Israeli attack. Each time they returned to Rashidieh, their house had been shelled and they had to begin again the process of rebuilding. Finally, in 1980, the family bought a house in Shatilla camp; there was less bombing in that area. During most of the Israeli assault on Beirut in 1982, Nabil's family stayed in Shatilla camp. When the Israeli army came very close to the camp, they fled to other parts of the city, but after a short time they, and some 10,000 others like them, returned – even though many houses had been destroyed. The family found that the bombing had damaged their house among the rest. Still, it provided shelter. It was one of two in the whole neighborhood that still had enough walls and doors so the families could live indoors. Conditions were primitive – no running water, no electricity – but there was no other place to go. The family started to reconstruct their lives.

Rumors spread that the Israeli army was making frequent visits to the camp entrance. Nabil watched as soldiers blew up sandbags and landmines that had been placed at the entrance by Palestinians trying to defend themselves during the invasion. They were clearing a path. The Palestinians in the camps were very afraid. The Isareli invasion was sucessful in forcing the PLO to evacuate from Lebanon and that left the Palestinians – mainly women, children and students – defenceless.

Early on September 15, the day after Bashir Gemayel's assassination, Nabil heard Israeli warplanes flying at a low level. Israeli tanks entered West Beirut and surrounded the camps, stopping people from going out. Nabil managed to get away to a friend's house, where he spent the night, but next day he returned. By early afternoon on September 16 the camp was being bombed and people said the Phalangists were just outside the entrance. Nabil, his family, and some neighbors stayed in a shelter until the bombing stopped early in the evening. Soon after they came out, a woman came running to them screaming, 'Go away! The Phalange have gotten into the camps – they're killing anyone they see!'

That evening Nabil, his oldest sister and her husband, and a cousin escaped to Sabra camp. Dodging snipers' bullets, they made their way to a hospital for the mentally handicapped where his aunt worked. Nabil went to the roof of the hospital and saw Israeli planes in the sky illuminating the camps with flares. He could see the tops of houses, although he could not see inside the houses or see what was happening in the streets. He heard shots, but no screams. The next night, he again watched the light from the planes, but he heard a new sound. Bulldozers were at work. On Saturday morning Nabil met up with a relative, who asked, 'Did you see your brother? They brought one of your brothers to *Gaza* Hospital – he was injured.' Nabil began to search for his wounded brother. Thursday evening, after Nabil left the shelter, Mounir, his brother, remained there with his mother, three sisters and two brothers, his uncle's family, and his neighbors. The bombing soon ceased. Shortly afterwards, Phalange militiamen discovered the shelter and ordered everyone outside. When they had rounded up everybody they could find, the Phalangists put all the males age 14 and over against a wall and shot them. 'Twenty-five men, in front of the wall outside of my house,' Mounir recalls. 'My uncle and cousin, people I was with a few minutes before, were killed.' The militiamen led the women and children, about a hundred in all, to a large garage. Mounir's 13-year-old brother escaped from the garage. The Phalangists shot him in the back, but he managed to get to another Palestinian hospital, Akka, where he was treated. After that, Phalangists entered the hospital and asked, 'Who is Palestinian here?' When he responded, they took him away. Two days later his body was found beside the hospital. He had been killed with a hatchet.

Once inside the garage, the Phalange began harassing their captives. One asked Nabil's 15-year-old sister whether her earrings were gold or zinc. She replied, 'Zinc'. The militiaman cursed her, beat her, and then shot her in the head in front of everyone. Mounir stayed close to his mother. The Phalangists shot many more in the garage, but not all died instantly. The militiamen announced that Red Cross workers were coming to take the injured for treatment and asked those still alive to raise their hands. These people they shot again. Although Mounir had been shot in the leg, he did not raise his hand. He hoped he would be mistaken for dead; everyone around him was dead. The militia took the jewelry from the dead women.

Throughout the night Mounir remained, motionless among the dead – one of these was his mother and he stayed close to her body. At one point, militiamen walked around with flashlights shooting anyone who stirred. Mounir was hit again, in his arm. The militiamen returned again in the morning and shot Mounir a third time. He was protecting his head with his hand; the bullet severed a finger. The Phalangists brought sheets and covered the bodies and Mounir heard them say, 'Let's go and bring the bulldozers and destroy the houses on top of the bodies.'

After they left, Mounir escaped and made his way to a neighbor's house where he found some shorts. Blood covered his body, and it took him more than an hour to change clothes. He first went back to the original shelter – passing bodies on the street. One of them was his uncle. Finding the shelter still empty and silent, he went on to a neighbor's house. There two militiamen found him. One made a move to stab him, but the other intervened. 'Are you Lebanese or Palestinian?' he asked. Mounir said he was Lebanese. When he saw them hesitate, he begged 'Please, you killed my brothers, you killed my sisters, you killed my family, my uncle, his family, please don't do this.' 'If you were Palestinian, we would have knifed you' was the response. The militiamen ordered Mounir to stay in a corner. When he was sure they were gone, he went to a nearby house. No one answered him. Another house – nobody answered. He made his way to another side of the camp and found some Palestinians who took him by car to *Gaza* Hospital. It was late Friday afternoon.

On Saturday, Nabil learned that Mounir had been transfered to a hospital in West Beirut, outside the camps. The hospital was far away – he needed to get past a dangerous area in order to get to taxis or to find small sheltered alleys to walk through. Instead, he made his way to a friend's house away from the camps, in a building that had been settled by refugees from Tal Zaatar camp. But in that neighborhood a rumor was spreading that the Israelis were coming that way to take away all young people. Nabil and his friend escaped. They couldn't find any kind of transportation to the hospital, which was three miles away, so they walked, taking small streets and avoiding militiamen. As they tried to enter the hospital area someone warned them to leave quickly: every young man, especially Palestinian, was being picked up. There were checkpoints manned by Israeli and South Lebanese Army at the entranceways around the hospital. They tried to return to the friend's house the way they had come, but they couldn't get back because checkpoints had been set up on the way. At last they found a cab and offered the driver as much money as he wanted to take them to the hospital without having to pass through checkpoints. When they arrived, Mounir was not there.

Rumors were spreading that teams of Israeli intelligence agents and Phalangists were driving around arresting young men. Nabil and his friend decided to go to the Red Cross. There they found several hundred people who had escaped from Sabra and Shatilla. The Israelis tried to enter the shelter, but the Red Cross staff kept them out. The shelter quickly became overcrowded, and everyone was moved to schools in the area. For two days, Sunday and Monday, the Red Cross provided shelter for them. Nabil again tried to enter the camp and again failed; the Israelis still surrounded it. Then the Israelis withdrew, and the Lebanese Army replaced them. But the Phalange had placed explosives under bodies so that anyone who moved them would be blown up. The Lebanese Army would not let anyone in until they had removed those explosives.

When Nabil finally entered the camp, he saw bodies everywhere. When he went to his neighborhood, he found the bodies of the friends he was with just before he left the camp a few days before – twenty-five young men. When he came to the garage where his family had been held, the building was being bulldozed on top of them. Before he entered the camp, Nabil had believed his family was alive and hoped to meet them there. After he entered the camp and saw all the dead, he still hoped to at least find their bodies. Nabil remembered that the Red Cross had designated an area where people could come to identify some of the bodies. It was filled with corpses – more than 200 of them. 'There were bones, the bodies changed color, they got dark, black – you couldn't identify them.' Some relatives were able to recognize loved ones by their shoes or their clothes. For two days Nabil searched without success for his family and relatives. Then the bodies that had not been identified were buried in a mass grave because of the sickening smell. The weather was very hot.

Nabil never learned just where his family's bodies were. He searched, found parts, pulled a head, a hand, out of the tangle of corpses. He found hair – someone's hair came out when he tried to pull a body from the heap. There were more than 100 people, and the garage had been bulldozed on top of them. 'The number of bodies, the way they were killed . . . the children. After they've been four or five days under the rubble you cannot identify anybody – the bodies dissolve. But even though I could not identify my family, I knew they were somewhere in that place. I found lots of parts of bodies, but not what I was searching for. My youngest sister was 6 years old, another was 8, another was 15, one brother was 13, another was 11. And my mother. My uncle's family was 11 people. The youngest was a few months old and the oldest was my age. All 11 of them were killed there. And our neighbors also.'

Between September 16 and 18, 1982, more than 800 Palestinian and Lebanese men, women, and children living in the Sabra and Shatilla camps were massacred. Days later, Nabil did find Mounir. Together, they left Lebanon and now live in the United States. Nabil is finishing a degree in computer science, and Mounir is a sophomore in high school.

As a Jew, I believe as I always have, that my people have a right to be free of the persecution that plagued them for so long and a right to live in peace. At the same time I hear Nabil: 'From camp to camp, nothing changed – the same tragedy repeats itself – in Rashidieh, in Tal Zaatar, in Damour, in Sidon, in Burj el-Barajneh, in Ein el-Hilweh, in Shatilla. We got used to the fighting, the revenge, the massacres, the death, all these things. We accepted it, because for us Palestinians, with each new day we expect that something else will come, more than what we have already been through.'

The Palestinians also dream of security and peace – of a homeland.[5]

After the Israeli conquest and occupation of the West Bank during the Six Day War in 1967 a second exodus took place. In the next twenty-five years forty per cent of the remaining Christians fled the harsh life under Israeli occupation, that is another 19,000 people. The latest figures now show that there are only 170,000 Christians remaining inside Israel and the West Bank totalling less than a quarter of one per cent of the population of Israel and the West Bank.[6]

Israel's Iron Fist policy in the Occupied Territories of the West Bank and Gaza is one reason for high emigration and it also led to the popular uprising: the Intifada. During the first two years of the uprising 800 men, women and children were killed in the streets, among them over 200 children under fourteen years old. Numbers of these were new babies killed by extra-potent teargas (labelled not to be used in confined places) shot inside their homes as they lay in their cots. Other babies were hit by teargas and rubber bullets as they were carried in the streets. In the first nine months alone 1,800 cases of spontaneous abortions were reported. Thousands of Palestinians were gassed and maimed, and the jails filled with indiscriminate collective arrests. A special law sanctioned routine torture for all Palestinian detainees. This meant anyone arrested in these collective arrests and held without charges could expect to be tortured. Torture became one of the shared experiences of this current generation.

A Western politician's wife at a dinner party blamed the Palestinian parents for the trouble: 'They should not allow their children to be on the streets throwing stones.' A journalist reminded her there was nowhere else for West Bank children to be outdoors, except in the dusty streets. Although the Intifada is over, parents and schoolteachers still need to tell their children 'Don't run in the street or you may be shot.' One West Bank pastor dreams for the day 'when it will be safe for our children to run and play in the street in safety'. We could ask the diplomat's wife, 'What would drive children to attack an occupying army with stones?' The answer would be incidents like the following one.

'On a single day in April, thirteen homes were destroyed in the village of Beita. This act of collective punishment was ordered after the death of an Israeli girl who was on a school hike in the village's outskirts. Official Israeli investigations later concluded that the girl was shot by an Israeli settler's bullet. A Palestinian who had sheltered the Israeli schoolchildren in her own home during the settlers' shooting rampage saw that home demolished with the rest. As a result of the destruction, the foundations of scores of other homes in Beita were damaged beyond repair. Children have also witnessed Israeli soldiers rounding up young men and women from their homes and chaining them; they have seen them gassing them in enclosed areas. From places of hiding they have watched the beating to death of a neighbourhood youth in some isolated alleyway. Their fathers and mothers (some pregnant), and older brothers and sisters have disappeared into some jail where thousands continue to survive without charge or trial.'[7] Curfews meant children were confined to crowded houses for days on end, often with no food. But even staying at home did not mean families were safe.

Years after the Intifada we stood with the family in their living room on the spot where their teenage son was killed. The room was decorated like a mausoleum and Palestinian colours draped his photograph. They considered him a war hero. As they related the story, through many tears, grandma fell into a chair unable to finish it, but it helped them to talk about him because their story would be told to the world bringing them some sense of justice. It was during the uprising and Palestinians were demonstrating in their streets, throwing stones at Israeli tanks. The tanks drove through the suburb firing willy-nilly. Muhammed heard the noise and came and stood in the heart of his house, on the threshold of the living room and kitchen, and warned his mother 'Come away from the front of the house. It's not safe.' Mother stopped washing the dishes and turned to speak to him. Before she took a step the bullet smashed through the window hitting him in the forehead and he fell in a pool of blood. He never knew he was hit. Witnesses said the Israeli soldiers did not kill him. A settler did. The settler stood at their front fence and fired into the house. The Israeli military authorities in control of the town made no attempt to investigate. Troublesome Palestinians were being shot every day.

The Intifada was confusing to Western Christians. A Christian pastor in Bethlehem explains: 'The Intifada, or uprising, was a sign of the people's total frustration. It was a united cry from Muslims and Christians to the Israelis to stop the Iron Fist policy of the occupation. But they responded with denial of more rights. Our College was closed for two years and when we were allowed to open curfews made it impossible for many students to continue study. The Bethlehem University was closed for four years. The Christian community here is as patriotic as any other. During the Intifada, Christian youth were in the front lines throwing stones and were shot. Christians paid a high price as their families are small and many were only sons. As Christians we have to find alternative ways to be patriotic and yet obedient to God. We use non-violent means to do our part. We have the power of prayer and we use that. We visit hospitals and do other things to show our patriotism.'

Palestinian Christians are suffering today for a reason similar to a situation faced by Eastern Christians during the Crusades. They were invisible to the West. Many Western Christians are surprised to learn there are Arab Christians. The Palestinian Christians suffer the most from the faulty images believed in the West about Arabs and are the most invisible and neglected.

One of the tragedies of the Crusades was that they weakened the presence of the Eastern Christians in their own land. The Pope sanctioned the sacking of Constantinople, the seat of the Eastern Church, to pay Crusade debts and this was one of the deathblows to the Byzantine Empire. It was left too weak to survive the Muslim Turk invasion. Eastern Christianity has never regained its original strength and the East-West breach in Christian relations is still not healed. Just as the first Crusaders didn't recognise the Eastern Christians from the Muslims and pillaged their resources and killed them, today Eastern Christians suffer because of the Western Church's actions. They are discriminated against by some of the Church that gives unconditional support for the State of Israel, thus supporting its anti-Arab policies designed to rob them of land and resources and force them from the land.

In these Western churches people have a suspicion (and are sometimes told) that Palestinians are the enemies of the Jews and God's purposes. This is based on a particular view of prophecy that is wrongly used against Arabs. In fact, the self-styled *Christian Embassy* to Jerusalem has claimed that the Palestinians are not really Christian – they just pretend to be Christian to gain Western sympathy. The so-called *Christian Embassy* was not elected by Christians to represent them. It has a Zionist political agenda and was birthed in a political event. Israel's sovereignty in Jerusalem is not recognised by the international community, which keeps almost all embassies to Israel in Tel Aviv. The Israelis seized the whole of Jerusalem by force, one half in 1948 and the other half in 1967. The government destroyed a band of Arab suburbs to make the dividing area between East and West Jerusalem. Today Jerusalem is basically separated into two areas – Jews living in the western side and Arabs continuing to live in the eastern side. East Jerusalem was declared an occupied territory in the UN Security Council Resolution 242, which specifically emphasised 'the inadmissibility of the acquisition of territory by war'. Thus Israel has no claim of sovereignty to East Jerusalem and its claim to sovereignty over West Jerusalem is also called into serious question by international law, which is why Tel Aviv hosts the embassies. The Christian Embassy to Jerusalem established itself as a statement of support for the State of Israel when the world refused to acknowledge Israel's illegal occupation of Jerusalem. The Christian Embassy to Jerusalem is one of the *proofs* for Muslims who think Western Christians hate Palestinians.

One of our friends, who heavily supports the Christian Embassy to Jerusalem, irrevocably terminated our fifteen-year relationship because we dined with Mr Arafat and had a friendship with Mrs Arafat. He sent us pamphlets denouncing Arafat as the anti-Christ and denouncing all the Middle Eastern leaders involved in the Oslo Peace Agreement. After I related my first-hand impressions of Mrs Arafat, gained over a six-month acquaintance, he wrote: 'If you believe that Mrs Arafat is a practising Orthodox Christian then you have lost all sense of spiritual discernment. Our relationship is severed from this time on.' He has never met her. I don't believe he has ever met any Palestinian Christians, but he chooses to believe propaganda reports.

* * *

Christians in the entire Middle East are an endangered people, particularly in the Holy Land. Unless something dramatic happens we could be the last generation to know a time when Christians live in the land of Christ. The major contributing factors have been Israel's occupation of the West Bank and treatment of Palestinians as second-class citizens within Israel, and the Oslo Peace Agreement disintegrating into the brink of collapse.

Z. Zoughbi is the director of Waim Conflict Resolution Center. He says, 'There is a great sense of apathy and hopelessness in our society. We feel as if the politicians of the world are playing chess with us. The sense of initiative and struggle is gone. We wanted to create a centre with space for youth to create and act, so they do not only react to negative events. Not only manage conflicts but to prevent them. People are giving up and leaving the land, particularly the Christians. Bethlehem has traditionally been a major Christian town. In 1967 there were 85 percent Christians, while today we are down to 35 percent of the 40,000 inhabitants. The emigration started in the beginning of the century and has continued since then. Today the main reason is lack of confidence in the peace process. There has been a Christian presence maintained here through 2,000 years of empires, unrest and war. The youth is the link to the future and if the emigration continues, there is a real risk that our churches become museums or some kind of Disneyland.'[8] Recent surveys show that a fifth of those remaining Christians hope to emigrate. They have lost hope in the peace process.[9]

We set out to visit the Christians of the Holy Land while it is still possible, beginning in northern Galilee, Israel. As we alighted from the bus the driver told us that 'everyone knows Father Chacour and his school: there will be no trouble finding it' but there was no sign of the village the sign boasted about. We dragged our heavy luggage from the bus and put it on the dusty road. After travelling for most of the day from Jordan by buses and communal taxis and footing it from station to station, this final leg of arriving home was disappointing. The day continued to be too hot for travel. Dusty hills splattered with grey olive groves filled the view. I was disappointed in the landscape. I had expected the lush green hills depicted in Bible story books of my childhood and I recalled the first Crusaders' lack of enthusiasm in the Promised Land. It was the wrong time of year for green hills. There was no sign of the famous Prophet Elias School and no sign of public transport leading anywhere. I understood Nathaniel's remark, 'Can anything good come out of Nazareth?' This area was still a backwater. One of the young Arab men who left the bus with us passed and we asked after our destination. 'Oh you're going to Abuna. That's a long way to walk. Wait here and I'll bring my father's car and take you.' He soon returned and drove us through the winding roads pointing out the village landmarks until the next bend revealed the school complex nestling in a brown hill.

We found Abuna (Father) Chacour walking among the olive trees spending time with the Lord after a busy day. Although he wore a peaceful expression he looked very tired and his clerical robe was splashed with sweat. His surprise at finding us in his olive garden also told us he had forgotten this was the day he was arranging transport for us from Haifa! However, we were soon enjoying a cool drink on a shady balcony while the fatted calf roasted on his barbecue.

He explained that our visit coincided with the opening day for college level classes. For the first time in history a college level education is now available for Palestinian youth in the Galilee. Prophet Elias (Elijah) College has a student body of 3,500 Muslim, Christian, Druze and a handful of Jewish students. Children travel up to seventy kilometres a day to attend the school. It would not be possible without special deals arranged with transportation companies. Chacour's dream is to have dormitories for students, empowering girls to study full time.

Seven of the 171 teachers are Jewish. Two teachers reclining in the living room said, 'We all work together realising our dream of a future pluralistic society united in diversity. We are proving that we can live in peace together.' One teacher is Palestinian; the other is Jewish. Chacour is in continual conflict with Israeli authorities whose programme to Judaise the Galilee region conflicts with his determination to assist Palestinians to stay in their land and bring it out of the backwaters into the modern world. He has a criminal record with the courts for his building activities and peace efforts. Only one building of the five on campus had electricity due to obstruction by the government. Chacour received the municipal permit for the new hook-up during our visit, along with a bill for $17,000 for the privilege. 'Israeli public institutions do not have to pay anything. This is because we are Palestinian and do not have equal rights.' 'How do you explain your vigorous battle for rights yet claim to be a pacifist?' we asked. Rubbing a finger over his long grey beard he explained, 'We are second class citizens in a Jewish state. Pacifism is the hard struggle for your rights without annihilating the other person.' His struggle may finally be productive. In 1998 the government gave permission to open an elementary school, thus completing the circle through to University.

Christians in the Holy Land are often asked when they converted from Islam, but they proudly trace their roots from the ministry of Christ and the apostles. 'You know that the first Christians to exist were my forefathers,' Chacour's smile beamed. 'They were a mixture of Jews, Gentiles, Arabs, Greeks and Romans. Today, through the gain of power and money in the West people started thinking that they are the real Christians forgetting that we transmitted the good news to them about the Living Lord and Risen Man from our Galilee. People ask us when we Palestinians were converted to Christianity. We converted when the first missionary came and preached to us. His name was Jesus Christ.'

Nawar is a Palestinian Christian who teaches Maths and Religious Instruction in schools. She is from an old evangelical Anglican family originally from the West Bank. 'My great-grandfather Suliman (Solomon) was a well-known missionary and pastor. He left Zababdi riding on horseback to evangelise in the Galilee region. The people attended church and prayed, but his heart was to teach them the Gospel. He settled in Ibillin and married a local girl and became a home teacher. The entire village would come to hear him read the daily news and teach the faith. He is the great uncle of my cousin, who is the director of Chairman Arafat's office. Many leaders and people behind the scenes and decision-makers are from Christian families.' Although Christians are only three (or today less than one) per cent of the population, about twenty-five per cent of the intimate circle of decision-makers around Yasser Arafat are from Christian backgrounds.

I had met Nawar's cousin on a few occasions in Tunis and was intrigued to learn of the family history. When Nawar told me this story she had not seen her cousin for twenty years. 'Our family was separated after the 1948 war and we could not see each other. We were in Israel and they were under Jordan and we were in a state of hostility. When Israel annexed the West Bank our families saw each other for the first time ever in 1976.' Her cousin later returned to his homeland with Arafat's staff after the Oslo Agreement.

Nawar took me to see the biblical sites in the area and as we drove past fields outside Nazareth she pointed out the field believed for centuries to be the village where Mary was from. Mary's village lies under dirt. It is one of the villages bulldozed by the Israeli government in order to prove their claim that Palestine was 'a land without a people waiting for a people without a land'.

Galilee is in Israel and so the Israeli Palestinian Christians are free to visit Jerusalem. Nawar said, 'I love the holy city of Jerusalem and go always to visit the Holy Places. When I enter the church I feel like I am with Christ in actuality and I am there walking with him. I give guided tours to anyone through the city, Muslim and Christian, and show them where Christ walked. I feel that he is walking hand in hand with me.'

However difficult life is for the Arabs in Israel, it is much worse in the Occupied Territories. Bethlehem on the West Bank has been under occupation by the Israelis since 1967. The symbols of life are barbed wire fences, heavily armed soldiers and armed settlers. There are no parks or places for children to play. There are no job opportunities or industries and the military authorities block new industrial initiatives. Unemployment is forty per cent. Locals refer to the Palestinians as a cow that Israel has milked to the skin leaving the economy near zero growth. Since 1967 Israel has illegally confiscated sixty per cent of Bethlehem's land and surrounded the town with Jewish settlements; it continues to confiscate land all over the West Bank.

In spite of the bleak situation a building in Hebron Street proclaims 'Christ is Lord'. The Bethlehem Bible College is an evangelical school providing training for Palestinians to minister the gospel to their own people. It co-operates with Bethlehem University, enabling students to gain a Bachelor of Arts degree and usually has about twenty-five students. The President, Rev. Bishara Awad, a mild-mannered pastor, described life and faith in the birthplace of Christ. 'The hardest thing is that the closure of the borders does not allow people to work. Their jobs were given to Russian Jewish settlers. Since the Gulf War we are denied access to Jerusalem so cannot celebrate Easter or Christmas there. Our students study the Bible but cannot visit the sites. In Jerusalem we are denied employment, family members, good schools and good health care. The road to Ramallah (the up and coming new Palestinian business city) goes through Jerusalem. There is a back by-pass that is so long and dangerous we call it the valley of fire, but we are forced to take it.' Awad poured a demitasse cup of strong coffee. 'Many families in our church lost their lands. The Christians used to be the upper and middle classes. Now we are among the poorer.'

Centuries ago the events of the Crusades caused Christianity to become entwined with the Western world's battles and thus Christianity was seen as an enemy and a tool of Western imperialism and oppression. This cemented a change in Muslims' attitudes towards the Christian minority groups in Islamic countries. A similar situation is happening today over Christian indiscriminate support for the State of Israel.

Some Christians believe that if we can just get all the Jews into the land of Israel, Christ will return. Part of this plan includes projects bringing Russian Jews to Israel. These plans remind us of the time when the disciples asked the Lord, 'Is it now that you will bring back the kingdom?' Jesus told them, 'It's none of your business, but the business of the Father. You preach the good news to the entire world.'

Pastors in Israel told us of the plight of the Russian Jewish immigrants and problems caused by them. Many are helped to Israel by Christian organisations but there are unforeseen problems. Their passage is paid for by the Zionism scheme and they are given all appliances and necessities tax-free on the condition they stay. But many cannot find work and want to leave. They discover they cannot return home to Russia because they cannot pay back their debt and are forced to stay. Young girls were turning to prostitution to survive. Some pastors estimated that approximately fifteen per cent of the Russian Jews immigrating are actually nominal Christians. They seek out the clergy confessing that the chance of a better life in Israel lured them. They are afraid to openly declare their faith or they will be penalised and have to pay back all benefits and could be deported. Israel is a Jews-only state. Only Jews can immigrate to Israel, unless they have converted to Christ. These Jewish-Christians then forfeit the right to immigrate and live in Israel. On Christmas Day 1989 the Israeli Supreme Court ruled that Jews who believe in Jesus are not entitled to automatic citizenship in Israel.[10] There are forty existing Messianic Jewish congregations from a grassroots movement in Israel. Although these Jewish Christians who were born in Israel are permitted to keep their Jewish citizenship, gained through their Jewish mothers, they suffer similar discrimination to the Arab population and feel cut off from the Jewish community.

Elias Chacour explained how Christian support to bring in new settlers affects Palestinians. 'If the Russian Jews are coming to confiscate more land to become new settlers, that means they will become a new additional obstacle to the peace. And doing so it hurts the Christian community and our testimony to our Muslim brethren. They ask us, "Why are you Christian when they are killing us all?" And they are right. We have to ask this of our brothers and sisters in the West. We are not against Christians supporting Israel. Everyone has the right to a homeland. We are against Christians giving unconditional unilateral support no matter whether that support goes to oppress or to prosper. Some Christians believe Israel has sole right to the land. If the Jews have any right to the land this does not mean they have the right to deport the Palestinians. We Christians have to stop dealing with the Jews as tools to practice our faith. It's time that we treated the Jews as simple human beings who are able to do good and evil. We do not believe in the priority of the land. Jesus said that the time will come when the true worshippers will need no more the temple of Jerusalem, but they will worship the Father in spirit and truth. Our God as Christians is neither a regional nor tribal God. He does not discriminate.'

Rev. Bishara Awad of Bethlehem experiences discrimination when he goes to the West to churches for support for the College. 'I am not welcome as a Palestinian in many churches. If I were a Jew it would be much easier. I believe that the chosen people and the holy nation is those who believe in the Lord Jesus Christ, that is the Church. We are all sons of Abraham through faith. My great-great-great grandfather was the Christian Palestinian governor of Jaffa when it used to be eighty per cent Christian. Today it is Jewish Tel Aviv. The church must re-evaluate its policy of bringing settlers to take our land and livelihood. We are hurting and struggling for survival. The West has listened for so long to stories that Palestinians do not exist and that there is no Church. It will soon be true.'

A Christian Arab visited a church in America. When a lady asked him where he was from and he answered 'Bethlehem', she embraced him exclaiming 'Oh, how wonderful – a Jew from Bethlehem.' When he told her he was Palestinian she recoiled in horror. An English Christian mentioned how she enjoyed hearing the 'lovely Jewish students' choir from the Bethlehem Bible College'. The students are all Palestinian Arabs and usually sing in traditional Palestinian dress. It is easier for Christians to ignore the fact that Palestinian Christians exist, for then they would have to listen to their cries for help to survive in their ancestral land. Western Christians need to realise that to be a friend to the Jews does not necessitate being an enemy to the Arabs.

The variety of Christians in the Holy Land can be confusing for Western Christians. Suha Arafat typifies this mystery and I am often asked about her nationality and religion. Her fair colouring and chic style does not fit popular images of Palestinians or Arabs. People express surprise when they learn that she is pure Palestinian and was born in Jerusalem. The next question is always about her religion and then more confusion enters. How can an Arab belong to a Greek Orthodox Church in Jerusalem? Does she speak Greek?

The Christian churches in the Holy Land have their roots in the day of Pentecost. Since then they have developed various traditions and today we have the following groups represented. *Eastern Orthodox*: Greek Orthodox, Russian Orthodox, and Romanian Orthodox. *Oriental Orthodox*: Armenian Orthodox, Syrian Orthodox, Ethiopian Orthodox, and Coptic Orthodox. *Roman Catholic* called the Latin Catholic, Melkite (Eastern/Greek) Catholic, and the *Protestant*, including Evangelicals. So there are thirteen different denominations, from churches of the East to the Protestants from the reformation tradition.

The majority of the Palestinian Christians are Orthodox. They pray through singing or chanting usually Scripture passages. The Greek Orthodox is the largest denomination with 6,000 members. It traces its roots back to James, the first Bishop of Jerusalem. The Patriarch and Church hierarchy is Greek while the priests and lay people and congregation is Arab. Arabic is used in the worship services. The Syrian Orthodox does not refer to Syrian Arab but to using Syriac Aramaic, a dialect of the language of Jesus. (Aramaic is still spoken in some Christian areas of Syria and Iraq.)

The Roman Catholic community numbers 5,000 in Jerusalem. It was established during the Crusades in the eleventh century. In 1342 the Pope put Franciscan friars in charge and for 500 years they were the West's presence in the Holy Land. The clergy and Patriarch are of Arab origin and daily masses are held in Arabic. The Melkite (Eastern Catholic) is the second largest group with 53,000 in the Holy Land, of which 50,000 are in Galilee. Its services are also in Arabic.

The Evangelicals are scattered between the major denominations. The Jerusalem dioceses of the Episcopal Church of Jerusalem and the Middle East and the Evangelical Lutheran Church in Jordan began in the nineteenth century missionary movement. There are two Anglican churches in Jerusalem: St

George's with an Arabic and English congregation and Christ Church with a Messianic Jewish congregation. There are thirteen other Arab Anglican churches in Israel, the West Bank and Gaza. The Evangelical Lutheran Church has six Arab congregations spread over Jerusalem, the West Bank and Amman. After World War Two other Protestant groups established congregations through missionary work: Southern Baptist, Christian Brethren Assembly, Christian and Missionary Alliance, Church of God, Church of the Nazarene, French Protestant Churches, Jerusalem Bible College, King of Kings Assembly and St Paul's Pentecostal Fellowship.[11]

After centuries of living together in peaceful coexistence, there has recently been growing insecurity among the Palestinian Christians with fears of a Muslim extremist revival pushing them out of the country.

Zoughbi (a Christian) said, 'We work with both Christians and Muslims. You find conflicts rather along social groups than along religious borders. Families can have conflicts regardless of religious affiliation. In spite of the difficult situation, we here have better relations between Christians and Muslims than in the neighbouring countries. The basic problem in our society comes from occupation. That does not mean that I want to demonise Israel or deny its right to exist within secure borders. It is the occupation and the expansionism that I oppose. The media is trying to enlarge the difference between Christians and Muslims, but that is like a broken finger compared with the cancer of occupation.'

Revd Awad from Bethlehem told us, 'We have close Muslim friends and we share about Jesus and salvation. Muslims are good religious people and they want to know. As a Church we should show them the love of Jesus and care for them. We must communicate with them. However, many Christians have a wrong attitude because of fear.'

However, the longer the process for peace and security to be realised the greater this danger becomes. With both Muslims and Christians disappointed in the failure of the peace process, along with unprecedented disillusionment in their leaders, they are losing hope for a peaceful future and the extremist movements, among both Palestinians and Jews, have fertile soil in which to grow.

In March 2000 the leading Palestinian intellectuals sent a letter to the Israeli and Jewish public expressing their despair in the settlement being forced on their negotiator and their fears that it would lead to future wars because it suffocates the Palestinian people and will not be accepted by them. The letter stated, 'You will have to choose between a settlement imposed by the balance of forces favouring your government and your military, and one that is just, which will favour both Israelis and Palestinians and which will provide the basis of a long-term coexistence on the same land. We are placing the choice in your hands. We are extending our hand to you to make a real and just peace, not the militant peace of coercion, the generals' peace.' The letter was forwarded on the Internet by an American Rabbi stating he had a moral obligation to bring this to their 'communities who care about peace to know what Barak is doing in offering Palestinians so little, so that we later don't claim we didn't hear from Palestinians who believe that the peace negotiations with Arafat are something like an apartheid-like bantatsu state, and that it will not provide any solution. This is an astounding response on the part of Palestinians who are quite decent, non-violent and serious people.'[12]

There remain six major obstacles to peace: Israel's policy for Judaising the city of Jerusalem, Jewish-only settlements in the West Bank and Gaza, expropriation of Palestinian land, demolition of Arab homes, non-issue of building permits and water restrictions.[13]

Jerusalem's Arab roots are as old its Jewish roots. When the Jews arrived in the Holy Land after the exodus of Moses, and again after World War Two, they found Arabs living there. Jerusalem is the largest Palestinian city and the centre of the social, economic and religious life of the Palestinian people and the question of Jerusalem lies at the heart of the Palestinian right to statehood and self-determination. Moreover, billions of Muslims and Christians around the world, as well as Jews, have a stake in the future of Jerusalem, the city where many of the holiest places of the three religions are situated.

Palestinian Jerusalemite families are treated as resident aliens by the Israeli government. At occupation, in 1967, residents were denied citizen rights and given 'residency status'. This status must be renewed each year and travel documents granted to enter the city. In 1998 Israel increased its efforts to rid Jerusalem of Palestinian residents by revoking their residency rights. They confiscated Jerusalemites' identity cards during the routine yearly renewal and sent written notices by mail informing Palestinians their residency in the city has 'expired'. The lives of tens of thousands of Jerusalemites are affected. Confiscation of their identity cards is followed by revocation of rights to live in the city and demolition of Palestinian homes. There was a 600 per cent increase of the confiscation of cards in 1997–98. Due to this a tent city of sixty families emerged camping under the hill of the Hebrew University with no water or electricity and two toilet blocks. These families' financial resources are exhausted and their choices are to stay in Jerusalem come what may or leave and risk losing their identity cards if they move outside the bounds of the city, as defined by Israel. They then lose the right to enter the city without a special permit. All Palestinian children born after their parents' cards are confiscated are not legally registered and cannot obtain birth certificates. They lose all citizens' rights, for example of education.[14] The Israeli government also confiscated papers of Palestinians with American passports holding dual citizenship claiming they cannot have dual citizenship and live in Jerusalem. All Israeli Jews are allowed dual citizenship. Palestinians are treated with fewer rights than tourists or foreign-born workers.[15]

Taxes are discriminatory. Jewish settlers in Jerusalem are exempt from taxes for five years and then pay a reduced rate. This bias means the Palestinians pay five times the tax of Israelis. Palestinian churches in East Jerusalem recently lost their tax immunity as non-profit organisations. The Israeli municipality of West Jerusalem demanded current and retroactive municipal taxes on properties and real estate belonging to the churches. The amounts being demanded could reach some NIS 110 million (Israeli shekels).[16]

We asked Chacour if he saw a solution to the problem of Jerusalem. 'It is a political problem between Israelis and Palestinians. It must be solved as a political problem first and then the religious problem will be easily solved. Palestinians without exception want Jerusalem as the capital of their country. The solution is to be under the joint control of Palestinians and Israelis. It must remain open to the three religions.'

Jewish-only settlements in the West Bank and Gaza areas are the most consequential roadblock to peace. Various land use agencies estimate that over 60 per cent of the West Bank and 40 per cent of Gaza have been expropriated to allow for the construction of settlements in breach of the Hague Regulations and Geneva Convention. This policy also required Israel to increase its military presence in these areas to provide security for the settlers. Israeli ring roads now cut the Arab section off from the rest of their countrymen and radical settler groups are buying up land. Settlers are given setting-up commodities tax free and special rate loans and grants and subsidised rent at one third of the cost. Many take advantage of the financial benefits by living in the settlement during the week and drive back to their town house for their real life at the weekend.

Jewish settler organisations are particularly targeting their energies to removing all non-Jewish influence from Jerusalem. The settlers have been successfully raising funds in churches in the West. They appeal to congregations to support them in their claims to take all the land and expel the Palestinians – of course they don't mention that Christians are among those losing their homes and livelihood. In 1922, fifty-two per cent of the population of Jerusalem was Christian. Christians still were the dominating influence in Jerusalem until the 1940s, but everyone now agrees there will probably be no permanent Christian presence in the future, unless Israel reverses its policy of Judaising the city.

Palestinian land is being continually expropriated by the Israeli government for Jewish settlements. The army, settlers and private companies have seized thousands of acres of land in Israel and the West Bank. Water rights are removed and the land is declared abandoned and land records are kept secret so Arabs are not able to contest them and modern Israeli settlements are built on it.

As we walked through the crowded streets of Sakhnin in Galilee, northern Israel, the barbed wire walls were ever present while we heard the story of the events here which began the Land Day movement in 1976. Sakhnin has 25,000 inhabitants but is not given city status and therefore receives less financial aid than a city. It has the highest birth rate in the Middle East. Both its Christians and Muslims here have large families. The Israeli government built wire fences around the last houses of the town and confiscated the remaining surrounding land. The city continued to grow and became extremely crowded. When the government declared its intention to expropriate 20,000 dunnums of Arab land in the Galilee area (one dunnum equals 1,000 square metres) there was a general strike. The Israeli army moved in on the first day and the soldiers were extremely nervous as they faced the morgue-like streets in Sakhnin. Six Palestinian collaborators with the Israelis had tried to talk the Palestinian authorities out of the strike but failed. They alone appeared in the street on the first day of the strike. The soldiers shot them dead on sight. Bishop Riah Abu Assal of the Jerusalem Anglican Church who was on the Land Day committee writes of the same incident and others across Israel as a 'landmark in the process of the Arab minority towards a willingness to stand up for their rights.[17] In the history of Israel I cannot point to one town or settlement that Israel has built for its Arab citizens, whereas hundreds have been built for the Jewish community.'[18]

Hand in hand with this policy is the demolition of homes on the West Bank and refusal of building permits for Arabs. Since 1967, 20,000 homes in the West Bank and Gaza have been demolished. Since Oslo another approximately 650 homes have been destroyed and 850 more families received demolition orders.[19] In Bethlehem the wife of an Orthodox priest showed us her father's home and mentioned that there were twenty-seven family members living in it due to refusal of permission to build on their land. We stood with a Muslim family in Bethlehem. The roof of their demolished home, built on their own land, lay shattered under our feet. The father sighed and said, 'How can I teach my children not to hate when they see this?'

Water is suspected to be the cause of the next wars in the Middle East. The Israeli Water Company drastically cuts water to Palestinian communities to meet increased consumption by Jewish settlements. The West Bank is particularly hard hit. Israel turns on water for twenty minutes every two weeks, enough time to fill one water tank on the roof that lasts about one week. Families must then purchase water from strained resources. Residents told us they limit showers to twice a week and only wash clothes when absolutely necessary. Lack of water is difficult for institutions and the Bethlehem Bible College stores it in bags on the roof and rations it. Whereas the Jewish illegal settlements on the other slope of the hill (built on land confiscated from the church's families) have unrestricted water twenty-four hours a day and their swimming pools are full. In fact eighty-four per cent of all West Bank water is plundered for Israel proper and David's Well near Bethlehem is dry.

Since the peace deal the Palestinian National Authority (PNA) has control of the town centre of Bethlehem, but the surrounding areas and suburbs are still occupied by armed Israeli forces. Palestinians are still refused building permits, denied freedom of travel and access to Jerusalem; their houses are still demolished to make way for illegal Jewish settlements. Palestinians are denied access to Jerusalem and they must apply for a special travel pass for medical or work reasons. No work passes are issued to men between the ages of eighteen and thirty. With Israeli bans on building up the West Bank infrastructure and unemployment at thirty or forty per cent, these men's dreams of employment in Israel are hopeless. It takes days to gain a special pass and it is valid for twenty hours. Moreover it is not uncommon for patients to die while kept waiting at the checkpoints with their medical passes in their hands, particularly at the Gaza crossing. The highest fatality rates are among dialysis patients and newborn babies.

It is a ten-minute drive along the main Hebron-Jerusalem Road from Bethlehem to Jerusalem. It is difficult to tell where the suburbs of Bethlehem end and the suburbs of East Jerusalem begin except for the checkpoint set midstream in the road outside Bethlehem. This is where Palestinians are denied access to the road and entry to Jerusalem. They are arrested if caught in Jerusalem or Israel without a valid permit. On 16 January 1998, eighteen-year-old Nidal Abu Srour was arrested as he left the Al Aqsa mosque after prayers with his family. He was held without charges for two days at the Russian compound in Jerusalem from where he was released to a hospital. He was unable to speak to his family and died as a result of 'injuries'. Israeli Chief Justice Barak has called for this prison to be closed. Other Palestinian detainees have died as a result of torture in this and other prisons. In 1997 an Israeli ministerial committee headed by Beniyamin Netanyahu extended the permit for Israeli security forces to use torture while interrogating Palestinians.[20] Finally in 1999 Israel made a landmark repeal of this law under the government of Ehud Barak.

But change comes too slowly for young Jewish soldiers who act in fear. There is another checkpoint on the road in Bethlehem half a kilometre from the first. The second protects Rachel's Tomb. Since Oslo, the Israeli authorities have turned it into a military-style fortress with machine gun toting soldiers and barricades blocking half of the main road and occasionally totally blocking it causing great inconvenience to local traffic. In 1998 during an expression of exasperation, seven-year-old Ali Jawariesh joined a group of children throwing stones at the soldiers at Rachel's Tomb checkpoint. The soldiers raced at the children firing on them. One soldier fired at Ali hitting him in the head. He was brain dead for four days and declared dead. Ali's father offered his organs to any needy donor, Arab or Jew. In another incident at the checkpoint Israeli police questioned seven Israeli border guards after they brutally beat three Palestinian boys aged fourteen to fifteen on 5 February. The beatings stopped when one boy passed out and had to be taken to hospital. Israeli police sources reported the soldiers would not be held on remand.[21]

The shame of daily discrimination and fear hit home during one of our journeys in Israel. Our bus approached the isolated roadside stop where an older lady, distinguished by her Palestinian traditional embroidered dress, stood leaning on her shopping bags of produce. Two men stood near her. The bus driver pulled up fifteen feet ahead of the group causing them to run in order to board. The two men reached the bus before the lady who was struggling with her heavy bags. As soon as the men stepped on board the driver shut the door and drove off. One of the men protested pointing out the lady still running for the bus. The driver shrugged him off saying, 'There will be another Arab bus soon.' Everyone on board knew there would not be another bus. The comments were in Hebrew so I did not find out what happened until the lady was far behind us. I noticed the bus passengers avoided each other's eyes. I think I will always remember her and feel ashamed that I didn't do something. I believe Jesus would at least have gotten off the bus to walk with her and help carry the bags, but I am not sure that I would have had the courage to react that quickly on impulse. I realised in that small incident how much courage it takes to be a peacemaker and to stand up for the oppressed. No-one on our bus did.

During our recent visit both Palestinian police in central Bethlehem and Jewish soldiers at Rachel's Tomb blocked the road. We had to divert our paths from the blockade at Rachel's Tomb in order to reach the second Israeli checkpoint to Jerusalem. The problem was compounded because we had intended to travel by public transport that was now no longer to be found and the car left at home did not have the special plates required to permit it in Israel. The whole town was scurrying around like ants splashed with hot water. After running between empty bus stops and finding that taxis refused to stop, finally a minibus took us on board and drove in all directions trying to find an open road. Drivers of cars coming from the other direction yelled to us that the roads were closed at their end and we spun around and took off in another direction. If we didn't get to the Jerusalem checkpoint in time we would be caught in Bethlehem and unable to keep our appointment in Jerusalem only fifteen minutes away. Maybe it would be a general closure lasting for days. Our Swedish friend, a resident in Bethlehem, made twelve cellular phone calls as the minibus raced over the dusty potholed roads throwing us from side to side. Her four-year-old daughter was on the other side of the barricade and she was trying to find someone who could collect her from school. As we raced pell mell around the outskirts of the town through the alleys of the refugee camp I discovered that if I clung to the seat in front when we hit potholes, my head did not hit the roof so hard. When we reached the other end of the main road we emerged from the dust and turmoil of the Bethlehem mini grand-prix complete with armed soldiers into a normal day. People walked leisurely in tree-lined streets bathed in calm sunlight. The difference between the two worlds was as sharp and sudden as a slap in the face. How unfair that these two different worlds co-exist in the same street.

We visited Bethlehem again in January 2000 and life was worse. Our bus got caught in a traffic jam due to students holding a non-violent protest against insufficient financial help. Students raced between the cars with Palestinian police chasing them with swinging clubs. Bottled anger raised the temperature in the silent bus and finally one man stomped his foot on the floor and ground an imaginary gnat bursting out 'We are treated like this – dirty gnats – with both Israel's and our own leaders stomping on us. What kind of peace is this!'

But our greatest shock was in Gaza which we understood from the press was now under Palestinian control. We stood with a Palestinian farmer next to his field of crops, hothouses and trees. Next to this was his land confiscated two weeks earlier by Israeli settlers. He told us they arrived with guns and uprooted everything and ploughed the field back to sand. There were tractor marks in the sand. The settlers lived in sight in modern town house settlements, not farms. While we were standing talking, the settlers arrived in a jeep carrying automatic guns. When we asked why they had taken this farmer's land they replied, 'We have the right because of what the world did to us in Germany.' A British lady asked these twenty-year-old youths (with American accents) who were too young to be alive then, why Palestinians have to pay for the West's guilt. 'The world has to pay,' they answered. We reminded them that the world did give them half of Palestine, and that they still received enormous financial assistance to build new lives; there was still plenty of vacant land in Israel. Why did they want this family's farmland? But the settlers were not living there in order to farm. They were there in order to prevent Palestinians living in what they see as a land only for Jews. Within ten minutes two Israeli army vehicles arrived to back them up, with the soldiers also brandishing automatic weapons. When another two military jeeps appeared on the road behind us we were sufficiently intimidated and left. We left the farmer and his family standing alone and unarmed in the remains of his farm in the midst of the settlers and soldiers and their weapons.

The incident highlighted the situation of Gaza – a done deal and *returned* to Palestinians. Gaza's population is close to one million – all Muslim except for 2,000 Orthodox, 200 Roman Catholics and a handful of Baptists. 716,930 persons are refugees from the conquered middle and north of Israel. Many were displaced twice – in 1948 and again in 1967. Five thousand Israeli settlers have occupied the best agricultural areas and over one third of the seaboard. In twenty-two military-guarded settlements they occupy forty per cent of the land of the Gaza Strip and use sixty per cent of the water. There are sixty-one persons per square mile in the Jewish area and 6,173 persons per square mile in the Palestinian areas. Declared 'security areas' near the settlements are still under Israeli control and Palestinians are denied permission to build any structures: houses or schools. They live in tents and the children walk five kilometres to the nearest school in Khan Younis. Palestinians are forbidden to use the 'Jews only' roads that run through to the West Bank. They are denied rights to the seacoast and cannot export their fish and restrictions limit their agricultural exports through the checkpoint into Israel. Unemployment runs at over sixty per cent. Those employed in Israel are a cheap source of labour and are being paid less than Israelis. They begin lining up to get through the long wait at the checkpoint to enter Israel at 4 am and return home about 6 pm. During a general closure (collective punishment by Israel) Gaza is effectively locked up like a concentration camp – behind barbed wire fences encircling it, Alsatian guard dogs and guns. In 1997, during eighteen days total closure in July, $24 million were lost in earning opportunities for Palestinians. A pastor told us he couldn't preach on faith, hope and love anymore. 'Love . . . you see what we are surrounded by, there is none. Faith – has taken such a beating it's out there somewhere. I can only speak to my people of hope. We must maintain Christian hope that God is with us while we are suffering. One day hope will bring us back faith and love.'

Change comes too slowly for the frustrated young Palestinians who joined the militants and kidnapped an Israeli soldier. The crisis was escalating as our taxi returned to the Jaffa gate in

Jerusalem with thousands of Jews gathered at the Wailing Wall to pray for him. Police barricades blocked the entrance into East Jerusalem and a stream of people surged through the narrow gate onto the main road filled with police and army vehicles. Our Palestinian taxi driver was nervous of finding himself in trouble and dropped us on the road, afraid to go further. His children came for the ride from Bethlehem and were sleeping in the back of the car. He was worried the Israeli authorities would close the checkpoints and they wouldn't get back home tonight and it was already after 10 pm. He lamented, 'I wish I knew where the poor kid was and I would go and get him myself. God help him and all Palestinians if they don't save him.'

The narrow street inside the walls was buzzing with Jews in skullcaps, long black coats, long curls and prayer shawls. A group of modern young people linked arm in arm took over the street, swaying from curb to curb. Their singing and chanting overwhelmed all other noises. It seemed that most of the people were armed. A father in a skullcap propelled his baby in a pusher while a toddler clung to his trouser leg. The father's pistol holster occasionally smacked against the little boy's head. The night felt hostile and the crowd's nervousness invaded me. Once in a lifetime photo shots paraded past me but I was too nervous to produce a camera. These fanatical looking Jews were intimidating and I couldn't understand their language so I didn't know if their chants were menacing. I stepped back in the shadows keeping the camera out of sight, but Mazhar approached a young man in the long coat and sash garb. I was relieved to note that he did not have a gun. At first he was very reticent and suspicious but after fifteen minutes, when the crowd's had almost dispersed, the night found them still in conversation. He looked for the Messiah to come and bring in justice and peace and believed the Jews should live by justice and equality and allow room for the Palestinians, and any other non-Jews who want to live there. But when asked if he knew any Palestinians he replied, 'I have never spoken to one. I am only visiting here and they told me it was dangerous to have contact with them. I am afraid to walk in the Arab areas – like this street.' Suddenly a Palestinian man behind him yelled to someone across the street. Our new Jewish friend tensed every muscle and sweat poured over his suddenly pale face. Reeling around with eyes popping out, he cried 'What's going on? They will kill me!' We were surprised. We had not noticed anything unusual, just someone calling out to his friend, 'Good night. God protect you until the morning.' I recalled my reaction earlier to the young people chanting and wondered how often does ignorance breed unnecessary fear and violence?

The extremists murdered the kidnapped soldier and the Israeli government closed off the Palestinian territories for another round of crippling economic punitive measures for millions of Palestinians. The papers featured the typical 'Palestinian terrorist' headlines. How ironic that a whole race of people has come to be thought of as violent terrorists. The Irish, Germans and Sicilians are not all lumped together with their violent extremist elements. The vast majority of the people I met in Israel and Palestine were kind and peace loving – mothers, fathers, grandparents, brothers and sisters who love their homeland and yearn to live out their lives in peace – both Jews and Palestinians. Jews told us they were afraid of Palestinians and would not believe our reports of Palestinians who simply wanted peace. Palestinians told us they were powerless, exploited and afraid of Israeli powers and incredulous of Jews being afraid of them. I left Jerusalem wishing they could talk to each other.

What would Palestinians like to say to Christians in the West? Zoughbi answers for them: 'As a Christian, I have to act upon the responsibility that Christ has given us towards this world. God wants righteousness and mercy and we have to strengthen the oppressed wherever they may be. But I would also like to draw their attention to Jerusalem. We need help to find a reasonable solution, so that we can have a part in an open Jerusalem. Here the Christian world could play a more important role, and such initiatives would connect them to the twelve million Christians in the Middle East. We Palestinians must struggle to get rid of occupation and to create an independent democratic state. Israel has to work on getting away from the occupant role and instead strive for peace and justice. The third party are Christians, peace groups and others who have influence and can point out that the two parties only have one real option: to live together and share the country and the resources. Without this vision, the future might be the worst of times.'

Awad and Chacour described ways Western Christians can encourage the Christian Palestinian community. 'First of all to acknowledge that we have the right to exist in Palestine as Palestinian Christians. Then try to encourage projects in education and aid that are now being built in the Arab milieu so that the Palestinians can become self-reliant. And whenever they come to the Holy Land, don't just see the stones and shrines but take some time to contact the living stones in the Holy land: their Christian brothers and sisters.'

We shared two illuminating taxi rides in Israel with reporters. The first reporter was from one of the prestigious international news weekly magazines that will have to remain anonymous. I asked him, 'If you wrote the truth about what is happening here would your magazine print it?' He replied, 'We must write within the understood limitations of this area. It's not like writing on other parts of the world.' The question begs to be asked 'Why not?' Why shouldn't Israel be held up to the same standards of justice as the rest of the world? His article, appearing the same week, dealt with the security problems and fears of Israelis and contained nothing about the insecurity of the Palestinians.

The second ride was across the desert from Jerusalem to Jordan with an American reporter who was flamed with indignation over the Israeli abuse of the Palestinians and the silence of the Western powers. She regaled us with stories of personal harassment by Zionist organisations in the USA after writing of incidents and told us 'how the Jewish lobbies have a stranglehold on the first amendment in America'. When I asked if she had any hope that the truth would ever be told in the popular media coverage she rolled her eyes in defeat, 'That's why I'm now writing travel books.'

A Christian who heard the Palestinians' side of the story for the first time cried out exasperated, 'How can we ever find out the truth if no-one will tell us?' Anyone who speaks out about these policies is branded anti-Semitic. Even Jews working with Palestinians to help them gain equal rights are called anti-Semitic. These Jews are quick to point out the difference between being Jewish and Zionist. They are proud of being one and deplore the policies of the other.

However, the violence has not been one-sided and Palestinians have also perpetrated violent attacks on Jews. I have not related any of these stories because they usually made front-page news around the world and I believe this will continue to be so. I have told the Palestinians' story because they are the oppressed whose voice is still not being heard.

South African Archbishop Desmond Tutu wrote, 'If I were to change the names, a description of what is happening in Gaza and the West Bank could describe events in South Africa.' The difference is that around the world Christians prayed and worked for peace and justice in South Africa by standing with the oppressed.

Palestinians and Jews both have a history of being oppressed and exploited. Palestinians are currently being oppressed in the name of Israel's God and Christ. Part of the Western evangelical Church is supporting Zionist policies and claiming that Palestinian Christians are not sincere believers and the Muslims are our enemies. I believe God wants to send ministers of his love to these people in the spirit of Francis of Assisi and the Master he followed. Palestinians are the wounded ones on the Jericho road and Christ is looking for his ministers of mercy to bind their wounds and give of our abundance to help them become financially independent, with no discrimination. Loving service should be given to all whether or not they respond to the Gospel.

If this kind of unconditional love and service is given, people will respond to the message this service exemplifies. The liberal Church has given loving service but sometimes failed to supplement works with life-giving words. The evangelical Church has given life-giving words but sometimes failed to demonstrate the message by deeds of love. We are called to combine the words of life of the Gospel with good deeds that glorify our Father and demonstrate his unconditional love to all. The Palestinians deserve at least justice. We should give them compassion and mercy.

Notes

1 16–18 September 1982. After the PLO were forced out of Lebanon their families were left defenceless. The Maronite Christian Militia massacred 3,000–3,500, women, babies and old men in the Sabra and Shatilla Camps while the Israeli Defence Force stood by enabling it to happen.
2 Romans 8:3 (*The Message* translation, Eugene H. Peterson 1993, Colorado Springs: NavPress).
3 Romans 9:14–16 (*The Message* translation).
4 Psalm 56:8 (*The Message* translation).
5 American Arab Anti-Discrimination Committee, Washington DC, USA, September 1999.
6 Dalrymple, W. (1999) *From the Holy Mountain: A Journey among the Christians of the Middle East*, New York: Henry Holt & Company, p. 317.
7 Boullata, K. (1990) *Faithful Witnesses: Palestinian Children Recreate their World*, Kuwait Society for the Advancement of Arab Children, Kuwait/Olive Branch Press, USA.
8 Mallouhi, C. & Gustafson, R. (1998) 'Little Batustan of Bethlehem', Issue 9/10 (The Open Veins of Jerusalem), *JUSOOR*, Maryland.
9 Dalrymple, op. cit., p. 317.
10 *Christianity Today*, 5 February 1980, p. 57.

11 Hilliard, A. & Bailey, B. J. (1999) *Living Stones Pilgrimage*, Indiana and London: Notre Dame Press, p. 42.
12 Rabbi Michael Lerner, Message to the Israeli Jewish Public, March 2000.
13 Smith, M. L. (1998) *Perspective on Peace*, Middle East Council of Churches, October 1998.
14 *Cornerstone*, Issue 10 (Christmas 1997), Jerusalem: SABEEL Palestinian Christian Liberation Theology Centre.
15 The Washington Report on Middle East Affairs: Sosebee, S. Dec 1997; Meehan, M. April 1998, Jan/Feb 1999 and June 1999; Gordon, N. March 1998.
16 *Palestine Report*, Volume 4, No. 34, 13 February 1998, Jerusalem.
17 Assel A. (1999) *Caught in Between*, London, p. 74.
18 Ibid. p. 79.
19 *Cornerstone*, Issue 10 (Christmas 1997).
20 Jerusalem: SABEEL, in memoriam for Nidal Abu Srour.
21 *Palestine Report*, Volume 4, No 34, 13 February 1998, Jerusalem.

Chapter Five

STILL CRUSADING?

O Thou who carried the pain of the world, How much the world
carried pain in your name.

Amed Shawqi: Egyptian poet

History left us a legacy of mutual prejudices. In the Muslim
world Christianity continued to be associated with Western colonialism and what was perceived as new military crusades against
Muslim lands. The Tunisian writer Mohammed Talbi describes
what this juxtaposition of Christianity and colonialism means
for Tunisians in the beginning of the third millennium: 'The
apostolic (traditional) church has a difficult history. All who live
humiliated by this colonialism carry memories never destroyed.
Many of us in Tunis recall the statue of Jules Ferry (Prime
Minister of France 1880–81, 83–85) in the capital city in the
main street which was named after him. (The main street and
place are now known as 7th November.) Ferry was one of the
greatest colonisers. Ferry's statue held an arrogant stance and
Tunis was symbolised by a Bedouin peasant woman at his feet
offering him the fruits of Tunis which he disdains. In 1930, May
8th, the Youth of the French Catholic church in Tunis dressed as
crusaders and staged a demonstration march to celebrate 100
years anniversary of France taking Algeria. At the other end of
the street was the statue of (the French) Cardinal Charles
Lavigerie (1825–1892). The Cardinal held a Bible in one hand

and a cross in the other. These two statues in the same street combined colonisation and Christianity and the demonstration of the power over Islam. In spite of this the (current) President Ben Ali invited the Pope to Tunis, although there is no (official) national church'.[1]

In addition to this, numerous contemporary political events in our lifetime confirmed our nascent suspicions that Muslims are our hostile enemies. 'Only Islam seemed never to have submitted completely to the West; and when after the dramatic oil-price rises of the early 1970s, the Muslim world seemed once more on the verge of repeating its early conquests, the whole West seemed to shudder. The onset of "Islamic terrorism" in the 1980s and 1990s has deepened and intensified the shock'[2] 'Islam has come to stand for everything that civilised rational people disapprove of. It is as if discrimination between religious passion, a struggle for a just cause, ordinary human weakness, political competition, and the history of men, women, and societies cannot be made when "Islam", or the Islam at work in Iran and other parts of the Muslim world, is dealt with by novelists, reporters, policymakers, "experts". "Islam" seems to engulf all aspects of the diverse Muslim world, reducing them all to a special malevolent and unthinking essence.'[3]

Modern Australia is 200 years old. We are so young we have had no time to become embroiled in the historical Muslim-Christian conflict. Until the latter part of this century Australia cocooned herself in the so-called White Australia Policy. We never had any obviously foreign immigrants living among us, so we never had to look at our prejudice. I was surprised to discover my generation did have a biased anti-Muslim heritage according to this article published in 1987.

The Origins of Australia's Virulent Anti-Arabism
When Australia first ventured into independent foreign policy a rich vein of Anti-Arab racism was already evident, built mostly on the experience of fighting two world wars on Arab lands. In the NSW

(New South Wales) parliament debate over sending troops to the Sudan in 1885, Sir Edward Strickland saw the expedition as a holy war, and called 'not upon NSW alone but upon all Christendom to crush the Saracens led by the Mehdi before they become as formidable as their renowned ancestors'.

While the rule of British Imperialism in the Middle East continued to produce numerous distinguished Arabists – Britons who learned the Arab language, loved Arab culture with its fabled hospitality, poetry and music, lived with Arab people and then betrayed them – Australians had no part in such necessary intimacy. The contempt felt by the Australian Light Horse for T. E. Lawrence, leading his Bedouin cohorts in Arab gear in the race to Damascus (and the racist comments quoted about the Arab population of Jerusalem) suggests that consorting with the inferior races was regarded as degenerate. There were certainly no counterparts to the British officers who used to 'sit cross-legged with desert sheikhs in their tents and discuss poetry in perfect Arabic'. Many Australians shot their horses rather than let them be sold to Arabs. . . The following sentiments, expressed in an army newsletter, was not atypical, 'those of you who were forced to sojourn in an area in Tobruk . . . will remember the gloomy, hang-dog, tremulous and pouch eyed inhabitants of that delectable spot'. . . .[4]

If this accurately portrays the attitude of the previous generation of Australians, then the ground was ready for suspicion of the Muslim communities that burst into flower in Australian cities later in the twentieth century.

There is a common unfounded perception in the West that Islam is inherently violent and therefore breeds terrorists and oppressive regimes. However even the most superficial attempt to understand modern events in the Muslim world reveals a complex situation intertwining religion with local and international politics and intrigue. It should be helpful to list some facts that may not be common knowledge to the average Western Christian who has not been following the relevant stories.

In the beginning of the twentieth century many intellectual Arabs were attracted to Communism, seeing it as the best vehicle to advance their countries from Western colonisation and topple unjust regimes. In Egypt Britain was the dominating colonial power and she encouraged the Fundamental Muslim Movement – led by Hassan Al Bana – using it as a buffer against Communism.

After the Second World War the USA became the dominating power and took over Britain's interest in encouraging the Fundamentalist movement against Communist influence. This threw the Fundamentalists into conflict with Egypt's first president, Gamal Abdul Nasser, who was friendly with the Soviet Union. The next president, Anwar Sadat, reversed foreign policy and became an ally to the USA. During his regime he gave the Fundamentalist Party freedom in order to use them against the remaining supporters of Nasser. However, they were opposed to his foreign policies which, they believed, contributed to the deteriorating financial crisis and they feared the growing influence of Western culture was polluting the moral and religious fibre of society. As a case in point, while the poverty-stricken masses struggled to survive, Sadat threw luxurious parties entertaining Western movie stars and planes ferried food from Maxime's in Paris for a family wedding. The extremists grew strong enough to assassinate Sadat. Since this time the Islamic extremist movement has been a thorn in the side of the Egyptian government.

The West's criticism of the Taliban government in Afghanistan is a similar case. It is extensively documented that the West, specifically America, bankrolled and trained the Taliban. When America bombed targets in Afghanistan in mid 1998 they knew where to hit, for the camps had been built by American intelligence for training the mujahadeen fighters against the Soviet forces. Osama Ben Laden listed as the USA's most wanted terrorist also worked with the CIA and he created a network of storage caves for the Afghan mujahadeen. At that time the entire world supported the mujahadeen, as did the Saudi, Pakistani and US governments.

Omar Abd al Rahman, who is currently serving a jail sentence in the USA for bombing the New York Trade Center, also worked with the CIA and recruited for them. Is it fair to lay the blame for the acts of desperate individuals working with, or against, the intrigues of Western subversion and espionage on the religion of Islam?

One of the main reasons the West came to see Islam as the enemy was the terrorism war of the 1980s. We can be forgiven for believing we were engaged in a bloody battle during that decade. It felt like it. Militant extremist groups claiming they were Islamic took out their retribution on the West. They blew up planes, shot travellers in world airports and indiscriminately took hostage any hapless Westerner who fell into their hands. Many of these hostages had given their lives serving the Arab peoples. Some of them were murdered. The fanatic treacherous terrorist came to be synonymous with Muslim in the mind of the ordinary Westerner who was digesting these atrocities regularly along with his morning breakfast cereal. Month after month the retaliatory battles raged. When Israel invaded Lebanon fierce radicalism and anger erupted at Israel and its supporters, mainly understood to be the United States. The American acting President of the University of Beirut was kidnapped and peace-keeping forces evacuated the PLO (Palestinian Liberation Organisation) from Beirut. Lebanese Christian militia massacred Palestinians in the Sabra and Shatilla camps while Israeli soldiers looked on. A car bomb destroyed the US Embassy in Beirut. The US navy bombarded Muslim, Druze and Syrian positions in civilian areas. Two retaliation suicide car bombings killed 243 US Marines at Beirut Airport and fifty-eight French troops. Two US planes were shot down. The US battleship New Jersey shelled the Shouf mountains around Beirut. More Westerners were kidnapped. Muslim militias seized Beirut and took control. More Westerners were kidnapped and the US Embassy was bombed again. The US bombed Libya and one American and two British hostages in Lebanon were murdered in retaliation. The Iran-Contra scandal broke. The US Vincente mistakenly shot down an Iraqi airbus killing 250 passengers, and the world was surprised when hostages in Beirut were not killed in retaliation. Meanwhile the Lebanese Christian militia group, the Phalangists, continued to hold four Iranians hostage which blocked deals for the release of the Western hostages. A new kind of terror emerged when a bomb blew up the Pan Am flight over Lockerbie, Scotland, killing 270 people. The war of terror waged by numerous brands of extremist groups from many different countries and causes peaked in the eighties. No embassy, airport, luxury ocean liner or even railway station or pub was safe. Terrorism even reached inside the Vatican when a Turkish nationalist tried to assassinate Pope John Paul II.[5]

Most of us lost track of who did what first and why, and we didn't really care. What most people cared about was the way that we, the ordinary people, were impacted by this strange war. We no longer felt safe in our world, and all we knew was that it was usually because of 'those Muslim fanatics'. The troubles in the Middle East stung many of us who thought it was nothing to do with us. During this time my family visited the United States. Australia was just one short flight away and I wanted to put our boys on a plane from Los Angeles to Melbourne to visit my parents. They had not seen their grandparents for four years. The boys were aged six and nine, but their age wasn't the problem. We were too afraid to put them on a Western plane. What if terrorists blew them up? We didn't send them and my father died the next year a few months before we were due to visit Melbourne.

The threat of violence permeated life in the Middle East. In the nineties our son was going on a special youth group ski trip to Austria from the expatriate church in Cairo. Faris and some of his friends worked all year raising funds to subsidise their expenses, but the trip was cancelled at the last minute because of the looming Gulf War. The church was afraid to send a plane-load of Western children into the sky in case terrorists blew them up. The possibility of being blown out of the sky was a real one. One of our friends was sitting two rows in front of a bomb that exploded over the Mediterranean. The plane managed to land safely, but passengers died from the blast and three generations of one family died when a grandmother, her daughter and grand-child were all sucked out of the hole. Arab Muslims were also injured in the blast. Real Christians, Muslims and Jews do not murder. Terrorists murder and terrorists do not discriminate for a terrorist's religion is hate and terror.

As long as the West sees Islam as an enemy it will not act impartially in the political arena. 'Zbigniew Brzezinski in his book *Out of Control* warns against ignoring conflicts in which the Muslim world is victimised. He asserts that had Sarajevo been Christian or Jewish, the West "would have acted quickly". Our failure to revoke the arms embargo against Bosnia "contrib-uted to an image promoted by extreme Muslim fundamentalists that the West is callous to the fate of Muslim nations but protec-tive of Jewish and Christian nations".'[6]

I disagree with Brzezinski. It is not only the extreme Funda-mentalists who think this way. The majority of my Muslim friends believe this, from the Fundamentalists to the ultra mod-ernists who do not practice their religion. Moreover, many of my Western friends living in the Muslim world also agree with Muslims and are embarrassed and angered by the West's policies in the Muslim world.

Iran is a case in point. Mossadegh was the first democratically elected prime minister of Iran but was overthrown by the CIA in 1953. The CIA also helped create the despised SAVAK which ran a terrifying police state. Sattareh Farmaian, Iran's first social worker, writes of very positive experiences with American Christian missionaries in her youth who gave themselves self-lessly to Iran, educating the youth and giving medical services. However, she relates: 'Iranian students, who were too young to remember the missionaries, saw the United States only as a harsh, militaristic power that was intervening in Vietnam, a small weak nation like our own. The Iranian security services who put down demonstrations rode around in American jeeps with a picture of clasped hands symbolising Iranian-American friendship. America threw away our affection. Thinking only of its fear of Communism and the interest of American oil companies, it had used its great power to stifle our nation's aspirations to independence and dignity. The way we felt about the United States would never be the same.'[7]

On 8 September 1978, Iranian police massacred a peaceful crowd demonstrating for freedom. Helicopter gunships hunted down demonstrators who fled and the killing went on all day until blood was running in the streets. On the day following the massacre the American President telephoned the Shah to assure him in person of America's friendship and future support. Many Iranians concluded from this that America supported the killings. In the following months the Shah's regime fell to Khomeini and, as the populace sought revenge for their sufferings, anti-American feelings grew. In this climate fifty-two Americans were taken hostage at the US embassy. This is the point at which the majority of Westerners entered modern-day Iran and were baffled by the intensity of animosity to the West and particularly to the USA. Television sets showed a country 'which seemed to be populated exclusively by black-clad, screaming mobs obsessed with reviling and humiliating innocent Americans'.[8]

In the Arab world the United States is seen as using double standards in its unilateral support of Israel against Arab states. It is not only Arabs and Muslims who are concerned about this. Western writers and activists are also calling for change. Graham Fuller, the Rand Corporation Middle East specialist, wrote in the Los Angeles Times: 'What do the Muslims perceive? They see a Washington unwilling to act even-handedly in the Arab-Israeli peace process and indefinitely tolerant of a hard-line government in Israel that denied Palestinians land, dignity and statehood. They perceive double standards that allow Israel to violate UN resolutions, but not Iraq; that Israeli nukes are OK, but not nukes in Muslim hands . . . (Muslims) see themselves routinely humbled by use of overwhelming Israeli power . . . Muslims are concerned that there are no Muslim Americans involved in high-level policy making in the Middle East, but that Jewish Americans occupy nearly every single senior position relating to U.S. Arab-Israeli policy.'[9]

Rana Kabbani, writing in 1989, says: 'Is the Western conscience not selective? The West feels sympathy for the Afghan mujahadeen, propped up by American intelligence just as the Nicaraguan Contras were, but feels no sympathy for militant Muslims who are not fighting its Cold War battles but have political concerns of their own. As I write, Palestinians are dying every day in the Occupied Territories nearly 600 dead at the last count, over 30,000 wounded and 20,000 in detention without trial – savage and prolonged curfews are imposed as routine collective punishments, homes are blown up, pregnant women gassed and beaten, and unarmed boys kicked to death by regular soldiers, yet Israel remains a democracy in Western eyes, an outpost of Western civilisation. What is one to think of such double standards?'[10]

Raymond Close, a retired CIA officer, addresses the same issue: '[more than one billion Muslims] see correctly, without doubt, that the US responds much more negatively against Muslim states than against Christian states or Israel . . . Double standard? Of course, without question. And yet we wonder why deep bitterness and disillusion are still breeding terrorism.'[11]

A few months later, the West was again punitively bombing Muslim countries (Afghanistan, Sudan, and Iraq) and British Muslims responded by citing double standards and outbreaks of Islamophobia fed by the media.

UN sanctions have been in place on Iraq since 1990. A UNICEF survey in 1999 on Child and Maternal Mortality shows a dramatic increase in child mortality since the Gulf War. The report estimates that there have been at least half a million child deaths which could have been prevented and that 'in the absence of the prolonged measures imposed by the UN Security

Council', Iraqis would not have suffered the malnutrition and disease resulting in the increased death rates. The report estimates that 20 per cent of Iraqi children under five suffer from stunted growth due to malnutrition. Criticism has been voiced by UN administrators of the Oil-for-Food programme, the Red Cross, and numerous religious leaders and human rights organisations. UNICEF officials have estimated that some 5,000–6,000 Iraqi children under five die each month. In spite of these statistics there is little evidence to suggest that the West cares about Iraq's children.

While Western governments and media paint Islam as an enemy, local Muslims and their communities are targeted in Western countries. Dr James Zogby, an American-Arab, writes: 'In the aftermath of that tragic event [the Trade Center bombing] I remember praying that its perpetrators were not Arabs or Muslims because I feared what would happen to my community if they were . . . we innocent Arab Americans are still feeling the impact of their hideous crime against not only fellow citizens but against our image and standing in society . . . our enemies have used the fear created by the World Trade Center bombing to push their negative stereotypes of Arabs and Muslims into legislation and public policies that threaten the civil liberties of our communities in the United States.'[12]

Richard Curtis, a retired USAI Officer, speaks on behalf of the Muslim community: 'to the world's nearly six billion people it makes no difference whether Bin Laden or someone else acting in the name of Islam blows up an airline in which they might have been travelling. Islam everywhere takes the rap. Millions of Muslims living as minorities in Europe, Asia and the United States become objects of suspicion.'[13]

Anti-Arab discrimination, stereotyping and hate crimes continued unabated during 1995. These ranged from the indignity of racial, ethnic and religious slurs to discrimination in the work place to life-threatening hate crimes. Arab-Americans are sometimes specifically targeted on account of ethnicity, but they also suffer the effects of the general anti-immigrant and anti-foreign nativism sweeping the country.

After the bombing of the federal building in Oklahoma City the initial news stories inaccurately reported that the suspects were 'Middle Eastern looking men'. The New York Times reported the damning fact that there were at least three mosques in Oklahoma City – implying that this could help to explain the bombing. A number of other prestigious papers ran similar columns. The response of the public to this irresponsible journalism was an immediate upsurge of anger and violence directed at Arab Muslim communities. Many people stayed home and avoided public places. Muslim women with head coverings were insulted in the street. Children were kept home from school. At least 222 incidents of harassment were reported in a three-day period. In one incident a pregnant woman huddled in the bathroom with her two children in fear, while angry crowds grew outside, throwing stones and other objects at her house. Believing the loud noises were gunshots and terrified for her children, she began haemorrhaging. Shortly afterwards her child was stillborn. In a little over a year, at least seven American mosques were burned down or seriously vandalised. In one attack the mosque was desecrated with satanic symbols. The home of a family from India was apparently mistaken for Arab and vandalised. The numbers '666' was sprayed on the door and obscenities about Arabs painted in their driveway. The ADC's (Arab American-Arab Anti-Discrimination Committee) Campus Chapter at a state college received a series of threats as a result of organising an 'Arab Awareness Week'. The chapter president was assaulted by two individuals in an effort to discourage them from continuing with the scheduled activities.'[14]

In March 1995 in Brooklyn New York, a demonstration was organised in protest of a 'militant racist teacher' who beat an eighth grade Yemeni student because of his ethnicity and religion. The boy was sent to the hospital. The teacher was accused of using racial slurs. Parents complained of other incidents of discrimination.

In Los Angeles, a Moroccan family is filing suit against a school for discrimination against their sons. The family moved to the USA from England for the father's executive career and the boys attended a junior high school in an upper middle class area with a very low percentage of ethnic students. They complained of racial and religious discrimination by the other students and occasionally by a couple of teachers. The insults denigrated their British accents, Islamic religion and Arab origins. When the eldest boy became withdrawn and his studies suffered, the parents removed him from the school. The case landed in court when the youngest son was beaten unconscious by a popular athletic student while others looked on. The boy claims he attempted to protect himself by picking up a rock but did not throw it when he realised that he was surrounded. He was left unconscious with broken bones and no-one called for medical help. The parents accuse the school of trying to cover up the incident, along with similar abuse other Arab students are citing. The school dealt with the incident by expelling the boy for using a rock as a deadly weapon. Nothing has happened to the student who beat the boy, nor has there been any investigation of the teachers accused of verbal abuse. The mother told me, 'We have tried every channel to have this looked into, but there is no chance of justice here. Why should anyone listen to us, after all we are the "terrorists".'

A number of people cited the lack of a suitable response in the courts where discrimination against Arabs and Muslims is not identified with the same gravity as discrimination against other ethnic groups.

In March 1999 Muslim leaders in Wisconsin issued a call for an end to alleged intimidation of local Muslims by agents of the FBI. 'While we support the need for law enforcement agencies to gather information, we feel that we are the target of "Islamophobic hysteria",' they said in an issued statement to a press conference. They cited several incidents of alleged intimidation in which individuals were threatened with deportation if they refused to provide information about specific Muslims or activities at local mosques. One computer engineer said he felt singled out solely because he was a Muslim and pressured to give the name of terrorist organisations outside the United States. Being a Muslim he is assumed to have connections to terrorist groups.[15]

However, on the other hand, some Muslims living in the West have contributed to Christians' fears by stated aspirations to gain political clout in the countries where they reside in order to bring in an Islamic government. In a market in a Swedish suburb a bearded Muslim wearing traditional Eastern clothes told another Arab, 'In five years we will take over this whole area.' He didn't realise the Arab he was addressing was an Iraqi Christian grandfather, who came to Sweden seeking refuge. He had experienced childhood horrors during one of the coups in Iraq and was fearful of belonging to a minority.

These troubled relations between Muslims and Christians permeate the world. In Morocco, a Muslim's father who ran a grocery store died. A middle-aged Greek woman, who was an old customer and friend, came to give her condolences. She spoke Arabic. The Muslim man brushed her aside and refused to receive her sympathy or recognise her shared grief. He stared at the ground quoting verses of the Quran about infidels until she sadly left.

An Iraqi Christian told us a Muslim had asked him many times for a Bible but he refused because 'We have a tradition in our church not to give it to Muslims.' A factor in this reticence is fear of being accused of proselytising Muslims, which is illegal in all Islamic countries. In some it carries a death penalty.

In Lebanon (where the population has experienced a civil-religious war) an Orthodox Christian woman said, 'Every time I see a Muslim I pray "May God destroy him".' The Christian who was told this said 'it breaks my heart to hear Christians talk this way about our Muslim brothers and sisters'.

At a friend's wedding in North Africa, I sat chatting with one of the teenage girls in her Muslim family. I had noticed the girl in the house during previous visits but she had never joined in the adult discussion. During our conversation she realised I was not Arabic and exclaimed in surprise, 'But of course you are Muslim?' When I told her I follow Christ her eyes widened in horror, 'How can this be? You are a good person! How can you follow that terrible religion!'

In an Egyptian market a Muslim saw a man with a Bible in his pocket and asked him to read a verse for him. The Christian took out the Bible, opened it and read, 'Don't cast your pearls before swine.'

Some Christians may wonder why we need to be involved at all in issues of social justice. Should we not just take the Gospel and try to stay out of local conflicts? This sounds like an easy option for those of us who live in peaceful countries. But for those living in places of conflict, anywhere in the world, their lives are daily impacted by local politics, and often international politics, and they are forced to understand the implications of living out their faith within their difficult context. How do I react to a government that does not treat me equally? Will I love an enemy who has killed my family? What should this *love* look like? How can I turn the other cheek when the government demolishes my family home without any compensation for *security reasons*? Do I remain silent while people are abused in a police state, or discriminated against in my own Western street? Did Jesus have anything to say about these issues of human rights and justice? I may not have to deal with many of these issues personally, but how will I advise those who do? Do I have the privilege to remain silent and inactive in a world that needs kingdom living? One of the ways we can build bridges to other faiths is by active mutual involvement in solving social problems.

Christian persecution watch groups report that countries ruled by Islamic-dominated governments continue to rank highest in Christian persecution. It is undeniably true that Eastern Christians are not treated equally in the Muslim world, and at times are persecuted and converts from Islam have been executed. We must ask Islam why it is afraid of Christ. Perhaps the question is not totally a religious one and the oppression is the result of the typical fear of regimes which too closely tie faith and politics. Whatever the answer is, and however Western Christians decide to support their co-religionists in the Muslim world, the solution lies in the hands of the Muslims in those countries to speak out for justice for all in their own lands – we appeal to them for their help.

However, sometimes Christian suffering is part of a general oppression or political instability in the entire country. When other people are also suffering, or persecuted, the accusations against governments for targeting Christians can therefore be unfair and not help the local Christian community in a time of turmoil. There is another problem in using the word *Christian*. It can be used indiscriminately and the reader does not know if it refers to the entire nominal Christian community in a country or individuals with personal faith in Christ. When we read that *Christians* burned and looted Muslim villages we presume this does not mean persons committed to Christ and peace. When we read that Christians are being persecuted in various countries how can we know if this refers to entire nominal communities caught up in civil or ethnic war, in which individuals committed to Christ are among those suffering, or if there is a specific campaign directed at those professing faith in Christ? There is a danger of using the same ethos as the secular media which needs sensationalism in order to sell and keep subscribers and viewers. Events can easily become blown up out of proportion or reported as a peculiarly Christian problem. There is also a danger of tunnel-vision: seeing only our side and how it affects us.

Emotional reports surged around the West when a group of Western Christians were charged with smuggling Bibles into a Muslim country and given suspended prison sentences. We lived in that country when the incident occurred and the Christian community was divided on whether it was persecution. Some saw the group as heroes: championing the Christian cause and being persecuted. However others were concerned about the incident and the stance of the Christian media reporting of the event along with the repercussions on the national Christian community which is struggling for the right to exist in the country. One national Christian explained, 'When I heard they did this under the cover of night they lost my support. We must have a clear testimony for our faith and conduct. We must walk in the light.' A responsible person in the expatriate Christian community told us the leader dedicates time each year to smuggling Bibles and had a number of previous warnings from the authorities. The reports included the men's description of the 'dungeon-like jail' and their harsh treatment. But they were treated more civilly than nationals have been treated in similar circumstances. Although none of those involved were American, the incident was dealt with via the US embassy because of pressure applied to Washington through the Christian persecution watch groups in the USA. This caused some staff in the embassies concerned to believe the whole affair was deliberately planned to cause an international embarrassment – an idea which I am sure was far from the Christian smugglers' intent.

At the same time another Christian organisation was blitzing the country with smuggled literature for children. Christian teachers in a local Muslim school expressed concern that it wasn't good for children to be targeted at a vulnerable age because, 'It is disturbing for them and these activities open doors for a reaction from Muslim fundamentalists.' Many Christians believed it was unethical to attempt to evangelise Muslim children in a culture where individual choice is not part of the culture, especially when it's a choice flying in the face of the family and community as a whole. In these cultures adults make decisions for their whole family. How did this children's campaign fit with Western Christian concerns for family values and respecting parents? How would we react if our children were evangelised in or near the school grounds by a group that we had reservations about, or strong objections to? Why would Muslim parents feel different? It seems that some Christians think that because we have the truth, the end justifies the means in how we get this truth out to the world.

Because of these two incidents a legal shipment of Christian literature destined for distribution in the secular market in the country was detained at the port. The authorities apologised to the publisher explaining that they were forced to forbid its sale due to the pressure they were under from the smuggling activities causing them international embarrassment. The Christian media quoted the smuggler leader claiming that the Bible is treated far worse than many other serious offences in this country. However, that is not a true representation of the incident when the whole scenario is considered. The government was allowing Bibles into the country within limits and was not reacting to the Bible per se, but to an aggressive Western illegal smuggling campaign.

The problems in Sudan have repeatedly contributed to headlines in Christian persecution reports. There is no doubt that ethnic Christians in southern Sudan have been suffering in the civil war between the north and south. Sudan is one case where civil war, ethnic tensions and claims of a deliberate policy to cleanse the country of its Christian presence all combine. However, there is another facet to life in Sudan that we are not hearing about. One of the problems in a warfare mentality is that we cannot afford to let any good light fall on the enemy. The story shared here of religious freedom is one of two identical reports sent to me from Arab Christian leaders ministering in northern Sudan whose names I have withheld. Sharing a story of unusual freedom for Christians in a Muslim city does not change the facts of the struggles of Christians in the south of that same country.

We are very thankful in spite of the political and economical situation of Sudan. We are amazed by the openness and friendliness of the Sudanese people. During 1998 in Khartoum the church had two Marches for Jesus, one during Easter and the second was during Christmas Eve. A few hundred believers marched through the three towns of Khartoum singing and holding banners, 'Christ Loves Sudan'. In about six different places of the city at each march they had open-air meetings with loud speakers. They also gave out about 30,000 Gospels to standersby. The same year we had around five Christian Book Exhibitions in central parts of the city where over 1,000 visited the exhibitions everyday. Videos where shown in a tent near the Exhibition. The locations were in a central street and the loud speakers presented different Christian songs and invited people to come in. One church was showing films three days a week on the street and having an open air meeting once a week for over a year. Lately they were stopped and there is a court case against the church. In spite of this, all the churches have government permission for programs on the National TV during Christmas and Easter with each denomination allowed about one hour. Public squares can be used for rallies and in January 99 we had five days of rallies in the Green Square not far from the Airport and around 15–25 thousand attended every day.

Stories of instances in recent years in southern Egypt regularly circulated in the Western and Christian press citing churches burned, businesses sacked and Christians killed. But it was not widely reported that some Muslims risked everything to protect their Christian neighbours from the extremists. Even the Christian media rarely reports the positives.

In some instances persecution is part of a greater problem and interference from the West can back up ideas that local Christians are agents of the West. There is a need to separate Christianity from the West and Western politics and allow it to truly be indigenous. The Coptic Church in Egypt admitted they were having problems with oppression by the government but asked the West not to interfere in what they considered an internal problem that they could handle better without outside help.

Bob Blincoe, an American Christian who lived in Asia for nine years, expressed concerns about this issue in an article in his newsletter entitled, 'The US government may impose sanctions on countries which oppress Christian minorities: The fault is partly our own'.

He cites the Portland Oregonian, 21 October 1998, stating that of the top thirty offenders of religious persecution, twenty-three countries have Islamic government. He writes:

> [M]any evangelicals have persuaded Congress and the President to punish the persecutors. The Senate has threatened to suspend some forms of aid and to ban US loans. Is this the way of Jesus? Constantine made Christianity the state religion of Rome. Result? Thriving missionary work in Persia (Rome's enemy) came to a screeching halt. I would like to ask the American Senate, who voted in favour of sanctions, to resign and take up residence in south Sudan or Pakistan, and beat their swords into ploughshares, and suffer alongside the poor and oppressed. This is the way Christ left his followers. That is the real revolution which will confront and overcome the world.
>
> Christians talk of the sword of Islam, but how does it seem when America rattles its sword against the *enemies* of Christianity? Have we moved away at all from the Crusaders vengeance? American evangelicals, feeling moved to do something, persuaded Congress to punish the offending governments. Results? Muslims get the message that Christians live by the sword after all. Is something wrong with this picture?

We are not too surprised to find Blincoe offering St Francis as a model for a solution. 'Until now the "do something" suggestion which evangelicals have made to congress has not been revolutionary enough to bring millions of Muslims into Christ's kingdom. We have Christ ("put away your swords") as our Lord, and St Francis ("a new knighthood based on love") as our example. Francis crossed a no-man's land to talk to the Sultan. Francis offered the Sultan a new knighthood which vowed poverty, chastity and the refusal of power. Can we not find leaders in our day who follow Christ as Francis did?'[16]

Christianity today is still perplexed about what to do about

Islam and how to encourage and support our co-religionists living in Muslim lands. However, Christianity will continue to be suspect while the West sees the Muslim world as an enemy. We must be fair in our reporting and not just publicise, nor sensationalise, the bad news. Even Christians sometimes act as if Muslims are evil people, rather than seeing that certain acts committed by extremists are evil, whether these extremists are Muslim, Jewish, Hindu, Buddhist, Communist or Christian. Defending the rights of all people should be integral to our faith. We call for justice and freedom of religion for Christians suffering around the world. We must also defend the rights of adherents to other faiths to hold their own religious and political convictions. We are therefore called to defend Muslims and others when they are persecuted or oppressed as is currently happening in some Western countries. The vast majority of Muslims are afraid of their extremist elements and deplore them. Moreover, Muslims whom the West perceive as fearful extremists – by their dress and devotion to Islam – are in fact, in my experience, often very sincere God-seekers. They are totally committed to serving God in the way they understand God's requirement for them. I have found very close friends amongst these Muslims because we share a similar religious worldview in opposition to a secularised one.

One current Christian view of Islam that has become popular again this century is that Islam is a religion inspired by Satan. Some of the ways Christian leaders have described Islam are: a pretension that sets itself up against the very knowledge of God; a stronghold of anti-Christian teaching; the last anti-Christ to be conquered before Christ returns, and it will be burned up in the testing fires of God.

The same feelings are reciprocated by some Muslims and their complaints reconnect to the Crusades. 'They call it the 10/40 window. To the modern day crusaders of the Christian missions it is exactly what China is to the Coca Cola Company – one billion people just dying to hear the message. . . . This region has

become the target of unprecedented efforts by Christian missionaries to convert the Muslims to their religion. Like a cancerous
growth, we are seeing Christians gain a foothold in the lands of
the believers. The first time these crusading forces came with
swords and suits of armour, this time they arrive with credit cards
and million-dollar aid cheques. Employing Faustian machina-
tions, these human devils are converting many Muslims to their
false religion and serving to inject a virulent poison into the
stream of the Ummah (Muslim community). The Muslim world
is under attack. Islam has spread all over the world rapidly and
with amazing acceptance. As such, the blasphemy of Christianity
is under threat. In response, they are "fighting back" through
escalated missionary activity. [The article quotes a missionary's
testimony criticising the custom of purdah which proscribes
women's veiling and staying in the home.] They are motivated by
their desire to mislead our brothers and sisters. They want our
sisters to walk round exposing themselves shamelessly in the
same manner that kafir (unbelieving) women do. They want our
sisters to leave their homes and wander the streets. They want us
to disbelieve in the Revelation and they want to extinguish the
light of truth that is Islam. They are calling us to the worship of
a false religion and thus they are calling us to hellfire.' The article
goes on in the same tone denouncing the Red Cross and Christian
missions and aid organisations accusing them of 'murder, sexual
assault, kidnapping and calculated deception. Weigh the effects
of drugs against the effects of apostasy and one finds that whilst
the effects of drugs are limited to the world, the effects of apostasy will carry a person all the way to the Hellfire.'[17]

Before we (justifiably) react, we could do better to endeavour
to understand what has made the author so angry. How does he
see Christians and our attitude to Islam? He claims, 'The meth-
odology of the Christian missionaries is reflective of the hatred
and contempt they hold for Allah and His religion.' He is saying
that we know you are Christians by your hatred of us and
contempt for our religion and culture. If there is any truth in this

statement we must bear the blame for contributing to his rejection of Christianity. He believes Christians are doing battle against him and the Muslim community. Therefore as an enemy in battle against his community, he suspects even our best acts of love and mercy. Is there any real difference between his view of us and the preceding Christian statements about Islam? Both statements refuse to recognise any light of God in the other's search and both condemn the other to hellfire for leading the elect astray by heresy. I sense Jesus' voice behind the smoke of the battle scene calling to us, 'You do not know what spirit you are dealing in.' Before we can bridge the gaps and in the spirit of Francis take Muslims the 'true Gospel', we will need to disengage from the battle by quitting our side of the rhetoric. When we share the Gospel in a kingdom manner it can never be perceived as hatred and contempt. 'When two cultures accuse each other of satanism, the only one who gains is Satan himself.'[18]

The World Prayer Center in Colorado is under the aegis of a local church which also runs the bookshop in the building. Their brochure states it was built in 'response to a vision for co-ordinating a global prayer ministry and plans to co-ordinate prayer requests with 50 million people from 120 countries. Outside 54 flags from different nations offer a visual representation of the nations and their need for prayer. About six miles of wiring and conduits are woven underneath the Center. Six hotel-style suites are designed as extended prayer rooms where people can pray overnight. On the ground floor a large prayer room views to the Rocky Mountains and hanging in the huge window a 2,200-pound world-globe hangs suspended. It was moulded from a giant golf ball on display at an Ohio golf course. With its dimples filled in by a fiberglass expert, the mould was cast transforming the giant golf ball into the globe that now rotates once every hour.' Local Christians use the room for conferences and told me the atmosphere was very peaceful and conducive to prayer and meditation. Three ministries are housed upstairs and all are committed to the 10/40 window mission philosophy.

One ministry conducts world-wide training conferences and seminars empowering Christians in their gifts and callings. A second related group trains Christians in church growth, deliverance ministry, prayer and spiritual warfare. It improves the quality and quantity of prayer by using the information super highway. The third group co-ordinates world prayer for nations in the 10/40 window. These three ministries are difficult to reach – each corridor leading to a ministry is sealed with a top security key-card pad device.

The group connected with empowering Christians to go on a prayer walk in the 10/40 countries invited us to their facilities and shared their vision. They put out a monthly prayer calendar which includes similar material as the other two groups on specific countries, demographical information, strategic towns, recent breakthroughs and spiritual bondages. It is all connected with the 10/40 prayer walks. One of the other three ministries in the Center encourages groups to engage in power encounters against territorial spirits and reclaim the land for Christ.

I met a number of Christians on prayer walks while I lived in the 10/40 countries and one group has become representative to me. A group of eight or so visited 'strategic cities' and walked around for a few days praying and receiving spiritual impressions for prayer material. They engaged in spiritual warfare by seeking to discover the 'territorial spirit' operating in the area that 'kept people in spiritual bondage'. Once identified they bound it by prayer in order to release the Holy Spirit over the land. This group then travelled inland to pray over the waters in a particular well. Their research into the country caused them to believe it was strategic because its water was 'connected to subterranean waters which go to Zamzam', the renowned well in Saudi Arabia. Muslims consider Zamzam a holy well and pilgrims take home its waters.

The theology behind these trips continues to concern me. One of the number of reasons is these groups unbiblical belief that they need to be in the region of the hostile spirits in order to confront them, and they need to be on the spot for their prayers to be effective for the country. The inherent militant vocabulary also disturbs me. In Colorado I was in the hub for the 10/40 philosophy and wasn't sure what I would find. What I did find in the office were two very sincere Christians. They believed prayer would open an outpouring of the Holy Spirit and blessing on the Muslim world. They advised groups on prayer walks to be careful not to break laws by overtly evangelising or handing out literature. They also expressed concern about the spiritual warfare militant language.

I asked if any Muslims come into their Centre and then realised it was too difficult for anyone to simply walk in from the street, but the secretary said they do receive abusive phone calls from Muslims saying, 'Go home you dogs! We know what you are doing. You raped our women and burnt our homes. Leave our countries.' The mild mannered man explained: 'They equate us with Western Christianity and the Crusades. It was nine hundred years ago but it is still as if it was yesterday with them.' He continued, 'I lived in a Muslim country and rubbed shoulders with them in face to face relationships. We made many friends.' He did not express any of the militant terms I had come to associate with groups focusing on spiritual warfare. He saw Muslims as individuals and had a genuine compassion for them as people. The comparison was simple. While he was perceived as one of a group doing battle with Muslims, he was a Crusader dog. When he was relating on a one-to-one human basis he was a friend. My meeting with him and the office staff had done the same thing. When I crossed the frontier and met face to face with the group, I gained a more sympathetic view and was reminded not to judge the whole by the eccentric few.

We left thinking that the 10/40 window groups are becoming well known, or infamous, among Muslims. However, as we left the building we discovered another reason for the abusive phone calls to the ministries upstairs. It was on the ground floor. *The Arsenal* is a surprising name for a bookshop, unless you remember that it fits the spiritual warfare jargon. But 'arsenal' is a fit description for the shop. On the display sale counter lay four heavy metal Crusader-style swords, three feet long and stamped *Made in Spain* (the last Islamic stronghold to be defeated). Next to them a numerous number of rams horns to sound the battle cry, still carrying the Hebrew tags *Made in Israel*, as did the Jewish prayer shawls next to them. To complete the Crusader image, modern and ancient, a life-size Crusader metal shield hung above the counter bearing the coat of arms for Richard the Lionhearted. Next to this was a painting – a burst of red flames pierced by a sword. Under the sword was an open Bible. The shop was festooned with Israeli flags decorating counters and with at least one menorah on top. The bookshelves featured titles on spiritual warfare which used militant language and war image dust covers. Many were blatantly anti-Islamic. A display cabinet containing what I can only describe as holy cosmetics featured products of 'Holy Anointing Oil from Jerusalem' made into roll-on deodorants and other products. Small vials of oil were on sale along with decorative golden holders for the vials priced at $15. All the products were packaged in ebony black and covered with gold Hebrew lettering. *The Arsenal* is the most easily accessible place to the public in the entire building. What message does this give to any Muslim who enters?

I do not believe the impression was deliberately anti-Islamic – in fact the salesperson had no idea that the symbols had any relationship to the Crusades! I think it is the result of living so within our own small framework and philosophy that we lose touch with the outside world and how it perceives us. It also epitomises the current trend to view the Christian life from a besieged battle mentality. The world is experiencing rapid changes which cause us to feel out of control, under attack and afraid. One of the common fear reactions is to try and stop the change by returning to the familiar past. Both Muslims and Christians are reacting this way by a new strengthening of rigidity and fundamentalism. We are digging deeper into our own community, creating a ghetto from where the outside world becomes an increasingly scarier place. We commonly hear statements about being in a battle, whether it is with the culture, with other religions, with secular education, evolution, abortion, the battle of the last day . . . the list goes on. I wonder if the fierceness of our criticism is the distance between our fears and our lack of contact with what we fear?

We also hear Christians (mainly Americans) complaining that they are victimised and warning that a state persecution is on the way. Christian militia fringe groups take this to its conclusion and build houses with secret tunnels fortified with weapons for the day of judgement to come. The problem is that we are the ones who declared the war and withdrew from society in order to fire artillery at it, and then complain that we are misrepresented and misunderstood. What good is the salt if it no longer fulfils its function? Jesus said that we *are* salt – we don't have to try and become salt. We are either salt that influences our environment in a positive way, or salt that has no positive effect. We are becoming so concerned about losing our saltiness that we are afraid to mingle with the food. The besieged mentality of withdrawing from secular life is evidenced by the plethora of Christian alternatives to any activity; how to do whatever you want to as a Christian and in a Christian environment without needing to be in touch with non-Christians. This embattled theology is fuelled by our fears. God's perfect love can cast out this fear and take us back into the world, where we belong to love and serve.

Muslims have also been known to engage in spiritual warfare. A Christian centre serving the local community, bringing together American and Arab Christians and Muslims, sponsored a cultural night inviting an Iraqi group to share their culture through song and dance. Instead of the expected colourful folk presentation the group of women arrived dressed in black robes. The centre's staff reminded them that the night was for fun and cultural events. The women marched around the room, waving flags as banners and chanting in Arabic. The Christian Arabs looked uncomfortable. The director of the centre surprised the non-Arabic speakers by loudly calling out something in Arabic and stopping the event. The Shia' Muslims were chanting to their prophet, 'Oh Ali, come and take this your place.' The director shouted, 'Stop in the name of Jesus.'

In the USA students from a large Christian university held a prayer walk on a nearby mosque. They stood in a group outside the precincts and prayed. The Muslims felt the action was done against them and asked the university permission to come on campus and in a public address to willing students explain their beliefs. The university refused.

We have to question our current approaches to Islam: fanfared reports of the battle skirmishes over the media and Internet, the typical war-status reporting where the enemy is villainised and we are the glorious victors, and where true statistics are accommodated to the war environment. There is an inkling of surrealism and the danger of losing a sense of reality and living in a deception of our own making.

Moreover, how can we continually paint Muslims as hostile spiritual enemies with whom we are engaged in the greatest battle of our century, and then be willing to go to our Muslim neighbours and share Christ's love with them? People do not normally reach out to enemies of whom they are afraid. And people rarely respond positively to those waging war on them. We need to lower the drawbridges of our battle towers that take us further from the frontiers of meaningful relationships with Muslims and others. Instead of raising the battle cry we could do better to demolish the battlement walls.

All through our lives we have repeatedly been told that we have enemies. We don't have to cross over to Islam or Communism to discover the power of these stereotypes. We have a lot of bridge repairing to do in our own house first.

The church was packed with over 1,000 worshippers for one of the four equally packed services held over every weekend. This was the young people's service. A number of the thirty teens joining the church shared how they had been brought to faith in Christ by the witness of school friends who then brought them to their church. The service bounced with modern praise songs, along with times of complete silence in awe of God's presence among them. Holy Communion ended with all in prayer on their knees. The priest's message exhorted the people to let go of their fears of allowing God to be in control and totally surrender to God and experience the joy and peace of total commitment. At the end of the service as the congregation left the building still singing, their songs strangled in their throats when they reached the car park. Every car's windscreen held a pamphlet urging them to leave their church because they were deceived and were following Satan and the anti-Christ. The pamphlets were served by a Protestant splinter group. The church was Catholic.

Instead of making war on each we would do better to make war on our ignorance and prejudices. It goes without question that the pamphlet servers did not go inside the church nor meet any of the worshippers obviously so in love with God. Just one foray into 'enemy territory' would have challenged their prejudices . . . and in this case blown them apart. Protestants were told the Catholics were our enemies, then the Communists and now Islam. During the Cold War, your Christian faith was suspect if you were not vehemently anti-Communist. Stories of Communist persecution were the only stories I ever heard. It seemed this was the only face of Communism. Prayer was an offensive weapon against it. I do not remember ever hearing anyone challenge us beyond the *ism* to love the individual Communist made in the image of God. It was an unthinkable thought. We were not challenged to think of the Communists as people, they were just the enemy Communist block.

So I was totally unprepared for the shock of the overnight train ride from Melbourne to Sydney in the seventies when I was trapped for hours next to a leader of the Communist party. I was twenty-one and had never met a real *commie*. I gaped at the man sharing my seat thinking, wasn't it illegal for these cruel tyrants to exist in our country? A finger of panic uncoiled in my spine. An anti-Christ was sitting next to me. My visions of us in another country with him dragging me to be beheaded were interrupted when he spoke despite my silence. He explained he had just left the party because he lost faith in its ability to make a better world, and certain practices of indoctrination had offended his sense of dignity. I was astounded that he had morals and that his reasons for becoming Communist were worthy. The anti-Christ turned into a decent and caring human being.

A while later he mentioned his grief over a failed marriage. He was feeling totally bereft. He had lost his family and his ideology that had been his reason for living. He wished he could have faith, but he could not put aside intellectual problems with Christianity. The anti-Christ underwent another transformation and turned into a sad child of Adam searching for Father and home. I silently prayed, 'Father lead this lost one home to you.' I got on the train with an anti-Christ and travelled with a human being in need. Neither of us moved seats, but I changed places. The change came when I saw a person, not an enemy monolithic block.

Teresa is married to a diplomat and their mission took them to the enemy territory.

When I was growing up in America in the 50s in the winter of the Cold War, I remember people in our church praying that Communism would fall, that democracy would triumph, and that we would win in the arms and space race. I knew little about Russians except that they were the enemy. I remember the day Stalin died: my friends and I were playing hopscotch and rejoiced that an evil man was dead in some far-off land called Russia.

My first encounter with a real live Russian was at a volley ball game at our ambassador's residence in central Africa during late 70s. The Russian men won and celebrated with American beer. The Russian women sipped their cokes and oohed and aahed over my 6-week-old Sarah. We American women covertly studied their over-done makeup and 50s dresses and felt thankful to be Americans.

None of us could communicate except with smiles and gestures. Russia was still far away.

To my great astonishment, twenty years later, Russia is close to me. Our back windows look out on the Russian *White House*. Today I served meals and wiped tables at a soup kitchen, shopped for linen from the Volga, walked through Red Square and ate a Russian ice cream cone. I rode on the fastest and most convenient metro in the world (or so they say) and felt thankful that I have two more years to get to know this incredibly fascinating city and its people.

Russia is full of paradoxes. The Bolsheviks blew up the Cathedral of Christ the Saviour in the 30s; Moscow's city government rebuilt it, at tremendous cost, in the 90s for the city's 850th birthday. And the people are a paradox at every street corner, in every season! The babushka selling her garden flowers near the metro station: perhaps even whether she eats next winter depends on those sales and the small vegetable garden she and her husband tend. The *new* Russian buying forty-five dollar shorts in the Nike store and paying a hundred dollars a ticket to hear a Russian rock star. Baba Nina, 78-year-old former ballerina, always smiling, loads piles of heavy dishes into an antiquated dishwashing machine at the student cafeteria where our soup kitchen is located: she wishes me 'health, prosperity and success' as she shakes my hand across the opening through which we shove the plates. The prima ballerina from Swan Lake at the Bolchoi Theater is taking one last curtain call: they say she may be paid in tickets which her family sell to foreigners in the metro station nearby. And there is the seemingly friendly woman who helped us communicate with a shop assistant when my Russian ran out. Was her son one of the men outside our embassy in April, throwing beer bottles and burning our flag?

When Teresa arrived in Russia she had already learnt enough Russian to be able to communicate and make friends. Within a few months she was responsible for opening the soup kitchen to give at least one hearty meal to hungry people with little hope for their next one. She did not find the *enemy* in Moscow, but individuals each needing to be judged by their own merits and personalities. Many Russians are now her friends.

Since the fall of Communism the West made Islam its new enemy. Islam is the *Green Menace* replacing the soviet *Red Menace*. There is little cultural exchange taking place with the Muslim world today such as happened in the middle centuries. The current view of Islam precludes any dialogue or exchange: what does darkness have to offer to light, error to truth, ignorance to knowledge, or Satan to Christ?

Our Scriptures warn us, 'Do not be squeezed into the world's way of thinking', yet the Christian attitude to Islam includes stereotypical secular ingredients: vitriol, hostility, culture assassination, exaggeration and hysteria. In these troubled times Christians have an opportunity to reach across the chasm to those being unfairly and unjustly treated and to be known by our love. However, Christians appear to be proud of their hostility to Islam – as if it is a sign of a vital faith – in the same way we dealt with Communism. I think that we should rather be appalled that even in the Dark Ages there were Christians showing more toleration and respect to Islam than today. Hostility forfeits the opportunity to share with Muslims the 'true Gospel'. A leading Sheikh in Jordan addressed a group of Christian seminary students on Muslim-Christian relations and warned both houses of faith, 'Missionaries of great causes have caused great disasters by their methods'. Another godly sheikh, Dr Mohammed Sayyid Al Tantouwi of the Al Azhar University Mosque in Cairo, calls 'human beings to co-operate with one another and to reject extremism, to reject terrorism and of course to reject killing and stealing and every evil deed. In Islam we believe all human beings come from one mother and father. And whatever their different beliefs and creeds their brotherhood is one. All human beings wherever they are living in Europe, Australia, America Africa, Asia and any part of the world, they are asked to co-operate with each other and make peace with each other for the good of love'.[19]

Bishop Kenneth Cragg, who has a long track record in building good relations, advises, 'There is an understanding, both

Muslim and Christian, that we should keep in mind. How you treat another party is likely to contribute to the response that party makes to you. If you are ready to assume a capacity that is positive and reciprocal, there's a better chance that you will find it. . . . The way we judge a person has a way of judging us. Our judgements must be based on perceptive honesty and a wide compassion.'[20]

The original source of Bishop Cragg's advice is Jesus. Francis of Assisi understood this principle and attempted to put Jesus' commands into action and Muslims received him and his message of the 'true Gospel'.

Notes

1 Talbi, M. & Othman, B. (1992) *Ayaal Allah*, Tunis: Dar Siras Al Nashr, p. 156.
2 Said, E. (1981) *Covering Islam*, New York: Vintage Books, p. 5, Reprinted by permission of Pantheon Books, a division of Random House Inc.
3 Ibid., p. 5.
4 Graham, C. (1987) 'Australia's War Image of the Arab', *Free Palestine* 43, January–February 1987.
5 Sis Levine, *Beirut Diary*, pp. 235–39.
6 Braibanti, R. (1995) *The Nature and Structure of the Islamic World*, Chicago: International Strategy and Policy Institute, p. 15.
7 Farmaian, S. F. (1992) *Daughter of Persia*, New York: Crown Publishers, pp. 201, 257. Rights and permission granted.
8 Ibid., p. 392.
9 Fuller, G. (1998) writing in the *Los Angeles Times*, 24 August 1998, cited in Words to Remember, Washington Report on Middle East Affairs, Oct-Nov 1998, p. 10–17.
10 Kabbani, R. (1989) *Letter to Christendom*, Camden, UK: Virago Press, p. 54.

11 Close R., The Washington Report on Middle East Affairs, Washington DC; Oct/November 1998, p. 16.

12 Ibid., Zogby J., p. 12.

13 Ibid., Curtis, R., November 1998, p. 14.

14 ADC Files quoted in JUSOOR, issue 7/9 1996, Kitab. Inc. Bethesda.

15 Agence France Press, 3 March 1999.

16 Blincoe, B. (1998) *The Blincoe Report*, November 1998, Mesa, Arizona.

17 Abdullah, A. *Nidau'l Al Islam*, 20, September/October 1997.

18 Cragg, K. *The Christian Century*, 17 February 1999, interview.

19 Unpublished interview, October 1998. (Used by permission of The Plough Publishing House, Philadelphia and East Sussex.)

20 Cragg, op. cit.

Chapter Six

A MUSLIM LIKE ME

'She was a lovely girl and worked for us as a house help for a number of years. One day she came to us saying she observed how we lived out our faith and was impressed by our prayers and witness and wanted to convert. We encouraged her, but when we explained that she would have to divorce her husband because he is not a believer, she wasn't able to follow through. Poor thing. She really wanted to become a Muslim.' Suad finished her story and poured more tea for us.

The other four women listening to this story about the Filipino Christian, who worked for Suad in Kuwait, agreed it was a pity and talked about the difficult situation she was caught in. I was the only Christian in the room and I sat silently watching the mental movies playing before me of mirror conversations where the Muslim house-help was influenced by the life of Christians and wanted to become a believer. Some of these people were told they could not marry the person their family chose for them because the intended spouse was not a believer and also found themselves in an impossible situation. This was one of those so numerous times that I was impressed afresh that Christians and Muslims both have missionary hearts at the core of their being and both want the world to see their particular light. There are two possible motives for this desire: to be the victors in a faith battle, or to share something precious with others. The motive can make the difference. I listened to the women discussing their expectation that their lives lived for God would cause others to desire to follow God more closely. And I thought once again: there's a Muslim just like me.

Ignorance is one of the reasons Christians fear Islam. As long as we see Muslims as people who are not like us this fear will lead us down troubled paths. One of the ways to dispel fear is to conquer ignorance with the truth. Christians and Muslims need to understand each others' basic beliefs and how this is actually lived out. We need to understand the fundamental teachings and practices of Islam. There are five basic tenets in Islam, known as the five pillars. The Creed (shahada), Prayer (salat), Charity (zakat), Fasting (sawm) especially in Ramadan and Pilgrimage (hajj). However, not all Muslims practice all five all of the time.

The Shahada

'God is Greater. There is no God but God, and Muhammed is his apostle.'

High in Morocco's Atlas Mountains the fiery fingertips of the setting sun stroked a clump of tents nestled in a remote valley. The long day of fasting in a Ramadan summer was about to end and the Bedouin Berbers prodded their goats and shag-tail sheep back to their pens. Families performed ablutions and sat down on rugs inside their black goat-hair tents to wait for the food the women had prepared. Patience hung silently on the air as they sat out the last few minutes before their meal. But there was no mosque or cannon within earshot to herald the breaking of the fast. The two Catholic nuns living among the Bedouin Muslims, and sharing the same rugged life and fasting with them, turned on their small portable radio at full blast. The hills echoed 'There is no God but God' and abruptly died. Muslims and Catholics then ate together in harmony with what was expressed and in harmony because of what was not expressed.

Islam means 'submitting oneself to God' and a Muslim is the person who has submitted to God. The cornerstone of Islam is belief in the one and only God who is indivisible. This concept is expressed by the term the 'unity' of God and it emphasises the unapproachable greatness of the one and only God. The word 'Allah' is Arabic for 'The God'. There is no other word for the one and only God in the Arabic language, so when someone uses this term, whether they are Christian or Muslim, they are simply saying 'God'. Therefore, I can join wholeheartedly with Muslims in this statement of faith and proclaim, 'There is no God but the one and only High God' who is attested to in the Scriptures.

'Allahu Akbar' (God is greater) is whispered in the new-born's ear so that these are the first words they hear. The words, 'Allahu Akbar' are better known in the West than the rest of the Muslim Creed and unfortunately it has come to be connected in peoples' minds with protest and violence. It often sounds to Christians like a war cry rather than a statement of faith. It's the cry we hear as Muslim protesters wave banners in the street and shout; it's the statement added to the Iraqi flag during the Gulf war; it's the cry of warring Islamic factions shouting as they go into battle.

Jonathan Kuttab, a Palestinian Christian lawyer, explains the meaning of 'Allahu Akbar' and why this cry is taken up in situations of social outcry. It is epitomised in the Palestinian struggle for recognition and justice. 'There is a tremendous internal spiritual strength that the Palestinians have in their struggle and they draw it primarily from their faith – whether they are Christian or Muslim – from a deep seated belief that justice will ultimately prevail and that God is sovereign, but they don't use those words. They say, Allahu Akbar. That literally translates "God is Greater", not God is the greatest. God is greater than the oppression; God is greater than your gun. God is greater than the power confronting us. So when Muslims yell, Allahu Akbar to the West, they are saying, "I am weak, you are strong. I don't have power, but God is greater than what is happening". It's not the army or the powerful rulers with the big gun who yells Allahu Akbar; it's the masses. It's the people with no power who are always yelling, "God is greater".[1] In this we understand Allahu Akbar is not usually a threat thundered against us, but a statement of faith and a protest at conditions and a voiced hope for a better future.

One becomes a Muslim by reciting the Creed, the statement of faith. Many times Muslims who are concerned that I am not going to heaven, and want me to be there, have urged me to recite the Creed. But it's here that even Muslims and Christians with the best intentions scrape against each other. In the second statement of faith, 'and Muhammed is his apostle', what is meant is that Muhammed is the seal of the prophets. God sent a prophet to each generation to make his will known to man and Muhammed was the last in this line and the final one. Each succeeding prophet abrogated the former prophets. So Muhammed is seen as the bearer of the complete and final revelation of God for humankind. Where his message contradicts former prophets, the revelation given to Muhammed is the correct one. So although Muslims believe in Christ and accord him great honour, Christ's message does not have the same place as the more recent message brought by Muhammed.

But Muslims do not believe Muhammed brought a new religion; he came as a reformer leading a revival of the original monotheism given to Abraham and confirmed by the prophets. The Quran contains stories from the Old and New Testaments and Muhammed believed he was calling Christians, Jews and pagans to renew the monotheist faith. He saw Christians worshipping Mary and statues and the trinity (which appeared to be three gods: God, Mary and Jesus) and he sent out a reformer's call to return to pure worship of God and leave all idolatry. This is the background for interpreting many chapters of the Quran that speak against the trinity. Muhammed's teaching on the unity of God is taken from Christianity and Judaism. The Shidaada, the statement of the unity of God, is the call of Deuteronomy 6:4,5. 'The Lord thy God is one.' Jesus stated this is the most important commandment with its ensuing obligation to put God first.[2]

Muhammed believed he was coming in the traditions of all the biblical prophets and was called to complete their message. He did not claim to begin a new religion, but to reaffirm the call to the original Islam (submission to God) that began with Adam. He heard the message of the Scriptures through a confusing variety of Jewish and Christian sects in the Arabian Gulf. These two faiths secured a strong place for Moses and Christ in Islam. The Christian sects included Nestorianism with a view on the nature of Jesus that he was partly God and partly man. Other Christian sects denied the divinity of Christ. The statement that 'Jesus didn't die' was not Muhammed's brainchild. Gnostic Christians and Jews were the source of this belief. Islam is often branded as an anti-Christ religion because of this statement, but we need to remember that Muhammed heard this from those claiming to be Christians.

Two cornerstone beliefs of Islam also have their roots in the 'people of the Book'. The Christian ascetics abounding at the time demonstrated that achievements are more important than grace, and the Jews demonstrated that the detailed obedience of the Law is the most important. The Quran reflects Muhammed's view that Christians are better than Jews because the Byzantine Church had some spiritual vitality at the time, but Judaism had lost vitality in the Jews he met. There had been no prophet recognised for 600 years. So Muhammed heard a confusing message. Some Christians have viewed his teaching as a compromise between Christianity and Judaism, with the main points being anti-idolatry and submission to God.

Why did Muhammed claim to be an apostle? He could have simply delivered his message or claimed only prophethood. This claim to apostleship is a key to understanding his declared links with the Christian tradition. It should also help us to grasp why the place of Muhammed and Islam is not simply dogma, but rooted into the deepest psyche of Arab Muslims. The apostles

held a very important place in the Eastern churches. Proof of
lineage and a genealogy is a very important aspect of Eastern
culture. The apostles divided the world between them and each
branch of the Church claimed their own apostle to prove they
were genuine: Thomas in India, Peter in Rome, Mark in Egypt.
But there was no apostle for the Arabian Gulf. Muhammed saw
himself as the missing apostle for the Arab world. As we previously discussed, Muhammed longed for a text he could totally
identify with in the Gulf Arabs' mother tongue and when he
delivered the Quran it stated, 'Now I have sent you an Arabic
Quran (Scripture)'. So his claim of apostleship is connected to
links with the historical revealed Scriptures and genuine authority for a people group to receive God's revelation in their mother
tongue.

Islam's roots in Christianity are recognised, but the extent of
its borrowings are disputed. One theory postulated is that the
word *Quran* (the Muslim Scriptures) has its origins in Syriac –
the language of many of the Arab Christians in the region at the
time. The Quran states that when Gabriel appeared to
Muhammed, he told him 'IQRA' – recite – and gave him the text
of the Quran. The Syriac word for *invoke* or *call* has the same
letters IQRA. Nouns are formed in similar ways in Arabic and
Syriac and *invocation* in Syriac is *Quran*. Scripture in the
churches was chanted, recited, or sung in the manner of calling
out an invocation, so it's interesting to note that the message
from God specifies there is now an Arabic holy Scripture to be
recited. The theory is weakened because the Syriac verb for reciting or chanting is different. But it is still a plausible theory
showing a possible relationship of liturgical roots. We also note
the Old Testament traditions reiterated as pure Islam: no pictures, no pork, halaal (kosher) slaughter of animals, and circumcision of boys relating to the circumcision of the Abrahamic
covenant. For all these reasons the early Church first understood
Islam as a Christian heresy and condemned it in the same category as the Donatist Christians of North Africa.[3]

The Church is split in its attitude to Muhammed. Some Christians assert Muhammed has no place worth discussing, others that he is indeed a true prophet and others claim he is the tool of the devil and even the anti-Christ. St John of Damascus has been accused of beginning the Christian tradition of ridiculing Muhammed. This continued when Islam conquered Christian Spain and the word spread that Muhammed was a licentious schemer, the antithesis of the self-sacrificing Christ. This view developed and Muhammed grew into the anti-Christ and this became the motivating slogan for the Crusades. In 1213 Pope Innocent III described him as the 'beast of the Apocalypse'.[4]

Rana Kabbani, a Muslim writer, notes: 'These stories have been used over the centuries to justify a depiction of the prophet as plagiarist, libertine and opportunist, a picture which is still with us. It was hoped a character assassination of Muhammed would discredit and bring down the whole of Islam. The implicit analogy was with Christianity, which is built around the virtuous person of Christ and depends crucially on his redemptive sacrifice. The only way to the father is through the Son. So to attack Jesus – to imply for example that he was a man with lusts – is to undermine the whole edifice. On this model it was supposed that Islam could be destroyed by destroying the reputation of its prophet. There seems little doubt that the long history of denigration and ridicule, fed by the church fathers, crusading knights, theologians, travellers, oriental scholars and contemporary novelists is in itself a formidable obstacle to tolerant understanding.'[5]

An analogy to help us understand how Muslims view Christ and Christians is to compare how Christians view Moses and the Jewish faith: the Jews have a light but in comparison to Christ it is dim. They have an old incomplete perception of the truth. They need to complete their faith, by accepting the Seal of the Prophets, whom the New Testament claims is Christ. Muslims tell me I should complete my faith journey by accepting God's final prophet. They are saddened that as a person of faith my journey will be lost. Nora, a Syrian Catholic, lives in North Africa and teaches at a government Muslim school. She is the only Christian on staff. One colleague told her, 'It's such a shame. You're such a good and respectable person and full of faith, but it's wasted. You're Christian.'

Fasting and Ramadan

Ramadan is a month dedicated to the spiritual pursuit of pleasing God by searching your inner self and putting straight what is wrong, reflection on the progress of your spiritual journey, purifying yourself from all evil and bringing the body into submission through struggling against the flesh by the denial of basic comforts. For one lunar month Muslims abstain from: all food and drink from sunrise to sunset, including swallowing saliva; smoking; marital sex; and women refrain from using make-up and perfume. Muslims attempt to abstain from all anger and gossip and from looking at anything religiously unlawful that takes the mind away from worship of God. The period of self-denial ends with the feast called Eid Al Fitr (Breaking The Fast), commonly called the Lesser Feast. It is celebrated with special food and new clothes for the children. It is followed after a few months by Eid Al Adha (Feast Of Sacrifice) commonly called the Great Feast. This feast, in which an animal (usually a sheep) is sacrificed, commemorates the great event when Abraham sacrificed the animal God provided as a substitute for his son. Muslims commonly believe this son was Ishmael, but the Quran does not state this, but says, 'the son'.

Ramadan is the most widely practised pillar of Islam, along with prayer. The Islamic calendar is lunar and Ramadan is the ninth month. The beginning of the fast varies from place to place. Even in these technological times it is still based on the physical sighting of the moon and astronomical calculations, but not all the Islamic world fasts at exactly the same time; Morocco usually begins one day after Saudi Arabia. So, although people can predict correctly the first day of the lunar month there are still a couple of days of anticipation in case the moon cannot be sighted on the predicted day. When the moon is officially sighted announcements are made on the media along with displays of fireworks and congratulatory messages. Everyone listens for the traditional cannon blast announcing the month has begun. This throws the Ramadan schedule into operation: schools and businesses open later and finish earlier and restaurants disguise their appearance or disappear from sight altogether during the day. Ramadan moves through the seasons as it follows the lunar calendar. The young, the elderly, the ill and nursing and pregnant mothers are excused. There is a great sense of jubilation when Ramadan begins and Muslims visit their friends or call those far away wishing them Ramadan blessings.

The year we lived in Damascus, Ramadan fell in autumn. Every morning the neighbourhood crier woke us at 4.30 am. He passed down the cold empty streets beating his drum and calling the believers to wake in order to eat their final dawn meal before the new day's fast. Lights burst into life and flickered around the opposite apartment building like a Christmas tree coming to life. Thirty minutes before dawn the mosque loudspeaker broadcast special readings before the call to prayer. The Syrian calls to prayer are beautiful and melodious. One mosque near our niece's house in the suburbs had a most unusual chanting which I have never heard anywhere else. Two muezzin (prayer callers) chanted passages from the Quran together in harmony sounding just like a contemporary Christian song. I was woken before dawn by melodious songs of praise to God wafting over the neighbourhood. A joyful peace touched my heart as I joined in prayer and praise and then went back to sleep, happy and contented, reminded I was in God's loving care.

At sunset a cannon blast, or a siren that sounds just like a war air raid alert, announces the 'breaking of the Fast'. In countries that are almost totally Muslim, like Morocco, any traffic still on the street roars to its destination. At intersections where lights are changing from orange to red cars gather speed to race the light. Everyone knows that in Ramadan, if the Fast is about to break, a red light has no authority. So one never assumes there is no car coming through on the red. Cars need to be sighted just like the moon. The few remaining pedestrians quickly evaporate indoors and in ten minutes there is not a soul, nor car to be seen. Standing alone in the middle of a ghost town shrouded in silence it is easy to imagine the end of all things came and somehow you got left behind, or everyone else has taken cover from an aerial attack and you alone are vulnerable in the open deserted streets. It's an eerie experience.

In countries where Ramadan is enforced, public life totally changes. All restaurants and coffee shops are closed during the day. Even the chairs and tables are removed or covered so as not to give even the appearance the establishment may serve food and hence be fined. All bars close day and night for the whole month and no alcohol is sold anywhere. Muslims face penalties if caught eating (one of our friends was jailed for six months), so they are easily angered if foreigners eat in public. You would expect non-Muslims to be sensitive and refrain from behaviour that offends, but the occasional tourist will wander in the street, chewing on something or smoking, or women will appear in revealing clothes. We could wonder why Muslims could be angry with someone who does not follow their religion; who does not need to abide by the rules. The problem is that not all are devout Muslims and some do not want to fast, but they must give the appearance of fasting or neighbours could report them to the police. For this reason they will keep a pretence of fasting in front of their children, so that they don't compromise them by giving them dangerous information that they could pass on innocently which will have serious repercussions. We have been in homes during Ramadan where the hot teapot was hidden under the table when the children entered the room. When the state forces people to live with this kind of hypocrisy, the citizens feel angry at their lack of freedom. So if a foreigner insensitively takes the freedom they are denied it is understandable that they are annoyed. Much of their anger is at their situation – anger which they cannot voice without reprisals.

Ramadan is not enforced in Syria and, apart from the morning crier and special sweets peddled by vendors, little else changes in daily life on the streets. Tunisia is an example of a middle model. Fasting is not enforced, but public life is voluntarily visibly changed. In Tunisia the coffee shops remove chairs and tables to the inside and cover the windows so that people eating are not evident. Alcohol is not served at all, nor on sale for the month, so people who drink stockpile before the Fast begins. Although fasting is not enforced most people choose to fast.

Ramadan has a social and religious significance similar to Christmas and Thanksgiving. It is a time for the family to draw together in unity and a special sense of community coming together. Celebration pervades the atmosphere. Women cook celebration foods for the night meals. Ramadan in Tunisia was the most wonderful time of the year. The Ministry of Culture organises musical events held in various locations in the ancient quarter of the capital city. Every night after the meal the old homes in the ancient quarter, now serving as museums and heritage trusts, fill with families enjoying performances from troupes from all over the world. We loved Ramadan because we spent most nights with friends breaking the Fast and then all went to one of the many events offered. The heritage trust homes are deep in the old quarter of the city and can only be reached on foot. As we arrived at a worn wooden door at the end of a cul-de-sac our guide reminded us to step up over the high threshold and bend our heads low under the architrave. We uncurled ourselves to emerge in a colourfully tiled courtyard open to the sky. The typical traditional Arab house is a rectangle encompassing an open courtyard in the centre. Two or three-storey homes have intricate wooden handcarved balconies (*machrabiyyeh*) entwining each floor like vines. The walls boast stuccowork picked out in gold leaf. Heavy doors in intricate designs and pastel colours look down onto the centre of the house where gigantic crystal chandeliers hang suspended over the courtyard. Here a fountain softly gurgles beside a lemon tree, but is drowned out by the chatter of the crowd sitting on the few hundred chairs placed on bright rugs. Small lanterns and candles grace the walls. These were the venues where we saw the whirling dervishes from Syria and listened to the Turkish National Orchestra, lute players and poetry readings.

Another memorable event at an equally interesting venue was a summer night at the Roman Amphitheatre at Carthage, open to the starry summer sky. It was filled to overflowing for a special type of poetry put to music. Jasmine wafted on the breeze. In summer many Tunisian men wear a sprig of jasmine over one ear and women don a threaded jasmine necklace. The artist was singing a famous poem by one of their great mystic-philosophers, Ibn Arabi, and cleverly throwing in some unexpected comments that kept the crowd glued to him. At every beloved line or quip the crowd let out one great long verbalised sigh, the famous Arab 'aahh'. The 'aahh' is a syllable expressing such deep and beautiful emotions from the centre of the heart it cannot be limited by a word. It's an emotive sigh. I will always remember those families and the hundreds of men of all ages, many with flowers on their ears, spellbound by beautiful poetry, gently swaying to its rhythm and expressing appreciation with far away looks and longing 'Aahhs'. The culture, refinement and beauty of the Middle East were epitomised in that fragrant starry night. I lay this memory beside televised images of Muslim countries which emphasise violence, and fanaticism erupting in dusty streets, and am deeply saddened that most Westerners will never experience a Ramadan summer poetry night heavy with jasmine and Aahhs and laughter. I am also saddened that so many Muslims in troubled spots may never escape the unrest and injustice to attain such a carefree night either.

Ramadan is the spiritual high point of the year and the time for the deepest and richest discussions about faith. So I was disturbed when a group of Western Christians in one country invited us to meet weekly to 'pray against the spirit of Ramadan'. I pictured every Ramadan event we were involved in with Muslims: family unity, the spiritual quest, heightened spiritual awareness, inter-faith discussions and community celebrations. From which one of these should I withdraw in order to pray against it? Jesus' teaching and example shows us to pray for people and for protection from evil. Christ did not teach us to pray against a religious culture. Groups connected to the occult are known to meet on religious holidays, but they are a small percentage of the population. When a person needed release from evil spirits, Jesus cast the specific spirit(s) out of a specific person and there was a night and day result of deliverance in that person's life. Unlike this, in this case, the Christians were praying against evil spirits they believed to be released in Muslim culture during Ramadan. It tied in with a belief that Satan permeates Islam. However, this topic depends on one's theology and I prefer to witness to the light rather than describe the darkness, so I declined. I invited them to join us with our Muslim friends for breaking the Fast and a concert, but they were unable to accept because it was a prayer night.

Our family is from the majority Sunni denomination. My sister-in-law was among the few in our family who didn't fast. When we sat down on the carpet to eat from the communal plates, Rowia winked at me remarking, 'No use fasting if your heart isn't pure.' 'Yes,' I replied, 'you are in agreement with Jesus. That's what he taught us. God wants to purify us from inside out, not outside in.' At the end of Ramadan month the street crier came to all his clients to collect his pay. He played his drum and sang in stairwells of buildings until the occupants came out and paid their dues. It was a good opportunity for the unemployed to make some money and students to gain pocket money.

When Ramadan falls in the summer months with long hot days in the hotter climates it is difficult, especially for those who are engaged in manual outdoor labour. In Australia the fasting day begins at 4.30 am and lasts until 9 pm. Huda, a Muslim university student in her early twenties, describes Ramadan in a Melbourne summer. 'It's a spiritual time and there is an awareness of accountability. No one else will know if I break the fast. Only God sees you all day. The nights are wonderful when it falls on school holidays. Ramadan brings people together and we share food and socialise at the mosque. The young people gather and talk about spiritual things.' In Australia congregations stay at their mosques for a communal dinner after prayers to break the fast at the end of the day. 'People feel on a spiritual high. It's a purely spiritual time. We are on our best behaviour. We try to be more generous, more sensitive and less selfish. We should be like this always, but it's easier when you are fasting. We should read the whole Quran in that month, but by attending prayers and hearing it read it's easy to finish it in that time. It is not just prayer that's important. There is no sense praying without good dealings with others.'

Tania is a Muslim from the minority Alouite sect that does not follow formal Muslim worship traditions. There is nothing to distinguish her from any other of the ethnic groups making up the tapestry of multi-cultural Australia. She anglicised her name after moving to Australia and does not wear any distinguishing clothing. 'I don't fast. In the summer time in Australia it's too hot and the day is too long to wait to drink. So I won't be a hypocrite and give the appearance I am fasting when I am not. Besides, I believe true religion is to live according to your conscience before God: be pure in heart, do good to others. Keeping rules about how to dress or pray or eat or not eat, or anything else, won't make us right with God if our heart isn't right. My fast is to fast from talk that hurts others or actions that harm others. There is no point keeping Ramadan, or praying all the time, if you still gossip or harm others. Everyone is different and this is how I see things.' Tania has had only positive experiences in Australia with friendly neighbours who helped her to adjust. 'I believe you get what you give. If you are kind and open hearted people will treat you the same way.'

The similarities between Ramadan and events in the Christian calendar are obvious. Our equivalent to Ramadan is Lent. The Christian Lent is a forty-day fast from a basic comfort. The Early Church in Proconsular Africa – current North Africa – fasted (in the same manner as Islam) during the daylight hours for forty days before Easter. This time of inner reflection and renewal and seeking repentance ends in the celebration of the feast of Easter commemorating God's provision of his sacrifice when he did not save his only son for us on the mount. Easter commemorates Christ as the fulfilment of the sacrifice of Abraham on Mount Moriah. Muslims celebrate Abraham's sacrifice in the Great Feast. Easter used to be the greatest feast in the Christian calendar and is still regarded as such in the Eastern churches. One of the reasons it became the lesser celebrated of the two feasts of Christendom is due to Francis of Assisi. Of all the events in Christ's life that Francis loved, the one he loved most was of the Christ child celebrated at Christmas. Christ vulnerable and lying in a poor manger that was not his own, but borrowed from the animals, epitomised the holy poverty of Jesus that Francis loved so dearly. He modelled his life and order on the poverty of Jesus. It's no wonder that Christmas was so special to him and he introduced one of the practices that endear the season to everyone: the nativity crèche.

I think this innovation by Francis is unfortunate for it changed the focus of the Western churches from Easter to the celebration of Christmas. Over the centuries and with the addition of consumerism the baby Francis placed in the manger is in danger of becoming Santa Claus. While Christmas is important, it is the prelude to Easter and although the events cannot be separated in God's redemptive plan for the world, the events at Easter are the cornerstone of our faith and hope. It is the culmination of Christ's obedience to the Father. He was born a baby, but then had to live a life of submission to God; no matter how he was tempted to put the cross behind him, he did not. At any point it was possible that we would not have an Easter to celebrate. That is one of the triumphs of Easter – although Christ was tempted as we are, he proved faithful to the end and blazed the trail where he will take us into God's presence. It is Christ's death on the cross that makes the reason for Christian and Muslim and any other fasting so different. The New Testament teaches that it is because of Christ's submission to the Father that we gain eternal life, not our own inadequate attempts to submit to God. Western Christianity could recover some vitality if we move the emphasis back to the celebration of Easter as our larger feast, but as things go in the West we then face the danger of the Easter bunny taking over! A Muslim told me, 'It's very sad to see the commercialism of Christmas. I think Jesus is not pleased by this.'

Prayer

Five times a day every mosque around the world calls the faithful to prayer by reciting in Arabic 'God is greater. There is no God but God, and Muhammed is his apostle. Come to Prayer, Come to good works. God is greater.' Muhammed brought nothing new in prayer, since praying a set number of times a day, prostrating oneself and ceremonial washing were Judeo-Christian practices.

There are four afternoon prayers through to night and the early morning prayer, Fajr, which is usually associated with a reading of the Quran. The four afternoon prayers are

Zuhr – immediately after the sun begins to decline in the afternoon
Asr' – in late afternoon
Maghrib – immediately after sunset
'Isha – after the glow of the sun has disappeared and full darkness has set in.

Morning prayer is singled out because the morning is a *Holy Hour* and special influences act on the soul after the night's rest.[6]

Although the five prayer times and ceremonies are not pro-scribed in the Quran, it is beyond dispute that they were well established before Muhammed's death. The worshipper must first take time to come to an attitude of prayer, or intention to worship (niyya). Each prayer consists of a certain number of raka': bowing from the torso followed by two prostrations with head touching the floor. Each raka' consists of seven movements along with a certain proclamation of faith while facing Mecca:

1. 'Allahu Akbar': hand open on the side of the face
2. Recite the Faatiha (opening prayer of the Quran): standing upright with hands open palms up in the prayer posture
3. Bowing
4. Straightening up
5. Sliding to the knees and prostrating with forehead to the ground
6. Sitting back on haunches
7. A second prostration

At the end of each prostration the worshipper recites the Creed and at the conclusion of the whole prayer, the salutations: turning to the right and left saying, 'Salaam Alaikum' (Peace be upon you). The proscribed prayers are two raka' at daybreak, four at noon, four at mid-afternoon, three after sunset, and four at the early part of the night. Because the prayers are conducted on the floor, special prayer rugs are kept for this use. Muslims also pray spontaneously when the moment decrees, usually recit-ing the Faatiha, the opening prayer of the Quran:

> Praise be to God
> Cherisher and Sustainer of the Worlds
> Most gracious, Most Merciful
> Lord of the day of judgement.
> Thee we worship
> Thine aid we seek
> Guide us on the straight path
> The way of those on whom

Thou hast bestowed Thy grace
Those whose portion is not wrath
and who go not astray.

What do Muslims understand about God in this prayer? We should let Muslims speak for themselves, just as we would like to be given the opportunity to explain our faith and not have a Muslim, or adherent to any other religion, interpret what we believe in a manner we don't recognise. The Muslim commentary on this prayer states this is placed first in the Quran because it 'sums up man's relation to God in contemplation and prayer. In our spiritual contemplation the first words should be praise. If the praise is from our inmost being it brings us into union with God's will . . . evil is purged out and our eyes are lifted above them to see God's attributes. This leads us to worship and acknowledgement and finally comes our prayer for guidance and a contemplation of what that guidance means. God needs no praise, for he is above all praise: he needs no petition for He knows our needs better than we do ourselves; and his bounties are open without asking; to the righteous and the sinner alike. The prayer is for our own spiritual education, consolation and confirmation. When we reach enlightenment they flow spontaneously from us.'

Children are taught this prayer early in life and told to pray it when they are afraid or confused or thankful. This was one of the first prayers our children learnt at school. It is memorised along with a rocking motion that keeps rhythm with the poetic meter of the verse. The Quran is very poetic and when chanted is beautifully melodious and has a powerful hypnotic effect on listeners. This is one of the reasons that Islam does not recognise translations of the Quran into other languages: it loses its beauty. The first and last rhyming refrains of the Faatiha often waft through my mind (along with pictures of our little boys singing it for homework) and I wish I could remember the rest to offer as a beautiful supplication to God. Some Christians were concerned our children had to memorise the Quran as well as learn Muslim doctrine as part of their curriculum. In fact if they failed these subjects they could not pass to the next class and they memorised a large portion of the Quran in primary school. Our friends thought those learnt verses would stay in their minds forever, thus threatening their latent Christian faith. I never thought to ask these concerned Christians if they had read the Quran.

Our sons' experiences in the Muslim community, as well as the fact that they were usually the only Christians in their classes at school, were only positive. The other children assumed they were different and assumed they were Christian. Their discussions taught them from an early age how to live in a world with different beliefs and celebrate it, while enjoying others who are different and yet keep their own faith identity. They knew how to explain their faith to Muslims when they were under ten years old in ways that mature Christians wished they knew. A Muslim education taught them respect for God and human authority, beginning with respect for parents and to protect the family unity, along with the necessity of a good moral life. When I compare their education with the problems experienced by parents educating their children in the West: struggling with secular humanism and a lack of respect for all values and authority, along with drug abuse and violence in the school ground, I am glad my children had the opportunity to be educated in a protected Muslim environment.

Most Muslims pray the morning prayer, but not all Muslims respond to the prayer call five times a day. Some Muslims told me they thought that eighty per cent of Muslims don't pray at all. I believe this figure to be highly exaggerated. Others thought that maybe fifty per cent prayed three times a day. The majority of Muslims I know in various places in the world pray three times during the day: at dawn, the middle of the day and the evening. However, I also know some Muslims who rarely pray even during Ramadan. Practice varies from country to country and also depends on how the state regiments religion. In Saudi Arabia, prayer times are enforced by the muttawa patrolling public places and forcing shops to close. However, in most counties life continues on unabated while the few faithful stop what they are doing in order to render to God what is his due.

Six women lounged on brocade sofa-lounge chairs in a fashionable apartment in a Muslim city drinking mint tea from small coloured glasses entwined with a gold-leaf design around the rims. We munched on cream cakes. The women were all dressed differently. One or two were wearing trousers and jackets and one wore a skirt above the knee. The others still had on the traditional long robes worn in the street as a body covering (djellaba) over traditional kaftans. In the midst of the conversation the one in the short skirt got up and stood to the side of the group and donned a djellaba and headscarf. She then rolled out a small velvet rug on the floor and began going through the various postures for prayer. She knelt, prostrated herself and returned to a kneeling position and repeated the motions a number of times all the time mumbling to herself the set prayer words. Right next to her the women took no notice and kept up their light-hearted conversation and laughter interspersed with tea drinking. When she finished she removed the scarf and djellaba and returned to the group and one of the others got up, put on the discarded scarf and took her place. Half of the women prayed in this manner. The others didn't pray at all and no comment was made about either.

The conversation turned to the hostess' teenage daughter who had not slept well since the father died eighteen months ago. The mother, who ran her own hairdressing salon, was at her wits' end and related that she went to the faqi (a sheikh) and got a charm to help her daughter. The sheikh gave her a small piece of paper with Quranic verses written on it, which she put in her daughter's tea and had her drink it. She used the charm and it worked and her daughter was now much better. Everyone gave their opinions on these folk Islam practices. A couple declared it was magic and was not allowed in Islam, but others believed in it because it had helped them in times of need.

I told them when I have trouble sleeping I pray, and since Satan doesn't want us to pray I usually fall quickly asleep! This was intended as a quip, but didn't have the effect I imagined. All talk stopped and all eyes were intensely watching me, 'Do you pray?' The question shocked me because the hostess, who was my friend, had introduced me to these women as a religious person and they had come to view me as living up to that reputation. How could they think I didn't pray? 'How do you pray?' Then I realised that they had never seen me perform prayers in the way they understood prayer. For a moment I had a ridiculous vision of me jumping out of bed in the middle of the night and performing prayer as the woman had just done – in order to fall asleep. No wonder they couldn't imagine falling asleep in the middle of all that activity. I tried to explain about extemporaneous prayer but could see that wasn't really true prayer in their eyes and it sounded lame to me too. It appeared to be a kind of waffling on at God when you feel it and not giving God glory by dedicating your whole body and soul in the process. It sounded especially suspect since I had just declared it put me to sleep! 'But what do you say?' I thought I had just answered that question so was at a loss until I remembered we do have a special prayer. So then I recited the Lord's prayer. The effect of this also took me by surprise. Not only were their spirits touched by its beauty, they were astounded by the implications of 'Forgive as we want to be forgiven' and with one voice they stopped me after that sentence to discuss it. In a culture built on retaliation (Islam along with Judaism believes in an eye for an eye and a tooth for a tooth) free and necessary forgiveness is revolutionary. Since that day I no longer rattle off 'Our Father' but notice how revolutionary the whole prayer is. I also learnt to pray with others in ways that they can recognise as prayer – whether it's receiving the blessing in Muslim prayer by wiping hands over face and chest, or making the sign of the cross in the Orthodox custom in recognition of living under the protection and covenant of Jesus' blood. Both have become very meaningful symbols.

When I met Aisha at her home in Melbourne she apologised
for the limited time of our interview as she was speaking at a
church group on Islam. She was dressed for the street wearing a
long dress, long sleeves and a veil: a large silk scarf falling around
her shoulders and covering all her hair. It was pinned under her
chin and decorated with a headband over the top. Her parents
are Egyptian and she was born and raised in Australia and
married an Egyptian Aussie. Aisha is a social worker and active
in Islamic awareness groups and a counsellor for the Muslim
community in Melbourne. She explained that she never took her
family's faith seriously, as it seemed to be mainly a cultural
expression. But during university studies when she researched
Islam she experienced an identity conflict, 'feeling neither completely Egyptian nor Australian. I found myself in being
Muslim. Islam was my saviour really. It helped me identify who
I was.' She prays five times a day. 'Non–Muslims feel Islam is
ritualistic, but there is another side. Everything in Islam is
worship. It's possible even for your sleep to be worship. It
depends on *the intention* (niyya) and this is something only God
can judge. For example, two people are praying. One prays
because God commands us to, but maybe the other is praying
because she doesn't want to look like the odd one out. Both
prayers go to God, but only God knows if he will accept the
prayer without the right intention. We can judge the action of a
person, but only God knows the intention. If I do religious acts
in order to gain approval from people I have already got my
reward. There will be none hereafter.'

I asked her about extemporaneous prayer and remembered
what had been one of the problems with talking about prayer
with the Muslim women at afternoon tea. I had used the wrong
word, so my prayer descriptions didn't make sense. When the
women asked me whether I prayed, they had asked, 'Do you
perform ritual prayers?' What I had unwittingly conveyed to
them was that I prayed ritual prayers extemporaneously without
any ritual. I should have used the word for *extemporary* prayer

for when I pray in bed, not liturgical prayer. Aisha explained, 'We pray all the time. We have two kinds of prayer: salat, the ritual of prayer, and da'wa, a calling to God from the heart. This da'wa can be any time and anywhere and you do not need to be ceremonially clean. Prayer is direct communication with God. Five times a day I am required to stop what I am doing (ritual prayer first requires ceremonial washing) and put aside everything and relate to God. If I telephoned a friend five times a day I would have a very close friendship! I feel very close to God in prayer. Also praying at regular intervals all during the day keeps me spiritually prepared for that time. It's not a burden. It's a wonderful thing. For five to ten minutes five times a day I put life back into perspective. I shut out the cleaning, cooking, children's demands, work's demands and recharge my battery. These times of prayer give me inner peace. I have a great sense of God's protection and safety and security.'

Muslims have difficulty with how Christians speak about their relationship with God. Terms such as 'God told me' are repugnant or just plain incomprehensible to them. I wanted Aisha to comment on this and even when I explained the question she shuddered when I used the term, so I asked her how did she look for guidance from God. 'The Quran is the main guide for living. But we actually have a set prayer for when we are ambivalent about a decision (istikha'). Then we look for the answer, maybe it will be dream or an incident.'

Nabila is also an Egyptian and a school teacher from Sydney, married to a Palestinian. She tries to pray five times a day 'but it's difficult to be consistent with the demands of home and work. If we don't have time during the day we make it up at home. We can add two prayers together. We actually pray more spontaneous prayers, for example I pray while I am driving asking God's help for the children or to keep them safe on a journey and I pray for patience when I am upset.' Huda is a law student from Melbourne and active in Islamic groups. She tries to pray five times a day, but faces the same time problem as Nabila. Huda describes prayer as 'a one-to-one relationship with God and without an intercessor we come very close to God'. One of Huda's friends pours everything out in a 'Dear God' letter. Although Huda feels very close to God she explained, 'You don't expect to hear something back. God hears and he sees and he listens and we feel close. We feel his presence and comfort and peace from being in his presence. If what I asked for doesn't happen I leave it to God's will. If you grow in trust, then you believe that God knows best and there is good in it. Every sigh on earth is not in vain. Suffering is rewarded in heaven.'

One of the problems between Muslims and Christians is their descriptions of their faith experience. It is not just anthropomorphisms that get in the way for Muslims. When I pray I do expect something back from God. I expect God will not only hear, but he will answer in more than circumstances. I expect to hear God's 'voice'. This can sound like borderline insanity for Muslims who believe God keeps at a respectful distance. But I believe God is about breaking through all the barriers of time and space and people's fears and reservations. God is the real seeker, not me. I pray to God because God stirs my heart to seek him out. This is the cornerstone Christian belief about God's nature. God seeks out men and women and children and makes himself known to us. I am limited by human language to describe this relationship with God and can only use words like see, hear, talk. Very human words for an infinite Spirit-God. I understand why Muslims, and others, balk at them. But the truth is that when I pray, I regularly hear God answering me and there is a reciprocal conversation between us. The warm glow that God's presence brings touches my emotions and my body. If I am emotionally hurting or physically ill this sense of warmth and well-being is so great I can get up healed and happy. But there is more than the sense of the presence of God – which Muslims also testify to. Christ says his followers will hear and recognise his voice. At times I have heard God's 'voice' suddenly prompting me to do something specific and out of my routine and subsequently discovered there was an important reason for obeying that impulse. At times the censure of God is so strong and the sense of relationship broken that it is impossible to get through the day without seeking forgiveness. Forgiveness is instant and there are very few emotions that compare with the soaring light and happiness of the knowledge of sins forgiven and everything right with the creator and sustainer of the universe. Christian belief that sins are forgiven through Christ here and now are difficult for Muslims, as they believe the outcome cannot be known until the day of judgement. Then there are those rare occasions when God almost demolishes the barriers and takes us into his presence in vision experiences when we see and hear in even more specific ways. For a person who believes God keeps a respectful distance my faith experience is alien, and I am too aware it sounds a little maniac. But I know my experience of God through Christ is not unique. Christians expect to touch, see, handle and taste God, because our Gospel teaches that God comes near through Christ. So if a Muslim were ever to ask me, why do I remain a Christian, I would not answer 'because I believe I know the truth about God'. I would answer 'because of the experiences I have of God through Christ. This is a personal intimate relationship and I am in love with the one who loves me.'

Huda's statement that she worships God simply because God is worthy to be worshipped and obeyed without expecting to hear anything back touches on the Muslim mystics' experiences of God. Many Muslims would answer they worship and obey God because they want to be forgiven and gain eternal life by obedience. Huda's statement impresses and challenges me. The times in my faith walk when God seemed distant and there was no sense of reciprocity in worship were dry times. It was like trudging through the desert until I reached the next waterhole. The difference in our views, expectations, and experiences of God do not need to put us in enemy trenches. They can be challenging and enriching. Being open to tolerance and dialogue does not mean we diminish our belief or pretend that there are no differences. It can mean that we give and receive from each other's experience.

Another way Muslims pray is with a rosary. Most men carry rosary beads, and in the Middle East both Muslims and Christians use them. Some men pray on them reciting the ninety-nine supreme names (characteristics) of God, and most men use them as stress beads. An Arab tradition says there are a hundred names of God, but only ninety-nine are known to men. Only the camel knows the hundredth name and that is why it walks so arrogantly with its head held high. The clicking of prayer beads being passed through fingers one by one is a common background soundtrack to conversations. The men also use them as a friendship symbol. For example, Ahmad notices Mustafa has an attractive blue stone rosary and asks for it. Sometimes they are given and sometimes they are lent for periods of time. Beads are regularly swapped around friends, so when they are praying with them or simply busy with them the person is reminded of his friend. We have prayer beads all over our house and stuffed in most suit coat pockets and most of them have a relationship to a friend.

The elderly usually become more religious as they approach the end of life and it is typical to see both men and elderly women reciting the rosary in public places. I was in the dentist's waiting room in North Africa and an elderly man was praying over his beads and droning on in a low voice for the whole hour. As I thought about Jesus' words on ostentatious public prayer and wondered if this fitted the bill, I had a sudden vision of my great-uncle Harry. Uncle Harry was a circuit riding Methodist lay preacher, and well into his eighties (in the 1970s) he still rode his bicycle around Buckinghamshire to preach on Sundays. He was known to sit in the dentist's waiting room quietly singing modern praise songs to Jesus.

The topic of discrimination inevitably surfaces for Muslims living in the West. Huda represents one of the Islamic Councils and explained that Muslims experience less discrimination on the university campus than on the streets. 'However, we feel excluded in university life. I was very excited to become part of the life at university but discovered nearly all the events involved alcohol. This climate of free sex and free drink is not how we live. The students look down on us because we don't join in. When they learn we don't believe in pre-marital sex or dating they are shocked. The see us as weirdos. Actually they have more acceptance about us going to pray at lunchtime, than not drinking or practising free sex. They cannot understand that we believe in sin and judgement.'

Zakat: Charity

There are two types of charity: 'zakat' (giving alms) and 'sadaaqat' (free will offerings). Charity is a beautiful loan to God. The Quran says, 'Who is he that will loan to God a beautiful loan which God will multiply to his credit and multiply many times?'[7] This is interpreted, 'Giving to God shows a beautiful spirit of self-denial; in other loans there may be doubt as to the safety of your capital or any return thereon, here you give to the Lord of all, in whose hands are the keys of want or plenty: giving you may have manifold blessings, or even lose what you have. If we remember that our goal is God, can we turn away from his cause?'

The Quran also states, 'Lit is such a light in houses which God has permitted to be raised to honour, for the celebration in them of His name, In them he is glorified in the mornings and in the evenings (again and again) by men whom neither traffic nor merchandise can divert from the Remembrance of God, nor from the practice of regular charity. Their only (fear) is for The Day when hearts and eyes will be transformed (in a world wholly new), that God may reward them according to the best of their deeds, and add even more for them out of his grace: for He doth provide for those whom He will without measure.'[8]

Charity is the outward sign of an inward faith and a means of salvation. Free will offerings are a means of expiating sins and are given to the needy, family and travellers. Traditionally there were no social services in Islamic countries as the rich in each community took care of the poor. There is still only a minimum of such services today. In traditional society in the Muslim world the rich and poor all lived together in the same streets and neighbourhood. This made it easy for the rich to care for the poor. Food was sent from house to house and those needing help could easily make their needs known; the rich would send a doctor at their own expense or pay for medicine or schoolbooks and so on. With the change in living patterns the rich now live separately in wealthy suburbs, and the poor live together without normal contact with the rich. The easiest way they can claim a handout is through begging on the streets. This usually happens on Fridays, the Holy day and communal prayer at the mosques, although there are always beggars to be found at mosque doors.

Small acts of kindness and charity are also offered as a religious obligation to the needy. Zahra and her family returned to her slum house in Cairo after a visit to southern Egypt. It was summer – with temperatures soaring in the hundreds. The journey had taken all day on public transport, including waiting for hours in the hot sun and travelling in a crowded bus with no air conditioning or fans, and with many of the men smoking. From the bus terminal they had to walk three miles over dusty paddocks carrying all their bags and staples brought from the family's village. She staggered through the front door and fell on the nearest bunk serving as a couch and sighed, 'Oh Lord if only I could have a big red watermelon.' A few minutes later a neighbour knocked on the door bringing them a big juicy red watermelon. She remembered this incident as one of the times God graciously met her needs.

Our youngest son was born at home in Fes, Morocco. Our landlord and his family lived upstairs and, until I was back on my feet, the landlady sent down a cooked meal for our family nearly every day, as well as cakes to offer the visitors coming to see the baby. When we offered thanks she responded with the customary reply, 'Don't thank me for my duty.' The service was offered to God and God will reward her on the Last Day. I was the means to enable her to give and thus receive a blessing.

The concept of neighbours being responsible for each other is still strong, more so in the poorer areas where they are dependant on each other. I heard about an uneducated and poor couple having marriage problems. The husband planned to take a new younger wife, divorce his current wife and send her back alone to her village, and take their five children to live with his mother. The first the wife knew about his intentions was when a removal truck arrived at her house to take the furniture. The neighbours heard the hysterical scene in the street and got involved trying to reason with the husband, without success. He had the right to take a second wife, but only if he treated them equally. Everyone who heard the story was very distressed and angry. I told my friend relating the story that God's righteous anger was against this man and I would pray in Jesus' name for God to help the wife. Two weeks later my friend came bursting in the door with the story of how God answered prayer. The leaders of the fundamentalist group in the neighbourhood went to the husband telling him he was acting against God and in an evil way toward his wife. If he did not reunite his family he had best beware of dark corners at night! He restored his wife and children to the home and she sent me a message that she was buying a lamb to sacrifice as a thank offering to Jesus for helping her. I should point out that I have only known of three polygamous marriages in the five Muslim countries where we've lived. In those countries monogamy was the norm and this atypical story illustrates the sacredness of the family unit. The community took action because the wife was living away from her family and therefore needed a mediator and protector. In case this story leaves the impression that Muslim men are wife beaters and worse, it should be noted that the men who did not allow this to happen were the black bearded, long robed, extreme fundamentalists.

Muslims give two per cent of their savings for zakat, usually to mosques or organisations. Charity is different. There are many ways to give sadaqa – from charitable deeds to time and effort and even a smile. At the time of the Feast of Sacrifice, Muslims in Melbourne give a donation of $50 to a Muslim aid group who buy a lamb on their behalf and send it to those abroad who are in need and cannot afford to buy their own, like in Kosovo or Palestine. Others gather together at the mosque for a bar-b-que and distribute food to the poor.

The Hajj: Pilgrimage

It is the hope of every Muslim to make the pilgrimage to Mecca once in a lifetime. It is obligatory for every person who can afford it. Once a person completes the pilgrimage they are henceforth given the honorific title Hajj or Hajja (for women) before their name. It is believed that if the hajj is completed properly the pilgrim's sins will be wiped out and the person will be clean like a newborn.

The pilgrimage includes a number of symbolic rituals and offering sacrifices. Pilgrims walk around the Kaaba (the building housing the black stone that fell from heaven) seven times, stone the devil (stoning three stone pillars outside Mina symbolising stoning the devil), say prayers at the station of Abraham, drink water from the well at Zamzam in memory of Hagar and Ishmael, and, among other things, walk seven circles around the mosque and run seven times between the small hills nearby. The ceremonies culminate in offering a sacrifice.

What do Muslims hope to gain from pilgrimage? 'The key is my intention to devote myself to worship. I want to forget worldly greed and trouble and dedicate myself to worship God.' There is also a 'unique experience of the community of Islam worshipping with people of many cultures, and languages. It's a place where rich and poor are equal. It's a fresh start to get away from the materialistic life that we are all influenced by.' I asked

Muslims, 'How does it change your life?' Their answers are summed up in this response, 'I feel complete. On pilgrimage I ask God for forgiveness and promise I will no longer sin. I reflect on myself and on repentance. I want to be a newly born person through coming close to God. Afterwards I feel like a new person refreshed to go back into the world and live God's way.'

A summary of the Muslims' replies evidenced that they were looking for, or actually experienced, a spiritual transformation through a time of repentance and closeness to God. They expected to be better Muslims afterwards. Some saw it as a time to obey God and thank him for his gifts. Still others saw it was a 'rehearsal for the day of judgement' through praying for forgiveness. Others saw it as chance to begin anew by asking God for a clean start.

The prophet Muhammed first set Medina as the pilgrimage venue, in place of Jerusalem, but after his quarrel with the Jews in Medina he changed the venue to Mecca. The pilgrimage is an old tradition and the Jews and Christians made pilgrimage to Jerusalem. Muhammed also claimed to have a miraculous visit to Jerusalem – a winged horse flew him to Abraham's rock that is now housed by the Dome of the Rock. So Jerusalem remains a holy city in the succession of prophets from Abraham to Jesus to Muhammed. Some Muslims try and go regularly to Mecca for pilgrimage. An Alouite Muslim told me, 'Once is enough, but I don't go. It's terrible to spend so much money continually going on pilgrimage. I take the equivalent of this money and give it to the poor. God accepts this as an equivalent pilgrimage. I think it's better.'

The Diversity of Islam

As we have seen, all Muslims do not believe alike, nor look alike, nor act alike. There is as great a diversity within Islam as within Christianity. The Muslim world is basically split between Sunni and Shia'. Sunni Muslims follow the model of Muhammed's life and consider the Quran and the Hadith as final authority. The Sunni could be approximated to Christianity's Protestants.

Shiite Muslims believe in extra-biblical events and persons and have doctrines not found in Sunni Islam. They could be equated closer to Christianity's Catholic and Orthodox denominations. Shiites believe that 'Divine Light' indwelt Muhammed and was passed down to his son-in-law, Ali, and Ali's son, Hussein. It indwells each successive Imam and lives in the present day in the Shia leader, or Ayatollah. The line of succession in Islam changed when Hussein was martyred in Karbala in 680CE and the Shia continue to wait for this succession to be rightfully restored. Shias celebrate Hussein's death with plays re-enacting the martyrdom on the tenth of Muharram (first month of the Muslim calendar). These plays and street processions have a similarity to the Catholic processions in Spain during the Passion Week. But there are numerous other denominations in Islam as well as differing approaches to faith. Islam also has its extreme fundamentalists, militants, intellectuals, and nominal believers who rarely put any faith into practice but believe in God and themselves Muslim. They have the same problems accepting each other's differences as Christians with their differences.

Selwa is an Alouite Muslim from Syria and mother of young adults and lives in Australia. She is a very attractive woman with long black hair and trendy clothes, and wears a lot of eye make-up and jewellery. When I asked her if she was religious she replied, 'That is not a good question. What do we mean by religious? Does that mean you wear a certain type of clothing and pray a certain way? Actually I am very religious, but I am very open. Islam is not narrow and hard. It's certain Muslims who make it appear that way.' Selwa does not perform formal prayers, 'I pray wherever I am. When I am walking down the street I pray.' I asked her if she prayed by recitation. 'No,' she replied, 'I talk to God about what is in my heart.'

She reads the Quran regularly, but 'I won't lie and say it's every day. Usually I read after my shower at night when I am relaxed and clean.' (Muslims must be ceremonially clean before they perform religious exercises. Before they touch the Quran they ceremonially wash.) 'I also read on the weekend morning when there is no rush. When you read the Quran you become more open to people because you come closer to God. The whole world should read it and we would have more unity and more peace. But people don't bother to read what it says. Religion is fearing God and following his messengers' teaching that is the prophets. Help if you can and don't cause anyone any problems. It's not wearing a scarf and praying five times a day, yet causing problems for other people. Prayer is action. Prayer is helping people and building a strong family and society. It's not treating evil with evil, just like Jesus says, "Turn the other cheek". Never harm anyone no matter how he or she treats you. Muhammed says in the Quran we must look after our neighbours for seven houses each side and seven streets each side. What does this mean? It translates into peace everywhere. Muslims say "we are the best people" (quoting the Quran), but we don't know who is right and who is the best. The real Muslim is one who doesn't interfere with the other. Follow your religion and leave the other to follow his and we will have peace.'

Selwa's ideas are shaped by her collective history as her comments about communal prayer displayed. 'We don't pray in the mosques because in our history when we were gathered in the mosque we were massacred, so today we still don't gather together in prayer. It's not safe.' She then related an incident that occurred that month in her suburb in Melbourne when a group of young men, Sunni Muslims, came against the Alouite Community Centre after a statement by one of the sheikhs from Al Azhar (in Cairo) that the Alouite are not true Muslims. 'These Sunnis give Islam a bad name and make people hate Islam.' There has been a bitter historical conflict between the denominations and she does not differentiate between radical extremists and mainstream Sunni Muslims. She believes that the Sunni interpretation of Islam is too narrow and that they are the cause of the misunderstanding and problems Islam has with the rest of the world and within their own house.

Selwa admires the freedom we have in the West and left the Middle East in order to have that freedom. 'My sister is still in Syria. She's forty-five and unmarried' (not typical) 'and she still lives with my parents at home because she is afraid of peoples' gossip if she lives alone. I tried to persuade her to live in my empty home there, but she needed someone else to confirm the idea. They asked a couple, both teachers with Maths and Science degrees, and they said it's not acceptable for her to live alone. Where did all that education go? We make life hard for ourselves. The educated are still bound by the narrow confines of the traditional values of the uneducated. These people have a bad influence on our society. People want change, but are afraid of the opinion of others. My sister does not even go out to parties because she is single. She goes from home to work and back. She has put herself in this small box. She is fighting against God! God made us social creatures for community and we need fun. She is going against all natural desires.'

Selwa has overcome many difficulties and says that it's been possible because God helped her. She was very unhappy in marriage and her health suffered. She wrote home to her parents in Syria saying she wanted to divorce and return to them. They would not accept a divorce in the family and told her to be patient and work it out. She tried for another twenty years. After the divorce she lost everything except the children and received no child support. 'We used plastic spoons for two years until I could afford to buy others. Actually it was a very difficult time and none of my friends or neighbours came and offered help.' Her husband was forced to support them, but stopped again after two years. 'I don't want his money. I will trust God for our needs. Look how God has helped us. Now I have everything I need and my children are educated and employed. I just dedicate myself to giving them a good start in life. I am where I am today because there is a God who sees.' I noted her reference to God's name and character revealed to Hagar at the well when he heard her cries for help: 'The God who sees.'

Selwa and her Alouite friend Tania both sent their children to Catholic schools. They expected a higher educational level than the government school and were concerned that their children were in a protected and religious environment. Selwa summed up her philosophy in a proverb, 'Don't fear the person who fears God. Fear the person who doesn't fear God.' When an Islamic school opened Tania sent her daughter Nada there to finish high school. The school requires the girl students to be veiled. Nada had a very protected life. Her social life revolved around the extended family events and the ball-receptions in the wider community. She never contemplated dating nor was alone with boys, which is typical for Arab girls both Muslim and Christian. Nada became engaged while she was in year twelve. Her parents wanted her to marry young in order to protect her from the influences of a loose society and they preferred an Arab Muslim. While on a trip to visit the family in Syria, one of her cousins liked her and after she returned to Australia his family phoned requesting her hand. She married the same year and had a lavish reception at one of the ballrooms used by the Arab community. Her gown was the modern medieval style, sleeveless with very little around the shoulders, low cut and an enormous skirt and train. Her long black hair was piled high on her head with a tiara perched on it. She now works at the school's office and wears veils and long skirts to work during the day. During the evening she wears slinky evening dresses, or mini-skirts and lots of make-up.

On the other hand, Selwa is not pushing her children to marry. She prefers them to receive a good education and find vocational careers to be independent. Although one daughter has an Australian boyfriend their family life is no different from the other Muslim families we know in Melbourne. The teenagers and young adults do not socialise with their university friends if the events include drinking. Most do not date. The girls do not stay out late and do not go to clubs or discos. The whole family is usually present when the parents have guests. A number of families have the grandparents living with them.

A number of books have been written about oppressed women in certain Muslim countries. I have not lived in those particular countries, but have lived in countries where Muslim feminists were roundly criticising the lack of women's rights. The black picture has already been vividly painted. The West needs to hear the bright side of the story in order to have a balanced view of the reality of the Muslim world. For example, when we hear stories of Irish terrorism we don't label all Irish terrorists. We have a broad picture of life in Ireland in which to slot these incidents. But if the only stories we hear about the Muslim world are the negative scary ones then we have no framework from which to get a balanced view.

Tunisia is a small progressive and peaceful Muslim country sandwiched between two very different neighbours: Libya and Algeria. Tunis has been a pacesetter in the Muslim world for fifty years. Proud of their liberal heritage, Tunisians carefully watch events across their borders. They are polite and easygoing and dislike fanaticism in any form. Life in the capital resembles life in most European cities. Expansive social services and industrial gains have enabled a majority middle class to emerge. The previous president Habiib Bourghiba bulleted the country through centuries overnight in the early 1950s with universal education, women's emancipation, and law reforms, which included outlawing polygamy. Women were brought out of the veil, and seclusion, into education and employment. The current president Ben Ali continues on the same road and today women are active in all segments of public life, including the Parliament. Tunisia is the only Muslim country where monogamy is the law and women have equal rights.

It is impossible to describe a Tunisian in general terms, as is true of any race. A Tunisian can be blonde, blue-eyed and fair skinned, or dark with Negroid features and fuzzy hair, or any of the possible mixes in between. He can be modern and chic at the office and relaxing in a swimsuit at the beach, or traditional wearing baggy trousers, cloak and turban and would never be seen 'naked' in a swimsuit at the beach. They both may wear a sprig of jasmine over one ear. Likewise she can be seen racing to work in her mini-skirt, dyed blondetips in her hair, clutching her briefcase, or she minces along the street in open sandals, wrapped in a white sheet and clutching the edges between her teeth. They are all typical.

When I think of life in the Arab Muslim world the central thought is of socialising and parties. Families and friends take every opportunity to spend the evening hours together just enjoying each other's company. Arabic even has a special verb for this activity. The women love to dance and it was not uncommon for someone to break into impromptu dancing. They danced during family nights in Syria and danced during women's meetings in Tunisia. In Tunisia I met weekly with a group of women to discuss current issues. After failing to solve the problems in the world they loved to end the afternoon tea by dancing. Their best meetings were held in Ramadan when we met to break the Fast and had a girl's-only party. When people are allowed to get on with life in Muslim countries, life is fun!

Westerners ask for stories about the lives of Muslim women, but I often feel the request is loaded. The stories are required to fit the person's preconceived ideas of bleak and miserable lives. One Muslim woman told me, 'People see us as having no choices. If I wear a blue scarf I am asked, "Is that the colour Islam states you have to wear?" If I wear a skirt they ask, am I not allowed to wear trousers? They think I have no freedom and everything I do is dictated by religion. And they think we are abused by our husbands, who of course are terrorists.' Stories like the one I related about the abused wife are one of the reasons for these stereotypes. If I related the story without mentioning that Muslim men helped the wife it would leave a severe impression of Muslim men. Of course stories like this one are retold because they are extreme and rare examples. These types of horror stories are related about the Muslim world leaving the impression that this is normal life. It isn't. An Anglo-Saxon Australian lady told me many of her friends believe all Muslim women are circumcised and will not listen to data disproving this. They read stories of some cases and now believe mutilated women populate the Muslim world.

Some of the Christians asking me for stories had no experience of life in Muslim countries, but they 'knew' the women were wretchedly unhappy. They based this on stories they read describing Muslim women living as miserable prisoners in a life of bondage to custom and family. The assumption is also that Muslim women do not know Christ, therefore they are unhappy. There are pamphlets describing Muslim women's bondage to fear and hopelessness that are written in order to encourage Christians to pray. Yet anyone living amongst Muslims knows women, who Christians have described in blanket statements as miserably unhappy and prisoners in purdah, who are happy and content with their lives and would not trade their lives for a Western woman's style of life. In fact, they feel sorry for the Western woman whom they perceive has lost the most precious possessions in life: faith in God and a close family life. They so long for us to have their experience of God that they keep trying to convert us. We must ensure that we do not reduce the Gospel to equal the sum total of what we believe is happiness, and we need to refrain from stereotyping Muslim women as being insecure and fearful simply because they are Muslims and of pasting our labels on the lives of Muslims and summing up their lives in ways with which they do not agree.

This picture of a deprived life is probably close to the current situation in Afghanistan where Muslim women themselves are describing their lives in these terms. In this situation, and others like it, we can join with them lamenting the circumstances and find out whether there is any way we can lend our support to Muslim groups working to help them.

I asked Aisha, the veiled social worker, 'What keeps you satisfied with being a Muslim and staying on this path?' The question surprised her as she had never been asked that before, but she only took about fifteen seconds to spring back her answer, 'The absolute belief in the existence of God and that Islam is the right religion. I read the Quran and it makes sense and fulfils all my needs – social and spiritual. So I can totally commit myself one hundred per cent. If I have confusion in my life I find the answer in the Quran. I don't know how anyone copes with life without faith, any kind of faith. How do you make sense of tragedies and murders that are not solved without a faith that there will be justice on Judgement Day? Life here is short in comparison to eternity. When you view this world as temporary it changes your outlook. It's easy to sacrifice when you know you will be rewarded. It would be easy to be selfish if you didn't believe in the hereafter. You would be tempted to get all you could out of this world.'

Islam's veiling of women is a problem for Westerners and often becomes the focal point at which all the West's abhorrence and fear of Muslims is concentrated. When a woman covers her head she is singled out and often pays a price for following her religion. However, the custom of veiling did not start with Islam. From ancient times, respectable dress for Eastern women was veiling. Greek and Roman women veiled outside their homes, and the first-century Church in the Greco-Roman empire practised veiling. The discussion about head coverings during worship in the New Testament is rooted in the Eastern custom of veiling.[9] The problem was whether the choice of Christian women to use their freedom to remove their veils during worship would be misinterpreted and give the Church a bad name. Paul sums it up in an admonition, not to offend cultural mores by reminding the Corinthians not to remove their veils in case their freedom is interpreted as licence and the reputation of the Church is damaged. Early Church history bears witness that in Rome, Antioch and Africa the custom remained, or became, the norm because in those societies all respectable women veiled.

Women in Arabia, beyond the scope of the Roman Empire, did not practice veiling until Muhammed's wives adopted the

custom. Muhammed regularly visited Damascus and it is probable that he observed the custom there. It was an upper class privilege so it appears that Muhammed introduced it as a modesty
custom and to give public honour to Muslim women. The verse
states in the Quran, 'Tell your daughters and wives and the
believing women that they should cast their outer garments over
their persons when they go abroad; That is most convenient that
they should be known (as Muslims) and not molested.'[10]

The Muslim commentary on this states, 'The times were those
of insecurity and they were asked to cover themselves with a long
gown covering the whole body, or a cloak covering the neck and
bosom. The object was not to restrict the liberty of women, but
to protect them from harm and molestation under the conditions
existing then in Arabia. In the East and West a distinctive public
dress of some sort or other has always been a badge of honour
or distinction, both among men and women. Assyrian law in its
palmiest days (approx 7BCE) enjoined the veiling of married
women and forbade the veiling of slaves and women of ill
repute.'[11] There is also a story of a Muslim woman wearing a
revealing dress in front of Muhammed that links in with this
injunction to not expose the body.

In the early years of Islam, non-Muslim women were penalised in public dress by being forbidden to veil. 'Their wives must
not dress as honourable Muslim women and must wear clothing
that exposes their legs and must not cover their heads.'[12] Veiling
came to be associated with the ruling and upper classes, particularly during the Ottoman Empire when a face veil was included.
Over the centuries veiling came to be seen as a principally
Muslim custom and the prohibition against veiling for non-
Muslim was not enforced. Non-Muslims adopted it in order to
escape harassment on the streets, or simply to fit in and not be
recognised as a minority group. The pre-Islamic roots of the veil
were forgotten and urban Eastern Christians who practised it
abhorred it as a sign of their domination.

Eastern churches in societies where women still practice

veiling as a sign of respectability are still discussing this issue. An Arabic international newspaper featured an article on the Coptic Church in Egypt struggling over whether women should wear veils in church in 1992.[13] The point is that some Christian women (usually rural) still veil in public in a similar manner to Muslim women. Both see it as an expression of respectability and faith. Modern Muslim women are perplexed at Christian hostility to the veil. Aisha, the social worker in Melbourne said, 'After all the mother of Jesus dressed this way.' She was nervous about adopting veiling. 'I wondered how people would accept me. I knew I was making a big statement. Actually it gave me freedom not to conform to rules for women. I no longer had to present myself in a certain way and be judged on appearances. There is certain recognition on appearance and attractive women are treated differently. From the first day men no longer invaded my personal space with touch. They no longer put an arm around me when saying hello, and stopped other invasive touching that happens in the workplace.' Aisha laughed as she remembered, 'One man apologised for swearing in my presence. All the other women exclaimed, "Hang on! What about swearing in front of us? We don't like it either!" I received respect from colleagues.'

She receives a mixed reaction in the street. 'There is some harassment. I have only experienced comments and stares, but one of my friends who adopted veiling was so harassed on the street she removed it. Another friend was physically assaulted when someone tried to pull her scarf off her head. An Indian man whose wife was veiled was assaulted at the petrol station by a carload of youths yelling "go home". Melbourne is their home. When I feel someone is staring out of curiosity, I go and ask him or her politely if they would like to ask me questions, then I would like to explain to them. I prefer to be proactive. Sometimes I take up a challenging comment, but usually I just let comments go. Veiling is a reflection of my commitment.'

Veiling brings positive and negative reactions all in the same gesture. People usually assume that women wearing veils cannot speak English and will offer to help read a sign or ask if the person needs help. 'This is positive in that people are being helpful. It's negative because they assume a scarf equals ignorance or back-wardness. I was in the Family Law court and a doorman offered to help me read the lift directory. I thanked him and explained I was there in support of a case. He looked totally shocked.'

Nabila and Huda both wear veils only on certain occasions. Nabila works at an Islamic school and is required to veil for work. She also prefers to veil when meeting with Islamic relig-ious leaders and representing Islam in public. Huda follows a similar custom. So both women have dual experiences in public with and without a veil. Huda claims 'it makes a huge difference in how people respond to me. Usually people assume I am ignor-ant and illiterate.' Nabila also teaches part time with the Adult Education Centre and in addition is a public lecturer represent-ing Islamic groups. 'When I went to my doctor wearing a scarf and there was a new secretary, she offered to help me fill in the form. People generally assume I know nothing, and cannot speak English. I am often offered an interpreter before enquiries are made if I need one. When wearing a scarf people speak very slowly to me. Without a scarf they treat me normally. This shows a scarf is equated with ignorance.'

A number of women I spoke with mentioned hostility and dis-crimination in the universities and Huda also had a story. 'An Anglo-Saxon Australian girl converted to Islam and married an Arab. She adopted veiling wearing a large enveloping veil and immediately encountered hostility. Her husband became very ill with cancer and died. But while he was in hospital under treat-ment and his wife was feeling so shattered, her lecturers were not sympathetic and would not give her extensions or consideration. In one subject she chose an Islamic topic and the lecturer would not allow her to make any positive comment of Islam in her paper. He actually denied basic facts of Islamic history, failed her and refused to allow the routine appeals. She dropped out of the course.'

Muslims live in a kaleidoscope of political systems, from brutal dictatorships to constitutional monarchies. The majority of Muslims live in either developing countries, areas of conflict and war zones or countries prone to catastrophic natural disasters. Overwhelming masses of Muslims live in abject poverty, which is aggravated by high birth rates. A large number are refugees: in 1994 there were an estimated twenty-three million world refugees of whom eighteen million are Muslims. In 1995 300,000 Muslims fled Grozny, Chechnya, and 5.7 million Afghans fled to nearby countries. Recently, Muslim refugees poured out of Kosovo escaping ethnic cleansing. The oldest and second largest group of people still wandering the world as refugees are Palestinians now numbering about 2.5 million. There are also 200,000 Bihari Muslims trapped in Bangladesh who are citizens of Pakistan and speak Urdu.

In addition to these problems, Muslims are also challenged by their changing culture under the impact of modernism and westernisation and many of their publications deal with this issue. I solicited responses from Muslim women in Indonesia, the Arabian Gulf, North Africa, Afghanistan, Maldive Islands, Khazakistan and China, as well as Muslims in the West, about their felt needs. They all identified these same areas of concern: happiness in the home, marriage and divorce, raising children, coping with financial stress and illness and disasters, addictions (mainly men's to alcohol), providing good education for children, concerns about the influence of materialism and secularism on children and culture, feeling powerless, pressure of society, and employment demands versus home and family and a desire for rebirth and power for living God's way. The issues raised by these Muslims worldwide are no different to the issues concerning my Anglo-Saxon neighbours in Melbourne. Are these any different to the issues concerning Christians?

Fear and insecurity are not endemic to Muslims. Fear, insecurity and anxiety are rampant in our century. In my experience Muslims' felt needs and pressures are mainly due to their political situation, whereas in the West our problems are not necessarily political, but due to the changing patterns or breakdown of our society. Most Christians would lay the blame for this in our rejection of God and loss of values. Sociologists talk of the loss of a collective conscience which provided people with a clear idea of how they should think, act and feel. They see this the result of the loss of a strong communal life through the industrial revolution.[14] Muslim society typically still has a strong communal life that gives a type of security which we have almost lost in the West. However, this is now changing in the Muslim world and causing insecurity just as it does in the West.

At the beginning of the third millennium, if we compare culture to culture I believe Islam is coping better than Christianity. Christians may protest that not all the West is really Christian, but not all Muslims are faith-filled either. So if we are going to talk in generalities about the Muslim world, then we must talk also in generalities about the countries that call themselves 'Christian'. Any comparisons drawn should be balanced: Muslim and Christian with faith compared to Muslim and Christian with no faith.

How are Muslims coping with life? They cope the same way we cope. They turn for help in religion, education and supernatural forces. Firstly they look for salvation in God's mercy. Muslims have a great belief in the mercy of God. I think Christians overlook this. The Quran teaches that the road to God's forgiveness is through repentance – as does the Bible. God forgives the person who repents because God is merciful. This is one of the reasons Muslims have trouble with Christ being presented as an intercessor: God's mercy is so great that we don't need an intercessor between God and humans. The idea of an intercessor puts a limit on the great mercy of God. Many times during the day a Muslim calls to remembrance the great mercy of God by reciting Bism-Allah Al Alrahim: In the name of God the Compassionate and Merciful.

Muslims look for salvation in education. This may not be

stated as a belief, but it is diligently practised. Families expend great efforts and make enormous sacrifices to provide a good education for their children.

Muslims also look for help through harnessing the spiritual powers to work for them. This includes the quasi-Islamic magical practices of folk-Islam; like sheikhs writing charms, and the activities of the mediums dealing in the occult. Official Islam rejects these practices. In Egypt, the Al Azhar Mosque will not perform exorcisms, so lay practitioners offer their services to the public. They exorcise demons and treat unresponsive illness by the reading of the Quran. A television programme in Cairo held a forum on evil spirits and exorcism and the panel encompassed beliefs across the whole spectrum: from there is no such thing as evil spirits, to practitioners exorcising them. The entire panel was Muslim.

Women tend to turn to the occult practitioners – that is, mediums and dealers in 'white magic'. These practices are carried out to heal mental and physical illnesses, and for such things as keeping a husband's love, or placing curses on enemies. I was first exposed to this type of magic when I lived in Egypt and have seen it everywhere since, including Australia. A main-line Australian women's magazine runs a column on how to place spells. It gave a spell for an easy childbirth, for a straying husband, for a daughter with headaches. I am sure Christians reading this will be saying, but real Christians do not practice these things. It's forbidden in the Bible. Muslims reading this will be saying the same thing just as they have often told me, 'This sort of thing is forbidden in Islam. It's simply occultism. We trust only in the Word of God for exorcism and in God alone to be our help in times of need.'

Much in Common

Islam and Christianity hold many beliefs in common. One way we can remove fear and ignorance is by teaching the truth of what each religion believes. We will then discover that two-thirds of our creeds are the same. The foundational belief is that the one and only God is the creator of all things which are held accountable to him. Genesis tells us that God created the heavens and the earth and mankind and all living things. The Quran attests to the same belief, 'Of old We created the heavens and the earth.'[15] Both groups believe God began human history and will end human history and be the judge at the last day. The Quran speaks of the (Lord) King of the Day of Judgement,[16] and the New Testament states 'He has appointed a day in which he will judge the world in righteousness.'[17]

Both religions traditionally teach that people are resurrected to eternal life, either in heaven or in hell – the Quran, 'Hell shall be a place of snares, the home of sinners to abide there for ages'[18] – and the New Testament, 'When the Lord Jesus is revealed from heaven in blazing fire with his angels He will punish those who do not know God. They will be punished with everlasting destruction and shut out from the presence of the Lord.'[19] Muslims usually interpret the Quran in a literal manner. Thus verses about heaven, describing it as a place where all the pleasures denied on earth are freely given as rewards, are taken literally. But whether a literal place or a state of being in God's presence, both the Quran and the Bible agree that heaven is the reward in the afterlife for those who have loved God in the present life.

Although both Muslims and Christians are monotheists, Muslims view Christian monotheism with some suspicion. The problem is the trinity. The Muslim belief in the unity or indivisibility of God is what brings them into collision with the idea of the trinity. However, this is one of the major problems that could be bridged by understanding what trinity means to the two religions. Muslims think the term trinity means three gods. The Quran understands the trinity to mean God the father, the Virgin Mary, and the son Jesus. 'O Jesus son of Mary did you say take me and my mother for two gods beside god!'[20] 'They misbelieve who say God is the third of three.'[21] Thus trinity equals three gods. However, Christians don't believe in three gods. The Bible states that there is only one God. 'You believe in the one God and this is good.'[22] 'The Lord your God is one.'[23] Both Islam and Christianity agree that there is only one God and worship of any other is not sanctioned.

Both Muslims and Christians believe Christ was born by the virgin Mary and conceived by the power of God's Spirit. He is an honoured prophet sent to the Jewish people who performed the greatest miracles, and was bodily received into heaven where he waits until he will be revealed in power at the end of human history when God judges the world. The Quran states, 'Mary, God has chosen you above women . . . and God gives you tidings of a Word from him and his name shall be Messiah Jesus.'[24] 'She said, "my Lord how can I have a child when no mortal has touched me?" He (Gabriel) said, "God creates what he will. He says only to it: Be! And it is."'[25] The Quranic account mirrors the Biblical story, 'Mary you have found favour with God. You will be with child and give birth to a son, and you are to give him the name Jesus. Mary asked "how will this be since I am a virgin?" He (Gabriel) answered, "The Holy Spirit will come upon you and the power of the most high will cover you."'[26]

One Muslim told me, 'God had a plan for Jesus even before he was born. When his grandmother was pregnant she dedicated the baby to the Temple, but was disappointed when that baby was a girl. However, this girl became the mother of Jesus and gave birth to him while she was still a virgin. We believe Christ is coming back in the last days to kill the anti-Christ and he will be the ruler. During this time he will unite all the faiths together. He is the Messiah the Jews are waiting for, and he will reconcile Muslims and Christians who are all waiting for his coming. Some traditions believe he will then live a normal life and die, because the Quran states that everything must taste death.'

Muslims of the Shia tradition believe it will not be Christ, but a special prophet, the Mehdi, who will return. In the Muslim tradition regarding the second coming of Jesus, Abu Harira – a companion of Muhammed who is the main authority for the accounts of the prophet's life – relates that Muhammed said, 'I swear by God it is near when Jesus, the son of Mary, will descend from heaven upon your people.'[27] The New Testament states, 'For the Lord himself will descend from heaven with a loud command.'[28]

The word 'trinity' is not in the Bible. The Tunisian Christian theologian Tertullian coined the term in the second century to describe the nature of God. The one God reveals himself in the Father (creator), the Son (word), and Holy Spirit (presence and power). While Muslims may not agree with this description of the nature of God, they can find common agreement with Christians that there is only one God and we cannot define the great spiritual absolute in adequate human terms. We may have been better off if Tertullian realised this and left God to be indescribable! I enjoyed reminding Muslims in Tunisia when they objected to the trinity, 'Well I am sorry about this misunderstanding you have of the term, but it was one of you who gave this term to describe how God was in Christ, so when you give us a better one we will use it.'

In North Africa, Mazhar was visiting with a Muslim friend at his work place when another customer joined them and attacked Mazhar's belief saying he believes in three gods. His friend came to his defence, 'Have you ever asked him what he believes? I tell you he does not believe in three gods but the one true God. If I give you my word on something can you separate me from my word? Well that's what he believes about Christ. He believes Christ is the Word of God. Can you separate God from his Word? So the Word and God are one.' We prefer this Muslim's explanation to Tertullian's.

When we realise the disagreement on Christ actually centres on the question 'What is the Word of God existing with God eternally in the heavens that God sent down to earth?' we may be able to come to a better understanding. When this question is posed, the Christians answer 'Christ' and the Muslims answer 'the Quran'. So the equivalencies are Christ and the Quran, not the Bible and the Quran, and not Christ and Muhammed.

However Muslims also believe Christ is the Word of God. The Quran states, 'O Mary, God gives you glad tidings of a word from God whose name is Messiah Jesus.'[29] Jesus is called the 'Word' in the Gospel. 'In the beginning was the Word and the Word was God.'[30] Muslims believe God's Word eternally existed in the heavens and was sent to earth to guide mankind. Christians believe God's Word eternally existed in the heavens and was sent to earth to guide mankind. So when we ask the question, 'How did God ultimately reveal his will in history?' Muslims and Christians both agree that the one creator God sent his eternally existing Word to earth.

If we make this the comparison we will find the two religions can come closer together. Traditionally we have compared book to book and prophet to prophet. This is not helpful, as they are not equivalents. Comparing book to book has problems because there is a basic disagreement on the nature of revelation. This in turn hangs on the idea of inspiration. The inspiration of the Scriptures is a term used by both, but with different understandings. Christianity teaches that the Bible is the self-revelation of God. God can be known and wants to be known by man. In the Christian understanding of inspiration God works with man in revealing the Scriptures, so the personality of the writer is still evident and there is an acceptable place for various types of literature within inspiration.

However, the Quran states God is too transcendent to reveal himself or to be truly perceived by anything in creation. He does not work with man. Muslims understand that the eternal Word of God existed in heaven with God and was sent down to be recorded without any co-operation from Muhammed. In fact Muhammed was reported to fall into a trance and mechanically recorded what he was told word for word. Christians believe that the eternal Word of God – existing with God in heaven and sent down to earth to reveal God – was Christ, and the primary function of the Scriptures is to bear witness to him.

The Muslim attitude to their Scriptures is closer to the Jew's attitude to their Scriptures than to the Christian view. The emphasis is on God's healing law revealed through the text. For example the Quran states, 'We send down (stage by stage) in the Quran that which is a healing and a mercy to those who believe: to the unjust it causes nothing but loss after loss.'[31] The Muslim commentary on this verse tells us, 'In God's revelation there is healing for our broken spirits, hope for our spiritual future, and joy in the forgiveness of our sins. All who work in faith will share these privileges. It is only the rebels against God's law who will suffer loss. The more they will oppose Truth, the deeper down will they go into the mire – the state of sin and Wrath – which is worse than destruction.'[32]

The majority of the Jews regard their Scriptures as the mouth of God bringing the Law to the community of Israel. It is God's Law that brings life and health. The Psalmist states, 'The Law of the Lord is perfect, reviving the soul. The precepts of the Lord are right, rejoicing the heart. They are sweeter than honey.'[33]

Christians read the same Old Testament texts and personalise them – firstly as God's word to the individual Christian and the community, and secondly, personalised and attained through Christ the Word of God.

Muslims accept the Bible is a holy book, but believe they have no need of it because all the important parts are now included in the Quran. They also believe that Christians and Jews corrupted the Bible and that it is superseded by the Quran. However, Christians believe the Bible was the final revelation of God and so cannot be superseded.

Both religions believe God reveals his will through the prophets. Islam accepts the prophets in the Judeo-Christian tradition. Some of these prophets are Adam, Noah, Abraham, Jonah and John the Baptist. But we understand prophethood differently. Christians believe the biblical prophets were ordinary people who revealed God's will. They could and did sin and the Bible records their failures – the exception is Christ who never sinned thus proving his deity. In Islam all prophets are believed to be sinless, so Muslims have difficulty with the biblical accounts of prophets' sins and the Christian claims for Christ's deity on the basis of sinlessness.

Each group refuses to give the honour that the other group claims for their prophet. Christians won't accept Muhammed as a prophet and Muslims won't accept Christ as more than a prophet. Muslims believe that Muhammed is the Seal of the Prophets but Christians have the equivalent belief about Christ who is the final revelation of God. 'Therefore God exalted him to the highest place and gave him the name that is above every name that at the name of Jesus every knee should bow and every tongue confess that Jesus Christ is Lord, to the glory of God the Father.'[34]

The great parting of the ways is the Muslim belief that Jesus did not die on the cross and rise from the dead. To Muslims the death of God's prophet would show God's weakness. Evil would triumph over God. It would be a meaningless shame that God could not allow, so God substituted someone else to take the shame and Christ was gloriously taken into heaven 'yet they did not slay him, neither crucified him, only a likeness of that was shown to them . . . ; God raised him up to him.'[35] However, Christians believe the apparent shame of the death of Christ is the great triumph of God which he planned before the foundation of the world. This is not seen as God's weakness but his triumph over the forces of evil. 'I am not ashamed of the Gospel because it is the power of God for the salvation for everyone who believes.'[36] And Christ's death is not meaningless but demonstrates God's mercy. 'God demonstrates his love for us in this: while we were still sinners Christ died for us.'[37] Some Muslims understand the Christian belief that Christ died as a substitutionary sacrifice for our sins, but they cannot accept it. Rana Kabbani explains how many Muslims see the picture: 'Muslims believe in the unity of God, revere Jesus as a prophet whose virgin birth they acknowledge and hold the Bible to be sacred, respecting Jews and Christians as People of The Book. However the notions of the Trinity or of Christ's divinity are anathema, as they seemed to offend against the Oneness of God. Muslims could not concede that the Almighty would allow his Messiah to be crucified. The Christian doctrine that man was born sinful and could be redeemed only by the blood of Christ borders, for them, on pagan belief.'[38]

There is further disagreement about prophesies concerning Christ, Muhammed and the Holy Spirit. The Quran states that Jesus prophesied the coming of Muhammed, 'and when Jesus the son of Mary said, O children of Israel verily I am the apostle of God sent to you confirming the law which was delivered before me and bringing good news of an apostle who shall come after me whose name shall be Ahmad'.[39] Yet, Jesus does not make this statement in the Bible and it seems the Quran is speaking of Jesus' promise of the Holy Spirit in John 14:16. 'I will ask the Father and he will give you another counsellor to be with you forever.' And again in John 14:26, 'But the counsellor whom the Father will send in my name will teach you of all things.' Christians say these verses apply to the Holy Spirit and Muslims say Christians changed the text and it originally spoke of Muhammed.

However, in spite of many differences Christians and Muslims do have many common beliefs, especially about Christ, which place us in close proximity to one another. There is a meeting place for people of both faiths to come together in honesty and vulnerability. If we step beyond the 'isms' and theology and expose our human side, our common bond as God's creation made in the image of God, we can touch each others' hearts and encourage each other on the search for the right path and the goal of a love relationship with God.

Sheikh Saleh Khneifes is an elderly Druze leader in Israel. 'If we fight each other the problem will remain. The problem is where there is a Jew and a Palestinian they have to face each other. You can change the labels to Protestant and Catholic, Albanian or Serbian. We must go out in the street to meet each other and care for people. We Druze have followed the words of Jesus Christ for 2,000 years. You will be amazed to hear a Druze speaking about Jesus because our Christian brothers do not know anything about that. The words of Jesus still echo in my mind saying that the wise and righteous people are those who will suffer in the world. Injustice is rejected by every decent human being. Go and try to make peace, however difficult it is.'[40]

Going out to the other and making a relationship is the key to removing the fear of foreigners and foreign religions. Friendship is where the *other* meets Christ in us. But we must never think of friendship as a strategy to convert people. It is simply being obedient to Jesus' command to love your neighbour as yourself, without thinking of success or reward.

Francis reminded us that life speaks louder than words. The world respects the faith of someone who selflessly gives to all regardless of creed or colour. Mother Theresa lived by Franciscan values and the world loved her like the world loved Francis. Every religion was present at the funeral for Mother Theresa. The world recognises God's love in action when Christians follow the advice of Francis and live like Christ. Christians are then in a position to invite Muslims to the fullness of Christ.

An Iranian in Australia saw a verse on the wall in a public place, and after questioning colleagues discovered it was from the Bible. He purchased a Bible and was captured by it, telling a Christian colleague, 'Do you know it says to love your enemies. That is really amazing and it has deeply challenged me.' E. Stanley Jones asked Ghandi how the Christians could have a more effective witness in India. Ghandi told him the most effective method of seeing the Church grow was for Christians to put their faith into practice. Christians who believe that Islam is erroneous need to remember that Muhammed took those ideas from our forefathers. One of the reasons was poor communication and poor relationships between the two faith communities. The West today is expressing anger at the Muslim world. The Muslim world is expressing anger at the West. Anger is the instinctive human response to fear. When we cross the barriers of fear and come close enough to talk to Muslims face to face we find Muslims are just like ourselves. Francis of Assisi demonstrated how to control our fear and anger – by going out in unconditional love to meet the enemy. In doing so we will discover we have acted in accordance with God's grace. Imtiazi Dakkar, an Asian Muslim said, 'Grace is a place where fear is filtered out.' Isn't it time we listened to St Francis and filled in the battle trenches and crossed to the other side? When we do, we find Muslims are not the alien other. They are just people like you and me.

Notes

1 Unpublished interview 16 September 1998. (Used by permission of the Plough Publishing House, Philadelphia and East Sussex.)
2 Mark 12:29.
3 See Hamra, V. (1997) for all comparison with Muhammed and the Eastern Church.
4 Kabbani, R. (1989) *Letter to Christendom*, Camden, UK: Virago Press, p. 4.
5 Ibid., p. 8.
6 Ali, A. Y. (1989) *The Meaning of the Holy Quran*, Maryland: Amana Corporation, n. 2276.
7 Surah 2:245.
8 Surah 24:36–38.
9 1 Corinthians 11:4–10.
10 Surah 33.59.
11 Ali, op. cit.
12 Al Masri, S. (1989) *Khalf Al Hijab*, Cairo: Sinai Publishing House, p. 98.

13 *Al-Quds Al-Arabi*, 5 Dec 1992, London, p. 4.
14 Durkeim (1998) *Introduction to Culture and Control: Boundaries and Identities*, Study Guide, Deakin University.
15 Surah 50:37.
16 Surah 43:77.
17 Acts 17:31.
18 Surah 88:1.
19 2 Thessalonians 1:7,8.
20 Surah 5:116.
21 Surah 5:77.
22 James 1:19.
23 Deuteronomy 6:4.
24 Surah 3:45–47.
25 Surah 3:37–43.
26 Luke 1:29–37.
27 Mishkat 23:6.
28 2 Thessalonians 4:16.
29 Surah 3:45.
30 John 1:1.
31 Surah 17:82.
32 All quotes from the Quran and their commentary notes are taken from Ali, A. Y. (1989) *The Meaning of the Holy Quran*, Maryland: Amana Corporation.
33 Psalm 19:7–10.
34 Philippians 2:10.
35 Surah Women 1–56.
36 Romans 1:16.
37 Romans 5:8.
38 Kabbani, op. cit., p. 5.
39 Surah 61:6.
40 Unpublished interview, July 1999. (Used by permission of the Plough Publishing House, Philadelphia and East Sussex.)

Chapter Seven

FROM THE OTHER SIDE

'Mummy that lady is scary!' The small boy's remark about a black-veiled woman on a Western street voiced the meaning of many of the adults' furtive glances.

I shared this reaction in Damascus when we were surrounded by Iranian Muslim women in black chadors pressing against us as their large group surged to the Shia mosque for prayers. My two nieces pressed close to me grasping my arms in case the force of the crowd separated us. The women's dress was foreign and strange, their language was foreign and strange and their style of worship was foreign and strange. For a few minutes we were the foreigners in the midst of a black-clad Iranian sea and we felt insecure. We felt a bile of irritation rise and commented on the sad state of affairs when we are made to feel like foreigners in our own Damascus street.

Our sightseeing expedition to the Iranian mosque coincided with a special prayer night. Inside the mosque our party was amazed to see many men and women crying loudly with tears running down their cheeks remembering the martyrdom of Mohammed's nephew, whom their branch of Islam considered Islam's true leader. Mosque guards, carrying sticks, roamed the precincts looking for any women not properly covered. Our youngest niece (who normally happily chooses to wear a head covering) took umbrage at the foreigners telling her how to behave in her own religion and country and refused to comply with the stricter standards, deliberately allowing her scarf to slip back and show hair. The guard noticed her and we spent the next minutes escaping him through the sardine-packed crowd.

I had lived in the Muslim world for over twenty years, but the night in the Iranian mosque was an enlightening experience to discover I could still have a prejudice to foreigners. Of course I never thought about the incongruity of an Aussie claiming to own the street in Damascus!

Six years later in Melbourne we were entertaining an Iranian friend's family visiting from Tehran. I was very drawn to his mother, a refined and warm and pleasant woman – and for those who are wondering what she wore, she dressed in modern Western clothes while out of her country. We were discussing mutual places we had visited and I suddenly realised I could have seen her before. She was one of the black-clad Iranian women going to the mosque in Damascus.

Negativity and fear are common reactions to Islam and the media feeds this. Vicious distortions of Islam and Arabs have appeared with alarming frequency since the Arab oil embargo of 1977 and have resulted in a subliminal public consensus that Muslims are aggressors and therefore must deserve what they get: hostility, abusive threats, sanctions, quarantines and air strikes.

Muslims in the West feel misrepresented and misunderstood. Rana Kabbani, a Muslim from Damascus, is the daughter of a Syrian diplomat. She grew up in New York and Indonesia, studied at Georgetown University and Jesus College Cambridge and has a PhD in English Literature. She married Patrick Seale. 'The West', she writes, 'sees Islam as a barbaric alien culture . . . Such was the polarisation . . . that I began to question whether I could continue living in the West without committing cultural treason . . . against my own Islamic background.'[1] Kabbani notes how 'in the West the tendency has been to overlook the past as a direct influence on how we think and feel. Children are taught history as something separate from their own existence: they are only products of their individual circumstance and immediate environment. Only the here and now counts. For many Americans and West Europeans the present is so successful and all-engrossing that it seems to rule out any psychological need to connect with the past.'[2] Muslims, on the other hand, understand that history can determine present emotions. 'Most Muslims are too poor and insecure to afford the luxury of individual feelings: instead their reactions to events are strongly shaped by communal memories. Easterners have been saddled with history and it's usually a grievance.'[3] Kabbani's statement helps us understand why Muslims can feel so connected to the Crusades, which we view as dead and buried history. She believes there has been a 'transfer of contempt from Jews to Muslims in secular Western culture today. Now the West has made a new enemy of the Muslim world to the extent Muslims feel under a type of oppression and fear persecution. Dr Shabbir Akhtar wrote in the Guardian (27 Feb 1989) "the next time there are gas chambers in Europe, there is no doubt concerning who'll be inside them".[4] In Washington we as a family encountered a visceral antagonism to Arabs in general and to Syrians in particular. We found that our Middle East was viewed solely and exclusively through the medium of Israeli propaganda myths: that Israel was weak and the Arabs were strong; that Israel was in constant danger of annihilation; that it wanted peace and the Arabs did not; that its history was one of justice and of heroic settlement of the empty desert; that there was no such thing as Palestine or the Palestinians. There was no glimmering of understanding that it was the Arabs who were besieged, bombarded and driven from their homes by Israeli might, propped up by the United States. It was not easy to live in an environment shaped by the deceit of our enemies. It is not surprising that a Muslim upbringing includes a strong dose of anti-Westernism, given Western contempt for and ignorance about Islam.'[5]

Europe has had a more balanced political view of the Middle East, but Muslims have not found life easy there either. One of my close friends is a Tunisian Muslim high school teacher married to a German. She has olive skin and black hair. When she walks in the street in Germany she is jostled, verbally insulted and on some occasions women crossed to the other side of the street as she approached them, or grasped their handbags to their sides as she passed. Another Tunisian Muslim family, living an upper middle class life in Belgium, left everything in the mid-1990s and moved to Tunis without any guarantee of employment: 'We were afraid for our future in the face of the growing animosity and violence against Muslims in Europe.'

Edward Said, a Palestinian graduate from Princeton and Harvard, is one of America's most eminent literary critics. Said has won numerous world-wide awards and published in twenty-four languages. In 1981 he wrote *Covering Islam: How the media and the experts determine how we see the rest of the world.* It was republished with an-updated introduction in 1997 and is a must for anyone interested in this subject. Said writes in the introductory notes, '(in the past fifteen years) there has been an intense focus on Muslims and Islam in the American and Western media, most of it characterised by a more highly exaggerated stereo-typing and belligerent hostility than what I had previously described in my book. Malicious generalisations about Islam have become the last acceptable form of denigration of a foreign culture in the West; what is said about the Muslim mind, or character, or religion, or culture as a whole cannot now be said in mainstream discussion about Africans, Jews, other Orientals or Asians.'[6]

On the afternoon of the Oklahoma bomb attack Said received about twenty-five phone calls from newspapers and major networks, all assuming he had some connection with Middle Eastern terrorists: 'the entire factitious connection between Arabs, Muslims and terrorism was never more forcefully made evident to me; the sense of guilty involvement which, despite myself, I was made to feel struck me as precisely the feeling I was meant to have. The media had assaulted me, in short, and Islam – or rather my connection with Islam – was the cause.'[7] Said is actually from a Christian background in the Anglican Church of Jerusalem.

Ralph Braibanti, a professor of Political Science at Duke University points out the unfairness of terms used to describe Muslims. '. . . in Islam all believers are fundamentalists. They believe the Quran was dictated by God to the archangel Gabriel to Mohammed and the text has remained unchanged for some 1,400 years. To refer to those who commit acts of violence as fundamentalists is to insult the whole of the Muslim community. Further it displays an abysmal ignorance of Islam, or a deliberate effort to distort its image by linking violence to Muslims generally and to the quintessentials of their belief.'[8]

Christian fundamentalists defend their classification with pride, but Muslim fundamentalists are expected to feel shame for holding their Scriptures in the same esteem. When it comes to Islam, fundamentalism 'equals everything we-must-now-fight-against as we did with Communism during the Cold War'.[9]

The Gulf War exacerbated Western fears and distrust of Muslim communities and there was a backlash against Muslims in Western countries. In Britain, Australia and America, Muslims were subjected to insult and verbal and physical abuse. Women wearing headscarves were shouted at in the street and their scarves ripped from their heads, rocks were thrown at Muslim school buses and the Muslim community complained that people who were of Arab background were not given equal job opportunities. Muslim leaders called for an end to Islamophobia.

One of the American flowergirls at our wedding is now married to an Iranian Muslim. His family fled Iran the day before the Shah fell. They settled in America and began rebuilding their lives. They were suffering from the losses of wealth and assets, worried for their extended family left in Iran, and dealing with the insecurities of a new country and language. His mother did not successfully manage to learn English to a level where she felt capable to manage alone in many situations in public places. Before she could gain enough confidence the Teheran hostage crisis erupted. Angry demonstrators brandishing signs and yelling 'Iranians Go Home' took to the streets. Iranians reported violent incidents against them and the family was frightened to go out alone. The men went out together and the women never left the house without men to protect them. Ahmed explained, 'Our mother and sisters were so afraid they chose not to leave the home and became house prisoners for the first time in their lives.' In the two countries they considered home, they did not feel safe on the streets due to fanaticism, neither in hostile Iran nor hostile America: the land of the brave and the free.

The media image of the Arab terrorist has permeated our culture. Abdu, the son of Palestinian refugees to the USA, attended university in his state. One night he and a fellow Arab student were invited to a Halloween party where everyone was expected to arrive in costume. They both dressed in typical street clothes and then wrapped their faces up in the traditional black and white checked Arab headscarves. When they arrived the other guests froze in terror. Someone called the police and they were hauled off to the local police station before they could explain what was happening. Although they laugh about it today they were surprised at how deeply they misjudged popular sentiment.

One of my Muslim friends in Melbourne felt the need to explain that 'there are millions of moderate Muslims. Why does the press delight in writing only about the fanatics and building hatred against us? I am not like the Muslims the newspapers portray.' She has been a friend for over fifteen years so I was surprised that she felt the media reporting threatened our relationship. The media insists her faith and culture are a threat and associated with terrorism, violence, and backwardness. Islam is presented as inferior to the West in every way and because she remains a Muslim she is a suspect human being.

Hollywood rarely misses an opportunity to portray Arabs and

Muslims in negative roles. Even the film *Father Of The Bride 2* had an obnoxious male chauvinist exploiting the dad in the sale of his house. His name, clothing, facial features and foreign language classed him as an Arab. The image was subliminal and deviously placed in a family comedy. The original lyrics of the movie *Aladdin*, produced by Walt Disney, read:

> Oh I come from a land . . .
> where they cut off your ear
> if they don't like your face.
> It's barbaric, but hey its home . . .

After meetings with the American-Arab Anti-Discrimination Committee the lines were changed, but the word 'barbaric' was not changed. Even the *New York Times* (14 July 1993) editorialised that the *Aladdin* lyrics were racist.

Said and Braibanti both list influential anti Arab-Muslim media propaganda. American Broadcasting Commission's *20–20* broadcast several segments discussing Islam as a crusading religion inculcating warriors of God; *Frontline* sponsored an investigation of the 'tentacles of Muslim terrorists around the world'. The documentary *Jihad In America* by the Public Broadcasting System 1994 was cynically designed to exploit this fear and characterised Muslims as bent on destroying American institutions. It conveyed a message that Muslims are arriving at (US) borders with political agendas and congregating in mosques to conspire terrorist activities. *True Lies* (1994) with Arnold Schwarzenegger in a lead role is blatantly racist, anti-Muslim and anti-Arab. 'Its villains are classic Arab terrorists, complete with glinty eyes and a passionate desire to kill Americans. The main purpose is first to demonise and dehumanise Muslims in order to show an intrepid Western hero killing them off. *Delta Force* (1985) began the trend and it was carried forward in the *Indiana Jones* saga, *The Siege* and innumerable television serials in which Muslims are uniformly represented as evil, violent and above all extremely killable.'[10]

Movies slanted against Arabs or Islam are not a new phenom-
enon. 'Time magazine listed films starting with *The Sheikh*
(1921), *Protocol* (1984) and *Jewel of the Nile* (1985) – all of which
emphasised Arabs as exotic, sex-crazed lovers. *Lawrence of
Arabia* (1962) depicts the Arabs as a "political naif in need of
tutelage from a wiser Westerner". *The Formula* (1980), *Rollover*
(1981) and *Power* (1981) emphasise the Arab as an unscrupulous,
oil wealthy plutocrat. *Black Sunday* (1977) portrays the Arabs as
terrorists.'[11]

The public accepts these Hollywood stereotypes without realising a subliminal message denigrating Arab and Muslim people
has been planted in the subconscious. This message is that Arabs
and Muslims are treacherous, lecherous and dangerous.
Alongside this is a supra-positive portrayal of Jews, and since the
press portrays Arabs as the enemies of the Jews this elevated portrayal adds to the demonisation of Arabs.

Muslim is synonymous with Arab in the West's stereotyping,
but there are millions of Arabs who are not Muslim. Ray
Hannania, a Palestinian Christian, was born and raised in
America. 'One of my Jewish friends asked whose side I was on
"the Arabs or the Israelis". All I could think about was that scene
in *Exodus* where the Arab who was friendly to the Jews was killed
by his own people, hanging in the public square, a Jewish star
carved into his chest with a knife. Like so many people I learned
about being Arab from the movies. The movie *Exodus* was the
American textbook on the subject. The Arab was the villain of
course. Unshaven and dark skinned, he wore a dress, a towel on
his head and a rope around his waist and he murdered children
ruthlessly. He had a moustache and he looked like my Uncle
Fawzi. In fact almost every TV Hollywood Arab terrorist looks
like some uncle or aunt or cousin of mine. The scene where Fred
Dwyer pounces on a gaggle of terrorists in the movie *Death
Before Dishonor* looks like an assault on a Hannania family
reunion.'[12]

During the Gulf War a documentary television programme in

Australia contacted a group of Muslim women and asked them to appear on the programme, but stipulated the women wear black chadours. The women explained they don't normally wear them and chadours do not represent all Muslim women. The Muslims told me they would not co-operate with the media's stereotype so the programme was not made. Their real voices and real views were not allowed to be heard. They were not scary enough. In another incident another Australian programme contacted an Islamic Council requesting photos of Muslim women for an article. They also insisted the women wear veils and described the images they required. The Council reminded the photographer that Arab Muslims are a minority amongst Muslims in the world and suggested using a variety of Muslims for the photo. A session was set up at an Islamic school and the school secretary chose a variety of students from different countries, including Anglo-Saxons. Even though all the students were wearing large scarves the photographer still ignored blue-eyed blondes and only photographed less home grown looking Muslims. The brown-eyed olive-skinned secretary was surprised to find that in the end the photographer published a photo of her. The media demands its own version of Islam: foreign looking is preferable to familiar looking, scarves preferable to bare heads and veils preferable to scarves, and everything and everyone is better covered in black.

There are many prestigious books, newspaper articles and magazine dustcovers portraying Islam as the new foreign devil. But the shaping of images and fears has its genesis in higher places than popular arts. 'The most comprehensive and frightening treatment of Islam as a potential enemy of the United States is found in the work of Yossef Bodansky, former technical editor of Israeli Air Force magazine. He was staff director of the House Republican Task Force on Terrorism and Unconventional Warfare. The report viewed Islam as the successor to Communism, aiming to "topple the Judaeo-Christian new world order".'[13]

One of the most popular recent articles was 'The roots of Muslim rage' by Bernard Lewis, published in the September 1990 issue of *The Atlantic*. Said comments: 'It attempts to characterise Muslims as one terrifyingly collective person enraged at an outside world that has disturbed his primeval calm and challenged rule. In other words Muslims react today only because it is historically and perhaps genetically, determined that they should do so: what they react to are not policies or actions, or anything so mundane as that. What they are fighting on behalf of is an irrational hatred of the secular present which . . . is "ours" and ours alone. . . . [N]ot only are Muslims and "we" shut off from each other, despite centuries or borrowings and crossing over which Lewis totally denies, but "they" are as doomed to rage and irrationalism as "we" are to the enjoyment of our rationalism and cultural supremacy. To demonise or dehumanise a whole culture on the grounds that it is enraged at modernity is to turn Muslims into the objects of a therapeutic, punitive attention.'[14]

A news reporter covering a front-page crisis in Morocco asked an American family, 'How could you live so long in Morocco with these angry people?' The wife replied, 'You cover crisis events, conflicts and people shouting "Down with America" and burning the flag. This is a small window of the reality. You are not here to experience their kindness, hospitality and friendship. In my experience Moroccans are more friendly to me as a foreigner in their country, than the British were when I was a foreigner in their country. Moroccans' statements against America are in the political strata, not personally at me. The long distance media reports are usually negative. For example, some Moroccans asked me why we elected a president who is a cannibal. They read an article about the president's ancestors who were part of the Donner Party. The party crossed the Donner Pass into California and were caught in heavy snows. A few managed to survive by eating the flesh of their frozen party. They gained the impression Ronald Reagan and his ancestors were cannibals. If I don't know a Muslim personally, and vice-versa, there is no way I can discern the media reports. When we get to know Muslims personally we discover impressions of long distance reporting is a negative imbalance.'

In the West Islam is the enemy. In Muslim countries the enemy is Western decadence. Muslims looking at the West comment on the broken families, divorced couples, blatant sexual promiscuity, abandoned babies and old people *thrown* in homes and every person living to please oneself. The commonly-accepted Western idea that personal rights and happiness take precedence over responsibility to family or community frightens Muslims. This is not acceptable in Muslim communities and Muslims living in the West are afraid their families will be influenced by these values. Parents are afraid they will end up alone in old people's homes without their family caring for them until their last days. The problem of values is not simply Muslim versus Western, but traditional Eastern versus modern Western.

So one might ask why would a Muslim, or any Easterner, want to come to the West and face these problems? The main reason is the endemic problems of developing countries and war zones causing uncertainty for the future and the instability of regimes creating fear of the present. Muslims recounted similar personal sagas, but I have chosen a Christian's story to demonstrate that the problem of values cannot be labelled as a specifically Muslim inability to accept the West. He was born in Iraq, the son of a renowned musician and Lebanese mother, and his parents moved to Lebanon when he was twelve. Life became difficult during the civil war because they were Baptist Christians living in the Muslim side of Beirut. 'I was lucky. I found two jobs and worked from 5 am to 11 pm in order to survive. I worked in my profession on the newspaper in the day and drove taxis at night.' As a result of the Gulf War the family experienced racism against Iraqis from the Lebanese and they moved to a new area. It was difficult to find work and difficult to travel. Their Iraqi nationality was a problem as Syrian forces controlled the country and the Bath party factions, split between Iraq and Syria, are sworn enemies. 'We had to travel long distances to avoid checkpoints and borders under Syrian control. When I was stopped at checkpoints and they saw I was born in Iraq I was routinely treated badly: roughed up and punched in the stomach. I was really afraid they would keep me and kidnap me across the border and throw me in jail. It happened to many people. Many of them have never been seen again. I got trouble from both Christians and Muslims and I was afraid to tell friends that I am Iraqi. I can't tell them my father is the famous musician they love to listen to. My best friend is a Syrian Muslim, but he didn't tell anyone either because he is a refugee. Finally we both got Lebanese identity and I tell some people who I really am, but my Syrian friend has never told anyone. We have a close friendship, even though we had opposing religions during the war, because we share a secret life. He felt safe enough to visit his home and see his family on his new Lebanese identity papers, so I took him to the bridge-crossing and watched until he was safely across. I didn't dare to try and cross myself because my sister had trouble getting into Syria for Christmas, even though her father-in-law is an officer in the military.'

He married a Lebanese girl who was born in Australia and is an Australian citizen, and they moved to Melbourne. Sitting in their half-packed sitting room he explained, 'Everything is easy in Australia, life is wonderful. If I could find work I would stay. However it was disappointing here. The only way I could make it financially until I gained proper employment was to cheat on the government and take unemployment benefits, but I won't do that. I couldn't upgrade my English and computer skills enough in order to find work in my profession. I needed to go back to school, but I had to support the family. I was desperate for work and took anything, mainly low paying jobs that would not amount to anything in the future, nor be adequate to raise a family. Eventually I took a job delivering pizza, but most of the earnings went on expenses for the job: petrol and car repairs. We lived on our savings and have used all of our resources. Being unemployed was terrible for my self-esteem and it placed a big burden on my wife, as she was the only one employable. Neither of us coped well with this role reversal and it placed a strain on our marriage, but we worked it through.'

The main concerns the couple expressed were related to raising their family in the West with the pressure of a secular individualistic society undermining their religious and family values. They had one son ten months old. 'In the West children go separate ways. I am afraid of that happening to our family. There is no sense of family ties here and I want my son to always be a part of me. Family is so important.' He sighed, 'We have a lot of blessing in our country, but politics are a problem.' It was a seesaw decision, but they decided their family had a better future in Lebanon, finished packing their house and moved to Beirut. However, the economic situation in Lebanon was in crisis and they discovered there was little chance of finding work. After a few months they moved back to Melbourne where the husband eventually found suitable work.

Sarah Powell Jamali, the daughter of a respected Minnesota family, was now in her eighties and in failing health. She had lived in Tunisia with her husband, as a guest of the government, for thirty-five years after escaping the revolution that ended their life in Iraq. Fadhel Jamali, her husband, was Iraq's Prime Minister twice and its delegate to the UN. When we knew him in the nineties he was one of two surviving men who signed the original UN charter. His party was overthrown in a revolution in 1958 and he was arrested and condemned to death. He told us, 'There was a report in the paper that I was dead and a picture of my body being dragged through the streets of Baghdad. So some unfortunate person died in my place!' The Iraqi government exonerated him in 1961, but they never lived in Iraq again. Sarah, the girl who arrived in Baghdad in the 1930s by driving across the desert because there were no air services, never wanted to talk about her adventure stories. It was simply matter of fact that she regularly hid underneath a chadour in order to be driven through the Baghdad streets to visit her husband while he was in jail. Nor did she care to remember how hard those years were while she awaited his execution, but all the while encouraged him and their children. Sarah was no stranger to tragedy. Their eldest son contracted encephalitis after a case of measles and was left brain damaged. When Sarah discovered there was no medical care available for children in her son's condition, she set about establishing some. Although they needed to send their own son to an institution in Britain, future mentally challenged children in Iraq had schools where they found help. Sarah took up the same challenge in Tunisia and was awarded a medal for her work. We sat chomping on her famous ginger biscuits while the group who gathered every Sunday discussed current affairs, and she typically declined to talk about another story that surfaced, 'Oh nothing but wars and revolutions.' Sarah kept her faith in Christ and Fadhel kept his faith in Mohammed. And they kept a great love for each other through exceedingly tumultuous events. When Fadhel Jamali died, Sarah moved to live with her children in Jordan and we lost contact with her. We missed them on our last visit and prayed for her at her husband's grave. We often discussed religion and Fadhel echoed a statement he had also published, 'Arabs are afraid of everything unclear and secretive. Historically the Church has been hidden and Muslims have not understood Christianity. This is the reason Muslims have considered Christians enemies. Making Christ's message readily available is very important for Muslims. Muslims and Christians must understand each other.'

I remember one past afternoon at the Jamali's. The pot of tea sat bubbling at boiling point on the samovar in the Iraqi style. Next to it another elderly Arab lady drinking tea with us balanced her cup and saucer on her knee while she reminisced about past days. She searched for an elusive date by remembering the marker, 'Oh let me see, that was the year my husband was sentenced to death.' In surprise I noted another brave lady who had lived through terrible days of political upheaval and I wondered about the hidden lives of other apparently frail old ladies who drank tea with me!

Yussef looked over my shoulder seeing years ago, 'I remember the massacres. Our neighbourhood organised groups of ten men to rotate standing guard during the night to help protect us. Walking along the road every telephone pole held a corpse . . . corpses strewn along the roadside with birds and animals eating them. Everyone was afraid to claim relationship with them to bury them.' This story could have been related from any of the twentieth century's violent events in the Middle East. It was an Iraqi Christian's remembrance of one of his country's revolutions. The Christians felt especially vulnerable because they were a minority group in a time of upheaval.

Naema wanted her daughter to have the big white wedding she missed out on. She married in 1948, the year of Palestinian history called *the catastrophe*, the year they lost their country. And they had lost friends in Deir Yassin.[15] Her father said they could not dream of having a proper celebration while the whole nation was going through such suffering. Naema dreamt of one but wouldn't suggest it. So after a proper waiting period, the two families celebrated the marriage quietly at home. Her family lost their home and ancestral lands in that year and moved to Jordan. The chance for the big white wedding came again with Naema's eldest daughter. But fate took a hand again and this time it was the war of 1967. How could anyone celebrate in that year when they were under an occupation army and the nation was on the move as refugees once again? So her dreams shifted to her second daughter. But before the wedding took place the events of Black September[16] sabotaged it. So they had another quiet celebration at home. The new political reality in Jordan caused them to move to Kuwait. Finally it was the wedding of her youngest daughter and Naema was determined to have a wonderful wedding and reception. But, 'On the week of the wedding every Palestinian home in Kuwait was flying black. Black reams of material hung from balconies and we all wore black. There wasn't a home untouched. We couldn't face a celebration. We postponed the marriage.' One of the worst massacres in the Palestinians' story was perpetrated that week in the Sabra and Shatilla refugee camps in Lebanon.[17] Kuwait expelled the Palestinians after the Gulf War and so her family moved to their third country of refuge. Naema had no chance for her white wedding and hopes her granddaughter will have one. She finished her story with a shrug and resigned smile.

The events in the Middle East have kept the newspapers in good business since World War One. Fighting broke out in Palestine after the thirties and intensified in the next decade when the European Jews moved into the country and Britain attempted to prevent both Jews and Palestinians from gaining possession. After World War Two Palestine erupted and the Palestinian refugees poured into nearby countries. Since then four major wars took place trying to settle the problem (1956, 1967, 1973, 1982).

The surrounding countries were not peaceful enclaves or refuges. The early part of the twentieth century opened with the Kurds massacring the Armenians. Mazhar's grandfather took in seven Armenian families who survived and arrived in a pitiful state in our family's hometown. At the end of the twentieth century the Kurds were on the receiving end from the Iraqi and Turkish governments. Millions have died in these wars in the region. The Lebanese civil war raged for twenty years. The Iran-Iraq war was an eight-year battle. When peace came Iranians fled either the Shah's vengeance or Khomeini's men. The Gulf War took its toll in deaths and displacement of Arab residents within those countries. Since 1990, 1.7 million Iraqis have died as a result of sanctions, most of them children. Iraqi children are also dying from diseases believed to be caused from DU (depleted uranium) particles. When ordnance coated with depleted uranium strikes a target the DU burns and aerosolises – releasing a fine dust that is both toxic and radioactive.[18] Added to this we must remember that the Arab countries were the battlefields for the great World Wars. In addition there are the continuing internal wars or cross-border conflicts taking their toll of lives in Sudan, Morocco, Libya, Chad, Algeria, Yemen, Somalia, Israel and Lebanon. The Arab peoples have been suffering wars or oppression since World War One and a number of current regimes allow little freedom of speech or belief.

When we returned to live in Damascus in 1995, Syrians predicted we would last six months. We were determined to prove them wrong and make Syria our home. They were wrong. We lasted seven months! Arab governments are suspicious of the West using religion as a cloak for seditious political activities in their lands – a number of books written in Arabic and others translated from English make this accusation. Moreover Syria is still in a state of war with Israel and the government is nervous about anything it does not control or understand. Mazhar loves his country and cares deeply about it and is proud of his heritage. He does not consider himself to have joined the *Christian* West nor changed loyalty. He is simply an Arab who follows Christ. But Mazhar is someone they do not understand. Thirty years ago he was an active member in a political party that resulted in his old friends being on the wrong list today. There were warrants out for his arrest – one charge connected with his faith in Christ.

But God had impressed upon our hearts that we should return. On the day Mazhar was entering Syria, God confirmed his promise that he would be kept safe. I entered a church at 8.30 am on a weekday to pray and found a small group in worship. The Scripture text was the dialogue with God meeting Moses and commissioning him to return to his people. Moses objected saying he was a fugitive from the authorities and it wasn't safe to return. God answered, 'You are not going alone, nor on your own authority. I AM will with be with you and bring you safely from Pharaoh's court.' Mazhar surrendered himself to the authorities requesting the case to be investigated and the chance to prove his innocence. He was kept in solitary confinement for eighteen days in an underground cell with the usual thin blanket on the concrete floor. He was denied all outside contacts and his only companion was a rat and cockroaches. But God planned to transform this prison experience into a spiritual gift by teaching him to embrace the bitter until its piercing brought drops of sweetness. Mazhar felt he was blessed with sharing the sufferings of Christ. He describes it, 'I felt as if I was released from my dismal surroundings and from my personal internal prison. I drank deeply of the Father's love and suffering for us in Christ on the cross.' He was treated somewhat kinder than the usual interrogation meted out to political prisoners in order to get a 'confession', but lost all hope of being cleared. On the eighteenth day with no word of what had happened to him, concerned friends in different countries felt constrained to pray and the following day he was suddenly released.

After his release we continued to be harassed by certain authorities which resulted in severely restricted movements. We stayed in isolation from other Christians, made no friends and saw no one but family. Our life resembled and felt like house arrest. The isolation and pressure of knowing we were being followed everywhere and accounting for every word pushed us into paranoia. We were afraid to speak together of the situation, even in bed. In mid winter we put on the radio inside the house (for supposed bugs) and sat outside to talk quietly. Thus we were living like too many citizens of the Arab world: afraid that comments overheard could be used against us or others. Mazhar needed special permission to leave the country. When we wanted to join our family in Melbourne for Christmas it took two months of visits to obtain the treasured piece of paper. We had paid for the tickets in hope and God helped us by getting this permission to leave just in time. We were allowed to leave one week before Christmas.

Even then when we attempted to board the plane Mazhar's name appeared on the computer and he was declared under arrest. I was left standing alone while he was taken away to a small room out of sight. I knew what was happening in there; this same thing happened each time we left or entered the country. He always carried a sheaf of papers to prove he was theoretically innocent. In the room out of sight they were now reading those papers. At any time they could decide not to accept the evidence, or there could be a new warrant issued, and he would not return to me but disappear in an underground cell again. Each time he was 'arrested' I reminded myself not to panic, breathe slowly and pray as I did on this occasion. God had led us back and God would care for us.

When we returned to Damascus after Christmas the situation worsened. We were grateful to the authorities for giving us fair recourse to justice, and for theoretically declaring Mazhar innocent, but they were not going to leave us in peace to live our life. We requested permission for one more trip out. At the airport, after the usual 'You are under arrest', Mazhar was returned from the secret room and we boarded the plane with shaking knees. It wasn't until we were airborne that the tension in our muscles began to uncoil. With very mixed emotions we thus joined the millions of other refugees in the world.

We were more fortunate than others in similar situations. There was the Lebanese Cabinet Minister whom we met when he was visiting friends in Cairo. I never thought of him again until his face stared at me from the front page of the newspaper proclaiming he was 'Kidnapped in Libya'. His body has never been found.

In one family we know, the children's father is a political refugee and the family was living in Algeria. When the father's papers became outdated and he could not obtain new ones, he was classified an illegal immigrant. The government jailed him, leaving his family without a breadwinner and his children not permitted to attend school. When he was eventually released after two years of real hardship for the family, they fled to another country, possibly to go through the same scenario again.

A Muslim Kurd in Istanbul told me, 'God hates the Kurds.

Otherwise why would he ignore our cries for so long?' Pictures of the Kurdish atrocities on the Armenians flashed through my mind and I pondered on the biblical theory of divine retribution working through history. But this Kurd wasn't even born at the time of the Armenian slaughter and my theory wouldn't bring any comfort to his wounded heart, unless he could see that one day the perpetrators of injustice to the Kurds would also reap what they sowed. Ultimately, God's working through history remains beyond our solving and our part is to work for peace, pray for peace, speak out against injustice and comfort the wounded. Some of these wounded, whether the wound is physical or spiritual, are Muslims fleeing to the West. When news of the earthquake that devastated the population of Istanbul in August 1999 was broadcast during our evening meal, I wondered whether God heard that Kurdish man's cries or whether he was with those crushed under the rubble.

All of these stories highlight reasons why Muslims might flee their homelands looking for a new life in the West. However, when they arrive, many are suspected of being violent trouble-makers or undesirables, thus the terrorised are branded terrorists.

Where is the Church in the midst of this war of words and images? Is the Church witnessing to Christ by setting an example of Christian love and reaching out to the media-oppressed; treating others as we would like to be treated? Some branches of the Church have been striving diligently to minister Christ in the midst of these troubled relations with Islam. However, others have not only been lagging behind, but some denominations and leaders are noted for their hostility to Islam.

Huda, the Muslim university student, said, 'We love to meet people with strong faith. We have a lot in common. We see the difference in those who are strong Christians. There is a difference in their life and we immediately feel a connection with them. They are more open than others and have an appreciation for faith.' However another Muslim woman present at the interview said, 'We cannot understand why Christian leaders are too afraid to speak out on issues that they oppose. There was an art exhibition in Melbourne that blasphemed Jesus Christ. We were upset about this as Christ is an honoured prophet. I belong to an inter-faith kitchen table group and was expecting the Christians to raise the topic. I was surprised when none of them brought up the subject, so finally I asked them what they were going to do. They answered "We cannot do anything." I took the initiative and encouraged them to join me in complaining to the council and we managed to get the exhibition closed. The media is very negative to Christians as well as to us, and the Christians are too afraid to speak out on issues. Actually it's very negative to anyone with faith.'

Arabs and Muslims are also unfairly stereotyped in the Christian media and these stereotypes are believed in many Western churches. Most Christians have never met Muslims, but either see them as adversaries or are afraid of them. One only needs to look at the covers of books about Muslims in any book-shop: daggers, guns, black robes, black veils, shadows. In churches, when I hold up the black and white checked head-dress (kerfieyya) worn by Arab men asking, 'What image does this connote?' The answer is never Palestine, the birthplace of Christ, but 'Palestinian terrorists', 'Muslim terrorists', 'machine guns and weapons'. The demonisation of a culture continues.

A missionary couple invited to a church in Minnesota spoke about their life in the Arab world, and then asked if there were any questions. The pastor of the fellowship asked if they would talk about the fanaticism and ruthlessness of the Arab people. They responded, 'It isn't worth talking about because it's such a small per cent of the population. In fact, it would be like saying that most American citizens belong to the Klu Klux Klan.' After a few other questions, the pastor again asked them to share about fundamentalism and fanaticism in Islam. Since his question was essentially the same, they gave the same answer . . . which didn't please him. After the meeting, he didn't talk to them or thank them for coming and they were left wondering where they would be spending the night. It was the middle of winter, there wasn't a hotel in town, and the pastor had promised to find a place for them to stay the night. After most people had gone home, a Native American couple invited them for the evening. They were very glad that they didn't have to sleep in the car for the night because they had defended their Arab friends.

The Church in Francis' day taught that Islam was demonic and therefore it would disappear. Today there are 1.2 billion Muslims in the world, one fifth of the world's population, and Islam is one of the fastest growing religions in a number of countries, including those in the West. Islam is not likely to disappear. Muslims are not our enemy and we need to learn to live with Muslims in a Christian way. Maybe we will learn to do this in the new millennium. I believe it will depend on how sincerely we live out Christ's message. The only way most Muslims will experience Christ's love for them is through a Christian who cares enough to cross the barrier, and go over to the other side, no matter what the cost.

Notes

1 Kabbani, R. (1989) *Letter to Christendom*, Camden, UK: Virago Press, p. ix.
2 Ibid., p. 1.
3 Ibid., p. 2.
4 Ibid., p. 11.
5 Ibid., pp. 51–52.
6 Said, E. (1981) *Covering Islam*, New York: Vintage Books, p. 7. Reprinted by Pantheon Books, a division of Random House Inc.
7 Ibid., p. xiv.
8 Braibanti, R. J. D. (1995) *The Nature and Structure of the Islamic World*, Chicago: International Strategy and Policy Institute, p. 9.

9 Said, op. cit., p. xiv.
10 Said, op. cit., p. xxvi-vii and Braibanti, op. cit., pp. 5–7.
11 Braibanti, op. cit., p. 7.
12 Hanania, R. (1996) *I'm Glad I Look Like a Terrorist*, Illinois: Urban Strategies Group Publishing, p. 18.
13 Braibanti, op. cit., p. 7.
14 Said, op. cit., pp. xxxii–iii.
15 Deir Yassin was a village west of Jerusalem. Approximately 250 civilians were massacred on 9 April 1948 by Jewish irregular forces under the command of Menachem Begin, later Israeli Prime Minister.
16 In 1970 the Jordanian army defeated a Palestinian guerrilla force in a ten-day civil war.
17 3,000–3,500 Palestinians and Lebanese in the refugee camps, Sabra and Shatilla, were brutally massacred between 16–18 September 1982 by Lebanese Phalangists with the aid of the Israeli Defence Force. ·Cf. Chapter 4.
18 *Plough Reader*, The Spoils of War, Spring 2000, East Sussex: The Plough Publishing House, p. 30.

Chapter Eight

A CHRISTIAN IN THE SULTAN'S CAMP

The story of the monk and the Sultan is one intriguing link in a chain of amazing encounters and friendships leaping across the chasm of brutality during the Crusade wars. Those were the days for the making of legends and some of the greatest figures of history wove their golden thread into a breathtaking tapestry: renowned chivalrous knights in shining armour, great philosophers not seen since, great mystics not fully fathomed since. Among these glorious pages of Francis' story ride the great King Richard the Lionhearted and his, perhaps even greater, Muslim counterpart, Salahadin. Richard the Lionheart's subjects viewed their king in the same light as the Muslims viewed Salahadin: the good, noble leader who would put right all wrongs, a grand warrior and an example of chivalry and mercy.

Salahadin

Salah Al Din Yusuf (1138–1193CE) was the first Sultan in the Abbuybid dynasty and the most famous Muslim soldier of the Crusades. His name is remembered as Salahadin (or shortened in English to Saladin). Salahadin is remembered as the gallant Muslim leader who engaged in war without hatred and practised great compassion and mercy, often when the Christian armies did not. He was generous – in the best of Arab tradition – giving unstintingly to his own disadvantage, even allowing himself to be robbed and exploited. He was known to be cheerful, courteous and chivalrous to all. 'Rarely in the accounts of a defeated people has there been such a paeon of praise to the victor.'[1] His influence was so great that many Christians named their children after him. In the fourteenth century the priest of Nantes' name was Olivier Salahadin and French families today still carry his name.[2] Before his death, Salahadin divided his empire between his two sons, but seven years after his death his brother Sultan Al Adil (the Just) had gained power as sole ruler.

King Richard I and Salahadin shared a mutual respect and Richard showed great affection for Salahadin. Adil, who conquered Salahadin's kingdom, is remembered as a great warrior and an able diplomat who was always ready to make peace. He also won the friendship of King Richard, who wanted to make Adil his brother-in-law by marrying him to his beloved sister Joan. The objective was to create a Muslim-Christian kingdom in Jerusalem through the alliance. When it was suggested that Sultan Adil should convert to Christianity, he did not reject the idea outright, but politely asked for time to think about it.[3] But the marriage never took place, because Joan did not want to marry a Muslim.[4] Adil had three sons who inherited his empire: Ashraf took Arabia, Muazzam took Syria and Kaamil – whom Francis was soon to meet – went to Egypt.

King Richard, Sultan Salahadin and Francis all shared a common interest. They were all influenced by the troubadour songs and poetry. The troubadour songs have their roots in the court poets of the Arab world and are believed to be one of the mediums whereby Muslim mysticism influenced the West. King Richard's parents were both French and he spent most of his life in France. French was his mother-tongue and the language of the Plantagenet court where the troubadour songs and minstrels were welcomed. These were the songs Francis loved as a youth and sang through the streets of Assisi. They fostered dreams of courtly love, humane knights and noble sentiments. These humane ideals materialised when knights met on the battlefields. When Richard fell ill with a fever during the Crusades, it is said that Salahadin sent him fruit and snow. King Richard and Francis both loved to sing in French, and probably sang the same songs in their youth.

Francis arrives

The ruckus from the group gathered on the European wharf beside the Crusader ship bound for Egypt grew louder. The ship laden with soldiers and ammunition was ready to sail to relieve the army besieging Damiettia in Egypt, but a bunch of monks were insisting on boarding. Francis had arrived with an assembly of Brothers intending to travel together, but the sailors refused to take such a large group. Francis solved the problem and called a young boy on the wharf to choose twelve among them and he obeyed the unseen hand of God in the boy's random choice. The friars boarded the ship and duly arrived at the war front in mid-July 1219. They joined the Crusaders under Duke Leopold of Austria who led a motley array of men known by the misnomer of the 'army'. They were men flamed by religious zeal to kill God's enemies and mercenaries looking for loot and adventure. 'The licence and disunity reigning in this army was sufficient explanation of its previous failure.'[5] This army was camped outside Damiettia where they had been laying siege to the city for one year.

Francis set up camp within the camp and began waging his own battle – against the Crusades. He first preached to the Crusader army calling for peace and telling them they were fighting against God and to lay down their weapons. He initially had wonderful results and a number abandoned their arms to join the Friars Minor. Jacques de Vitry, a celebrated thirteenth-century contemporaneous chronicler with no ties to the monks, described the event:

Francis is loved by God and venerated by all. He came into our camp
burning with zeal for the faith, he was not afraid to go into the very
camp of our enemy. Colin the Englishman, my clerk, has also entered
this order along with two other companions . . . And I am having
difficulty holding onto Henry, the chanter and a few others.[6]

Another witness to Francis' preaching (in Europe) said, 'I heard
Francis preach . . . His whole manner of speech was calculated
to stamp out enmities and to make peace. His tunic was dirty, his
person unimposing and his face far from handsome, yet God
gave him such power of his words that many factions of the
nobility, among whom the fierce anger of ancient feuds had been
raging with much bloodshed, were brought to reconciliation. He
did not keep to the method of an expositor so much as a reviv-
alist.'[7] Francis did not try to win verbal victories over antago-
nists, but sowed the path to peace.

One month after arriving, on 15 August, Francis witnessed
what happened to eight Muslims who were discovered while
trying to infiltrate the camp. Four of them were sent back to the
Sultan with nose, lips and arms hacked off and the other four
sent to Damiettia in the same state.[8]

Two weeks later, on 29 August, Francis tried to dissuade the
army from a massive assault on the city believing they were
running into another defeat. They refused to listen and mocked
him. The assault was a catastrophic defeat and 5,000 men were
lost, either killed or captured. Francis gained a reputation as a
prophet. The camp was in a miserable state and both armies
exhausted, so a truce was declared. While the preliminaries of
peace were taking place between the Crusader leaders and the
Sultan, Francis exploited this truce to go over to the enemy
camp, much to the astonishment of the Crusaders. They were
incredulous and appalled that he would venture into the enemy
camp at all, much less unarmed. 'The idea of converting the
Saracens must have seemed singularly fantastic to men who up
to then had thought only of cutting their throats.'[9]

But more than this they must have been totally flabbergasted that he intended to preach the very same message to the Muslims that he had preached to the Crusaders themselves. The same message for those infidels as for the believers! Believer is an ambiguous term: it depends which side is speaking, as both sides saw the other as the unbelievers. Francis' contemporaries who had never met Sultan Kaamil described him as 'the savage beast'. This is all he could be for he was 'the other', 'the enemy', 'the son of the devil'.

Sultan Al Kaamil

But was Kaamil this savage infidel? The Crusaders would have been staggered to know that Kaamil was actually a knight of their beloved King Richard. In 1192 when Kaamil was a young adolescent he accompanied his father to the camp of King Richard during negotiations. Richard again tried to cement his friendship with Salahadin's family. He knighted Kaamil on the Feast of Pentecost! The ceremony posed problems for those writing up the liturgy as they had to work up a non-Christian service. The obstacles that were overcome highlight the depth of the relationship between the Western king and the future Sultans, the brother and nephew of Salahadin.[10] Thus Kaamil inherited a family tradition of fraternal relations with Christian infidels. Moreover, Kaamil the true knight of Richard the Lionhearted and nephew of the noble Salahadin who was so admired by the West, was a king where the best of East and West had embraced. This so-called 'savage beast' of a Sultan was also a cultured man with a love of poetry, especially the poems of the mystics which yearned for the true path of a deeper love relationship with God. Kaamil had a mystic attached to his court – Fakhr al Din al Farisi. The records tell us Fakhr al Din al Farisi was present during the conversations with Francis. In God's plan this was no coincidence.

The Meeting

With the Sultan and Francis both in Egypt the stage was now set for the encounter which would bring them face to face. Both men would be changed forever by their meeting and both would become legends in their own times and until today.

Francis and his companion, Illuminato, walked directly into the enemy camp, the field headquarters of Sultan Kaamil. The Muslim soldiers promptly arrested and harshly treated them and Francis' cries to be taken to the Sultan in order to convert him to the Gospel found a sudden reception.

We picture the Sultan reclining on cushions in a plush tent wearing long Eastern robes. The walls are lined with brocades and lanterns entwined like grape-clusters drape intricate designs over bodies and faces and silhouette slaves and retainers hovering. (I have seen beduin tents decorated in this manner and it's more interesting than picturing drab military tents.) When Kaamil heard that the monks were discovered in the camp the following story is recorded of his preparations.

The Sultan's voice rings out, 'Bring a carpet woven with patterns of the cross and place it on the floor. Then fetch that man who seems to be a true Christian.' Bodies sped to carry out the Sultan's order and set in place the trap for the expected monk. He deliberately and callously placed Francis in the situation he thought was impossible saying, 'If he walks on it I will accuse him of insulting their God. If he refuses I will ask him why he disdains to approach me.' (Presumably that could mean losing more than limbs or nose!) Is Francis sincere if he treats his religious symbol with such contempt? If roles were reversed the Sultan could not imagine himself profaning sacred writings or symbols in such a blasphemous manner.

Two dirty and dishevelled monks clothed in torn and patched woollen robes are manhandled into the tent in chains. The monk and the Sultan, great representatives of Christianity and Islam, come face to face on the battlefield – in the Sultan's territory under the sign of the crescent. Without more than a cursory glance at the carpet, Francis walks over it to the Sultan and hails him with his usual greeting, 'God give you peace'.

(The carpet story appears in chronicles in another following form. Salahadin gave a reception to the Western leaders in the tent – the floor of which was covered by a carpet with crosses and Christian symbols. The Muslim princes carefully walked around the carpet – avoiding stepping on it, but the Crusader knights strode over it without a glance. Salahadin sadly shook his head exclaiming, 'My own emirs would have been less careless of the symbols of their religion.')

Kaamil expected Francis to either be travelling under the truce flag in the name of the Crusaders, attempting to reopen the interrupted peace negotiations, or wishing to follow the example of a number of other Crusaders who deserted their camp and embraced Islam. The Sultan asked if Francis had come with the intention of becoming a Muslim or only as a messenger. However Francis surprised the Sultan by giving an unimaginable answer, 'I have a message to you from God.' The Sultan draws attention to what Francis has done, 'You Christians adore the cross as a special sign of your God: why then didn't you fear to trample it underfoot?' In an echo reminiscent of his bravado remarks to the brigands in the woods, Francis retorts, 'Thieves were also crucified along with our Lord. We have the true cross of our Lord and Saviour Jesus Christ: we adore it and show it great devotion. If the holy cross of our Lord has been given to us, the cross of the thieves has been left to you as your share. That is why I had no scruple in walking over brigands.' The Sultan answered, 'Your Lord taught in his gospels that evil must not be repaid with evil, that you should not refuse your cloak to anyone who wants to take your tunic, etc. In that case, Christians should not invade our land.' 'It seems,' Francis answered, 'that you have not read the Gospel of our Lord Jesus Christ completely. In another place we read: if your eye causes you to sin, tear it out and throw it away. Here he wanted to teach us that every man, however dear and close he is to us, and even if he is as precious as the apple of our eye, must be repulsed, pulled out, expelled if he seeks to turn us aside from the faith and love of our God. That is why it is just that Christians invade the land you inhabit, for you blaspheme the name of Christ and alienate everyone you can from his worship. But if you were to recognise, confess, and adore the creator and redeemer, Christians would love you as themselves.' The account then states that, 'All the spectators were in admiration at his answers.'[11]

The records tell us that as a result of this meeting the Sultan so warmed to Francis that he invited him to stay with him. In fact we know that Francis did stay for a prolonged time at Kaamil's camp and that afterwards Kaamil gave him and the Franciscans special written permission to preach in Muslim lands. Future Popes benefited from the monk's meeting with the Sultan and sent Franciscan brothers on diplomatic missions to different Muslim countries. And in 1244 another Egyptian Sultan chose a Franciscan brother as his messenger to Pope Innocent IV.[12]

In spite of the outcome of the actual meeting, what took place continues to tease and thwart those who would plumb its depths. Christian sources state that Kaamil received Francis very favourably, along with his message of the 'true Gospel'. Older Christian traditions state that Kaamil accepted Francis' prayer for him and was converted. Muslim sources state that Kaamil was a changed man after meeting Francis. One roaming legend from an obscure and forgotten source has Kaamil declaring, 'Oh Francis if I ever meet another Christian like you, I will become Christian.' On the other hand, more recent Christian rereading of the accounts claim that *Francis* was a changed man after Egypt and this has led to much speculation about what happened to both men. Francis never spoke about what happened. It is possible that all of these things did.

The Legend Grows

We will look at the first three original accounts of the meeting and note the differences and new strains they take in the re-telling. The first account, by Jacques de Vitry, is written one year after the event.

> Even the Saracens and men plunged into the darkness of unbelief admire their humility and virtue when the brothers come among them to preach to them without fear: they receive them very gladly and give them all they need. The founder Francis is a simple unlettered man, loved by God and men. Spiritual fervour and ecstasy moved him to such excess that . . . with no fear whatsoever he set out for the camp of the Sultan of Egypt. The Saracens arrested him on his way. 'I am a Christian' he said, 'Bring me to your master'. On seeing the man of God, the Sultan, that cruel beast, became sweetness itself, kept him with him for a few days and with a great deal of attention listened to him preach the faith of Christ to him and his followers. But in the end he was afraid of seeing some of his soldiers whom the effective words of this man would have converted to the Lord go over to the army of the Christians. He therefore had Francis led back to our camp with many signs of honour and with security precautions, but not without saying to him 'Pray for me that God may reveal to me that Law and faith which is to him most pleasing'.

The Sultan's words have also been rendered 'Pray for me that God will reveal to me the right path which to him is most pleasing.' This is a crucially important distinction which we will later return to.

One year after Francis died Pope Gregory XI canonised him and commissioned the Franciscan leaders, who had been Francis' companions, to write his biography. The Pope was the former Cardinal Hugolin who 'venerated Francis as one sent by God. Handsome, brave, robust, eloquent, a great traveller and scholar, with a warm and faithful heart . . . and a statesman, this Pope was likewise a man of God. He was happy only in the company of monks who he counted on to reform the Church.'

There is another intriguing adjective applied to Hugolin. He had mystic leanings which is no doubt one of the reasons he understood Francis and supported him.[13]

In the first biography written by Thomas of Celano the following emphasis appears:

> Francis set out at a time when great and severe battles were raging daily between the Christians and the pagans (sic): he took with him a companion, and he did not fear to present himself before the Sultan of Saracens. But who can narrate with what great steadfastness of mind he stood before him, with what strength of spirit he spoke to him, and what eloquence and confidence he replied to those who insulted the Christian law? . . . he was captured by the Sultan's soldiers, was insulted and beaten, still he was not frightened: he did not fear the threats of torture and when death was threatened he did not grow pale. But though he was treated shamefully by many who were quite hostile toward him, he was nevertheless received very honourably by the Sultan. He honoured him as much as he was able, and having given him many gifts, he tried to bend Francis' mind toward the riches of the world. But when he saw Francis most vigorously despised all these things as so much dung, he was filled with the greatest admiration, and he looked upon him as a man different from all others. He was deeply moved by his words and listened to him very willingly. Still in all these things the Lord did not fulfil Francis' desire for martyrdom.[14]

One generation later the Pope ordered another biography and St Bonaventure, the new head of the Franciscan order, wrote it. The legend took on additional hues.

> The Sultan had decreed that anyone who brought him the head of a Christian should be rewarded with a Byzantine gold piece. However, Francis the knight of Christ, was undaunted and had high hopes that he would realise his ambition. The thought of death attracted him so he decided to make the journey. They were fiercely seized by the Sultan's men, savagely ill treated and beaten and put in chains. Then exhausted by the treatment they had received they were dragged

before the Sultan. The Sultan asked them by whom and why and in what capacity they had been sent, and how they got there: but Francis replied intrepidly that they had been sent by God and not by man, to show him and his subjects the way of salvation and proclaim the truth of the Gospel message.

When the Sultan saw his enthusiasm and courage he listened willingly to him and pressed him to stay with him. Francis however was inspired by God to reply, 'If you and your people are willing to become converts to Christ, I shall be glad to stay with you for love of him. But if you are afraid to abandon the law of Mohomet for Christ's sake, then light a big fire and I will go into it with your priests. That will show you which faith is more sure and holy.' To that the Sultan replied, 'I do not think that any of my priests would be willing to expose himself to the flames just to defend his faith, or suffer any of kind of torture' (he had just caught a glimpse of one of his old esteemed priests slipping away the moment he heard Francis' proposal). Then Francis continued, 'If you are prepared to promise me that you and your people will embrace the Christian religion, if I come out of the fire unharmed, I will enter it alone. But if I am burned you must attribute it to my sins: if on the other hand, God saves me by his power, you must acknowledge Christ the power of God, Christ the wisdom of God as true God, the Lord and saviour of all.'

The Sultan replied that he would not dare to accept a choice like that for fear of revolt among his people. Then he offered Francis a number of valuable presents, but the saint was only anxious for the salvation of souls; he had no interest in the things of this earth so he scorned them as if they were so much dust. The Sultan was lost in admiration at the sight of such perfect disregard for worldly wealth and he felt a greater respect than ever for the saint. He refused, and perhaps did not dare, to become a Christian, but at the same time he implored the saint to take the gifts and give them to the Christian poor or to churches, for his (the Sultan's) salvation. Francis however did not want to be bothered with money and besides he could see no sign of a genuinely religious spirit in the Sultan, and so he absolutely refused to agree. Francis now realised there was no hope of converting the Moslems and that he could not win the crown of martyrdom, and so by divine inspiration he made his way back to the Christian camp.[15]

The Sultan's Conversion

We note that this record depicts Francis concluding that Muslims are a lost cause for Christ and gives up the mission. However, the great impact Francis had on the Sultan is confirmed in all secular and religious sources. The Sultan's reputed conversion seems to be an echo of St Bonaventure's report, based on interviews with Brother Illuminato who quotes Kaamil, '"I believe your faith is good and true." And from that moment he always had the Christian faith imprinted on his heart.' This is backed by the comment that his Arab contemporaries criticised him for not being a fervent Muslim.[16]

On the Christian side of the stage the legend grows until the great Muslim Sultan was cast into doubt about his faith and prayed with Francis asking to find the true path and was thus converted to Christ.

Many speculations were made and legends born that Kaamil promised to receive baptism before his death. The historian Matthieu refers to this when he writes of the death of Kaamil in 1238. When the German emperor Frederic II, who was a great friend of the Sultan, hears of his death, he begins to cry bitterly, 'The Sultan promised to receive the baptism, and the emperor hoped this way to increase the dominion of Christendom.'[17] Another legend circulated that in order to keep a promise Francis made to Kaamil, two Franciscans miraculously appeared and administered baptism to Kaamil upon his deathbed.

These accounts all leave us with many questions and a good dose of incredulity. It takes a great stretch of the imagination to understand how the Sultan's conversion could come out of such a mutually acrimonious first meeting. And was Kaamil converted? Bonaventure's accounts are contradictory. In 1260 he claimed that there was no sign of a religious spirit in the Sultan and then in 1267 that 'since that moment the Sultan had the Christian faith in his heart'.

Was Kaamil converted or was he someone without a religious

bone in his body? The circumstances of the meeting are depicted as more adventurous and more dangerous in each succeeding account. The Sultan develops into a cruel beast offering gold coins for the heads of Christians and thus Francis' venture is more daring. The beating is intensified to include chains and threats of torture and physical exhaustion. Finally with the bravado of an Old Testament prophet Francis is the only one in the camp ready to enter the flames in the test of faith. In addition to this, the effect of Francis' preaching is about to win over the Muslim camp if the Sultan had not intervened. Kaamil is only portrayed as the sinister foil to display Francis' godliness. No more events of this incredible meeting are known, and we can be forgiven for viewing some of these accounts with scepticism, but all the secular, Christian and Muslim sources agree that Kaamil received Francis with respect and wanted to hear more of his message. Even the Arabic sources mention that Kaamil was a changed man after the incident.

So it is certain that something positive happened. However, this certainty dwindles into a confusing uncertainty about *what* happened. So the tale has been interpreted many different ways according to the perception of the storyteller. This is my telling of the story and I propose that Sultan Kaamil was converted. Moreover, I also propose that Francis was likewise converted during their meeting.

The first problem is the representation of both Francis and the Sultan in the accounts. Their attitudes and remarks are out of character for both men. With what we know of these men it is difficult to imagine their conversation taking place in those tones. The accounts reflect a stereotype of Muslims as the pagan enemy under the reign of Satan who are anti-Christ in all their attitudes. There is also no sign of the qualities Francis is renowned for, nor his vision and mission in life. Francis is renowned for spurning confrontation, for attempting reconciliation – particularly in his preaching. He saw signs of God in every living thing from ragged lepers to wolves and birds. He even treated earthworms with great exaggerated respect. He looked for the image and light of God in all of creation and because of this he treated every person with respect and dignity. According to contemporary witnesses his preaching typically made peace and brought an end to hostilities and enmity. So why, when he finally reaches the foreign missionfield of his dreams, would he be so verbally aggressive – going so far as to insult him over the cross of Christ, the core of his message? The first account states Francis was about to win many of the Muslims 'over to the Christian army'. But Francis was trying to *disband* the Christian army.

We have already seen that Al Kaamil was nothing like the savage unbeliever he is likened to in contemporary records. Al Kaamil's name means 'perfect' and he is remembered as living up to his name. Moreover, rather than looking for ways to desecrate a Christian's faith, he was interested in interfaith dialogue. In the midst of the religious wars 'Kaamil's court included sceptics who liked to discuss the prospective merits of the Quran and the Gospel and who were chivalrous in their deportment'.[18]

Kaamil was a man similar to Francis. Francis set out on the road of his ambitions to become a knight, a noble, and a great warrior. What Francis began Al Kaamil accomplished. Both men saw themselves as knights for God. Both men were mystics and poets whose veins ran deep with faith. But whereas Francis' worldview caused him to renounce the world in order to follow God, Kaamil's worldview allowed him to intertwine religion and the world.

Islam practises two equally balanced hands of the faith: Din wa Dounya (Religion and the World). There was no need for Kaamil to renounce his position and wealth. He believed it was given and ordained by God. Where Christ teaches 'give to Caesar what is Caesar's', Mohammed taught 'the Kingdom of God and the kingdom of Caesar are one'. What is for God is for Caesar and this is why the Caliphate ruled in the name of God. It was a similar position to the Catholic Church at the time.

We note that Kaamil conducted courteous interfaith dialogue in his court and won the friendship and respect of Western world leaders. Therefore the carpet story is also out of character, as is the picture of the impact of Francis' presence immediately changing the Sultan from a rough pagan into a polite God-seeker. For these reasons I doubt that it happened. Some of the accounts written about Francis' exploits tell us more about the biographer and attitudes of the times than about Francis himself. There is no doubt that the meeting took place. In the fifty years that followed this event eleven authors wrote about it: only four were Franciscans, three were secular historians and one source is unknown. The question concerns what took place during the meeting. There can only be two conclusions. Either this conversation never happened and the words are put into Francis' mouth by contemporaries who could not understand his ethos or appreciate the Sultan, or it is true. If it is true then it reflects Francis' thinking before he entered the enemy camp – he did see Kaamil as an anti-Christian pagan. That then leaves us with the conclusion that after this face to face meeting with a Muslim, Francis himself was converted.

It appears from the historical records that both Francis and the Sultan were never the same as a result of this meeting, that is both went through a conversion experience. It appears to me that Francis' contemporaries could not fathom either man and wrote up the incident coloured by their prejudices. Until today the question still remains whether it was a success or failure.

The current General Minister of the Franciscan Order, Fr Herman Schaluck, sums up the event: 'Francis of Assisi wanted to cross to the other bank in order to meet with men who, despite everything, were brothers. He believed that when going to the Muslims one must avoid confrontations and disputes, submit to the legal authority while introducing oneself as a Christian. The encounter between Francis and the Sultan, considered as a failure, is in fact a great event which represents a source of inspiration and vision at a time when religious and cultural fanaticism suggests further clashes and confrontations if nothing is done to prevent them.'[19]

Captured by Islam

What did Francis hope to do? It was Francis' life ambition to convert the pagans and when he spoke of missions he meant the Saracens. So Francis hoped to convert the Sultan. Francis also hoped to put an end to the Crusade wars by converting the armies on both sides of the battle. His highest hope was to follow Christ's footsteps and win the crown of martyrdom through these attempts. Jacques de Vitry, his contemporary, says he went to Egypt in a vain attempt to put an end to the Crusades or win a martyr's crown. He longed to offer himself as a living victim to God by the sword of martyrdom. In this way he would repay Christ for dying for us and inspire others to love God.[20]

So Francis got a surprise if he went to the Sultan expecting to meet a hostile enemy. If he expected martyrdom at the hands of infidels he found a God-fearing man who received him with courtesy and even welcomed his message. As we have seen, the attitude of the age and the teaching of the Church was that Muslims were the anti-Christ. But Francis had a deep drive for reconciliation, so even if they were the enemy he had to go out to this enemy. However, instead of an enemy he found a friend – and possibly a soulmate. Francis and the Sultan were both people of deep living faith and therefore were secure in their faith and not afraid of the other. This lack of fear took them over the frontiers of prejudices and polemics.

When Francis left the Damiettia camp he placed himself beyond the Crusades by simply going to see the Sultan without any arms. If he went there with the least means of protection, that would mean he went as an enemy. All sources are unanimous that he went to the Sultan assuming his own responsibility, refusing any protection. In the heat of battle Francis renounced the raised fist and left behind everything except the Gospel in his heart. He crossed undefended and defenceless to the other side. There seems no doubt that he looked for martyrdom. It was highly esteemed and believed to be the highest way to follow in the steps of Christ. Hence he was willing to die for the message he took, not to aggressively defend it.

Francis' first words to the Sultan 'Peace to you', sum up his attitude and message. This greeting, which Francis declared was given to him by God, was an innovation in Europe and not always appreciated simply because it was new. Francis always greeted people and began sermons with this blessing. It happens to be the traditional and usual greeting in the Middle East still used today, 'Salaam alaikum' (Peace be upon you). It is the greeting with which Jesus greeted people (in Aramaic and Hebrew). A leading Imam in the Muslim world today explains the implications of salaam alaikum, 'It means "The blessings of God be upon you." When I say this, I feel that you are at peace with me, and I with you. I am extending a helping hand to you. I am coming to you to give you peace. And in the meantime, until we meet again, it means that I pray to God to bless you and have mercy upon you, and to strengthen my relationship with you as a brother.'[21] In the sovereignty of God, Francis greeted the Sultan with this peace. Yet today some Christians, Western and Arab, refuse to use 'salaam alaikum' because it is a term used by Muslims. Instead they say, 'Good day'.

Did Francis fail or succeed in his mission? It is obvious that he failed to end the wars, but was he successful in converting the Sultan? The change in Kaamil is witnessed and certified to by many contemporaries. After the Sultan's recovery of Damiettia he freed all the Christians he found in his prisons. Their number surpassed 30,000 and he ordered that they be treated with respect.[22] The letter of Oliver of Cologne (who was present at the siege of Damiettia), 22 September addresses the Sultan, 'when the Lord wished we fall between your hands, we did not have the feeling that we were in the empire of a tyrant, but in the hands of a father who surrounded us with care, helped us in times of danger, visited us when we suffered'.[23]

Muslim sources also testify to the impact of their meeting, 'The extraordinary importance of Francis is confirmed in Arabic chronicles. In the 15th century, an Arab writer Ibn Zayyat, gives evidence of the sojourn of Francis in Damiettia. He mentions a great mystic whose influence was known in Kaamil's court: Fakhr-el-din-Farisi. On the epithet of Farisi's tomb we read, "This man has a virtue known to all. His adventure with Sultan al Kaamil and what became the latter because of the monk, all this is well known." The monk is a reference to Francis. So the importance of this text is to show that the journey of Francis was not only a western event for Christendom but it was significant for Muslims.'[24]

These reports lend credence to the story that Kaamil was converted. However, he faced great obstacles to embrace the Christian faith. The biggest obstacle was the Church and Christianity. Christ was wrapped and trapped inside the Crusades and medieval Christianity. To be a Christian meant to be a Crusader. How could the renowned general from such a great Muslim lineage betray his people by crossing to the enemy camp and become a despised barbarian Crusader? The great tragedy of the Crusades is that the Church clothed Christ with a battle sword, filled his mouth with words of hatred and took him back to the Muslim world as an enemy. How could a Muslim fall in love with this Christ and follow him?

We know that Francis refused to be associated with the Crusades and redefined the meaning of Christian to mean 'not a Crusader'. He makes a point of taking the 'true Gospel' to Kaamil in opposition to what was being presented as Christ's message in his contemporary Christian world. It is Francis' gift and genius that he was able to extricate Christ from Crusader clothes and present him to Kaamil. The Sultan is then able to see for the first time that it is possible for a Muslim to love and follow such a Christ. Thus Kaamil is converted in his view of Christ. But we do not know the extent of his conversion.

We need to also look at how Francis viewed conversion. In a conversation with Brother Leo about perfect joy, Francis states, 'even if a Friar Minor could preach so well that he should convert all the infidels to the faith, perfect joy is not there. Above all the graces of the Holy spirit which Christ gives to His friends is that of conquering oneself and willingly enduring hardships, insults and humiliations for the love of Christ. That is perfect joy.'[25]

Who did Francis see as the enemy? Francis saw that the greatest enemy is self. One night after spending time alone in prayer Francis desired to sleep and could not. His mind was beset by fear and disturbed by suggestions from the Devil. He made the sign of the cross and went outside the church saying, 'devils I command you on the Lord Jesus Christ to make my body suffer. I am ready to endure everything, for I have no greater enemy than my body; in this way you will avenge me on this adversary and enemy.' The suggestions ceased immediately and he fell asleep and rested peacefully.[26]

Francis sees the conversion of self equally important as converting 'the other'. What do we mean by conversion? Christians commonly understand conversion as a once in a lifetime event when a person changes from going in one direction to going in another direction: from going our own way to going God's way. This radical change involves repentance and the decision to make faith a profoundly personal profession. In practice it becomes the greatest moment of repentance and faith in a person's life: light shines into the darkness, the issues clear and a decision is made to follow. It is a decisive watershed event never to be replicated in the same way. The new believer is delivered from the kingdom of darkness into the kingdom of light. Among Catholics (and many mainline Protestant churches) conversion is understood somewhat differently. Faith is made personal at the time of Confirmation when one's infant baptism is affirmed as a personal profession of faith. Rather than one cataclysmic event, conversion is understood as a lifelong process of responding to God. What is understood as *sanctification* to Protestants is part of the conversion process to Catholics. However, when it comes to those outside the Church, both branches of the Church understand conversion in the typical sense of embracing and following Christ.

The question of the nature of conversion is important to our understanding of what happened with Kaamil and what Francis expected from him. Did Kaamil see the difference between following Christianity (becoming a Crusader and joining the Western camp), which was impossible or following Christ (and staying in his own culture), which was not only possible but plausible? Was Francis able to explain what being a Christian did *not* mean? Did Kaamil have a cataclysmic watershed change of direction from going in one direction to going in another? Or did he make one more positive response in a series of life decisions seeking to know God more intimately?

Transforming Conversion

One theory posits that, because he was a Muslim, Kaamil highly respected Christ. When he asked Francis to pray that God would continue to guide him on the right path he was still following in the Muslim tradition and this was not a sign of conversion. Muslims pray 'Guide us on the right path' every day in the Faatiha prayer. The only way Francis' contemporaries could fathom a Muslim who was cultured, kind and positive towards Christ and Christians was to believe he was converted.[27] Surely a despised Muslim could not have such a positive character and could not pray with Francis in the name of Christ. The legends about Kaamil's conversion grew.

This interpretation is plausible because the same thing still happens today when Muslims agree to pray with Christians. The Christians claim they have converted the Muslims. If a Muslim is asked to 'accept Christ' he does not understand the implications of that cliché. Muslims already accept Christ as an honoured prophet. A number of Muslim leaders have been claimed as Christian converts in this manner, usually because they accepted a Bible and agreed to pray with the person. Yasser

Arafat is one such person. He has a Christian wife, is reported to wear a cross under his lapel out of respect for Christ, and has welcomed Christian organisations to the Palestinian territories. More than one Christian leader claims he 'converted' him when Mr Arafat accepted a Bible and prayed. But President Arafat does not claim to be a Christian and testifies to his faith in God as a Muslim. Similar stories have circulated about other Muslim personalities. The roots of the stories are in the Christians' lack of knowledge of Islam and Muslim belief and are usually accompanied by a battle mentality of winning heads to our side.

Francis challenged the Sultan not to fight against the living God who offers peace. In a recent interpretation of this the Sultan replies, '"If I seek Him in the camp of my enemies – shall I find Him?" Francis bows his head for it is a question he dares not answer. Finally he admits he challenged the Christian armies with the same words and he failed.'[28]

Sultan and monk needed each other. Francis' credo of life and God was confirmed and embraced in the Sultan. If Francis expected to meet an enemy, he found a friend and a God-seeker. Francis was either converted in his theology (and now was totally inclusive in his vision of finding the image of God in every person), or confirmed in his theology. In the Muslim Sultan, Francis found God – already present and working. Francis gave the Sultan God in Christ. The Sultan gave Francis affirmation of the God who is Compassionate and Merciful (Allah Al Rahmaan Al Rahiim) who searches out every human being for his grace.

Francis and Kaamil's meeting enabled both to be converted and they left as friends, but they failed to convert their own sides of the war and twenty years later (1240) the Muslim armies reached Assisi.

Frederick II

At this stage of the saga Frederick II (1194–1250CE) pops up again, and he deserves a special mention. He was King of Sicily and Holy Roman Emperor from 1220–1250. His court was one of the most brilliant in Europe and not only a rival to the Roman papacy, but probably its most formidable opponent. He posed a real military threat to the papal states and was their arch-enemy because of his liberal, anti-clerical religious policies. He further aggravated his opponents by using Muslims in his forces. His life was filled with wars and conflict and within twenty-two years of his death all his heirs were dead, victims of wars with the papal states.

However, Frederick also had another side. He was a social reformer and founded the University of Naples. But more to our point, he was a poet and he corresponded with Muslim Sufi (mystic) leaders and dealt with the Muslims in a different way to the popes. There is an Arabic saying that you have three friends: your friend, your friend's friend and your enemy's enemy. Frederick was a close friend of Sultan Kaamil, the Pope's enemy.

Frederick organised a meeting of Muslims, Christians and Jews in Palermo, Italy, and there were active dialogues and inter-faith discussions held at his court. Because of his openness to Islam, Frederick was suspected of having doubts about the Christian faith. In fact, Dante places him in hell with the sowers of schism. Yet the ancient legend to the contrary (previously quoted) depicts him weeping at Sultan Kaamil's death because he hoped for his baptism.

Frederick took a Crusader vow and then delayed for more than twelve years before going to war against the Muslims. Pope Gregory twice excommunicated him for the delays. When he eventually landed at Acre in Palestine, he conducted his own style of Crusade, almost entirely by diplomatic negotiations, with Sultan Kaamil. The two men produced a peace treaty which restored Jerusalem to the Crusaders and guaranteed a ten-year truce. Frederick was crowned king of the city. Despite this achievement the Pope refused to honour the treaty and excommunicated Frederick (a third time) for negotiating with an infidel, and proclaimed a Crusade against Frederick. The Pope raised an army, and proceeded to attack Frederick's Italian possessions. Frederick returned to the West to cope with this threat in May 1229 and, after he left, fighting broke out in Jerusalem and the Muslims ended up retaking the city.

Frederick showed little thought for the excommunication and continued fighting against the Pope, invading Italy in 1240. So the Muslim armies which arrived at Assisi were Frederick's troops, but Francis' lady saved the day. The soldiers arrived at San Damiano and scaled the walls of Clare's convent. The legend tells us that Clare boldly confronted them carrying the bread of the Sacrament in her hands and praying, 'Lord Jesus do not let these defenceless virgins fall into the hands of these heathens.' The soldiers promptly fled, climbed over the walls and left. Not only was the convent saved, but the whole city of Assisi. Another intriguing drop of information falls our way in the letter Clare wrote to the Abbess of Prague, Agnes of Bohemia, about the miraculous escape. Agnes had also escaped Frederick. She had been betrothed to Frederick II before becoming a nun! [29] We are not told if the betrothal played any part in her decision to take up holy vows!

One of the problems in getting to the bottom of the legends and myths to the historical encounter of monk and Sultan is Francis' enigmatic silence on the subject. He never wrote about it and made no public comment about it. Francis' closest contemporaries speak of his life's ambition to go and preach to the Muslims. He finally reaches the mission-field and his mission is successful in that he preaches to one of the greatest Muslim leaders of his time and receives an overwhelmingly positive response. Then he returns to Europe and never mentions it again! Is it because of his aversion to marketing God's doings that he followed his principles and kept 'God's marvellous doings to himself'? Or is it due to his understanding that the work of conversion is God's domain, mysteriously wrought in the secret places in prayer. Francis had a horror of God's people priding themselves on 'results' by their efforts and taking God's glory.

He wrote, 'There are many brothers who day and night put all their energy into the pursuit of knowledge, thereby abandoning prayer and their holy vocation. And when they preached to a few men or to the people, and learn that certain ones were edified or converted to penance through their discourse, they are puffed up and pride themselves on the results and work of others. For those whom they think they edified or converted to penance by their discourse were actually edified or converted by God through the prayers of the holy bothers who are completely ignorant of it, God wished it this way for fear it should be grounds for pride. Behold my knights of the round table, the brothers who hide in abandoned and secluded places to devote themselves with more fervour to prayer and meditation, to weep over their sins and over the sins of others, their holiness is known to God, but most often unbeknown to men. When their souls are presented to the Lord, He will reveal the effect and reward of their labours, that is the host of souls saved by their prayers.'[30]

But there may be a third reason for his silence. Was there such a great gap between Francis' experience of Muslims and the contemporary view of them that there was no way he could bridge it?

Europe believed Islam was a weak political power and would soon fall, Francis saw it was very strong and not likely to collapse. Europe believed Muslims were brutish infidels and anti-Christ: Francis found them cultured and open to Christ. Europe believed Muslims were totally beyond the pale of God's grace: Francis found some of them walking the same path and speaking the same language as himself. How could he convey this experience to the battle-crazed West, thereby telling them their greatest glory was their greatest failure?

The failure was the spirit of the Crusades. Francis was intensely loyal to the Catholic Church and his Church was blessing armed conflict against Muslims. In every situation where Francis found himself in conflict with his leaders, he eschewed battle and criticism and simply went out and did what he believed was right. He didn't lose time and energy attacking the darkness, but went out and lit a candle by sharing what he believed was the truth in word and deed through respectful relationships. This candle blazed into a bonfire that overcame the darkness in his personal relationships and finally in his Church and the world. Pope Innocent IV (1243–1250) saw the light and decreed that 'war should not be declared to the Saracens with the goal of converting them to Christianity'.

Francis practised evangelism without intolerance. The heart of Francis' gospel is that God does not discriminate: even if we are at enmity with God, God loves us. Francis sees no enemies, but every person is a child made in God's image. Francis said he preached 'the true Gospel' to the Sultan and explains his motive for always going in peace thus: 'Since you speak of peace all the more so you must have it in your heart. Let none be provoked to scandal or anger by you, but rather may they be drawn to peace and good will, to benignity and concern through your gentleness. We have been called to heal wounds, to unite what has fallen apart, and to bring home those who have lost their way. Many who may seem to us to be children of the devil will still become Christ's disciples.'[31]

Seven hundred years later we face the choice again – raise the battle cry against Muslims and launch a spiritual offensive against them, or walk to them carrying a Gospel of good news and peace.

Notes

1 Oldenbourg, Z. (1966) *The Crusades*, New York and Toronto: Random House, p. 431; Orion Books, London; Editions Gallimard, Paris.
2 Jeusset, G. (1996) *Recontre Sur L'Autre Rive: Francis d'Assise et les Musulmans*, Paris: Les Editions Franciscaines, p. 42.
3 Oldenbourg, op. cit., p. 459.

4 Jeusset, op. cit., p. 43.
5 Englebert, O. (1965) *St Francis of Assisi*, Quincy, Illinois Franciscan Press, p. 175.
6 Thirteenth century testimonies, *Omnibus of Sources for the Life of St Francis*, p. 1609.
7 A New Fioretti 52, *Omnibus*, p. 1877.
8 Jeusset, op. cit., Chapter 1.
9 Engelbert, op. cit., p. 176.
10 Jeusset, op. cit., p. 44.
11 Thirteenth century testimonies, *Omnibus*, p. 1615.
12 Ibid., p. 1614.
13 Engelbert, op. cit., p. 144.
14 Celano's First Life of Francis, *Omnibus*, p. 276.
15 Bonaventure's Major Life of Francis, Chapter 9, *Omnibus*, p. 701–704.
16 *Omnibus*, p. 1519.
17 De Beer, F.
18 Engelbert, op. cit., p. 176.
19 Jeusset, op. cit., Preface.
20 Bonaventure's Major Life of Francis, Chapter 9, *Omnibus*, p. 701–704.
21 Arnold, C. (1998) *Seeking Peace*, Philadelphia and East Sussex: The Plough Publishing House, p. 9.
22 De Beer, F. (1977) Francois que disait-on de toi? Paris: Editions Franciscaines, p. 81.
23 Ibid., p. 82.
24 Ibid., p. 83.
25 Little Flowers 8, *Omnibus*, p. 1320.
26 Legend of Perugia, *Omnibus*, p. 1000.
27 Jeusset, op. cit.
28 Houseman, L. (1935) *The Little Plays of St Francis*, Sidgwick & Jackson Ltd., London.
29 Engelbert, op. cit., p. 119.
30 Legend of Perugia, *Omnibus*, p. 1047.
31 Legend of the Three Companions, *Omnibus*, p. 943.

Chapter Nine

THE MYSTICAL INFLUENCE IN ISLAM

The person who catches the disease of Christ can never be cured.
Ibn Arabi, Muslim mystic

The common experience that brushed monk and Sultan with its strokes was the contemplative mystic spirit. Mystics have existed for thousands of years and are at home in every religion. They have generally been protected in Islam, but at times were persecuted for 'witchcraft' or 'pantheism'. Although mainline Muslims happily balanced the world and faith, the Muslim mystics practised renunciation of the world in order to enter the deeper spiritual path.

The first Muslim mystics wore woollen robes like Christian monks. They were named for their robes made of wool (suuf) and called *sufi – suufiyiin,* the plural, being expressed in English as *Sufis*. The patriarch of the Sufis was Hasan Al Basri (642–728CE) from Iraq. The Muslim community of his time was in a moral crisis through the corruption of riches and the abuse of power. Basri risked his life by brave public reproaches of the leaders including the Caliph, while staying loyal, calling for reform and never encouraging revolt.[1] His approach of bringing religious reform while remaining loyal to leaders is the path Francis also chose.

It is not too difficult to see the similarities between the mystics in Islam and Christianity. The growth of the mystics was a similar response within both communities – to bring spiritual renewal to a religious community in moral and spiritual crisis. The key of the mystic path is seeking consciousness of the divine presence, which is in everything, including man. Through a steadfast adherence to the doctrine of a spiritual path to move towards oneness, the Sufi strives for illumination of the divine essence. The Sufi mystery is to be in the world, but not of it: to be free from ambition, greed, intellectual pride or blind obedience to custom – in order to find a mystical union with God. The Sufis reacted to an era of dry theological debates about God. They wanted more than doctrine only and understood that knowledge of God is not to be found in collecting information about God, but in knowing God through experience. The Sufis sought the narrow spiritual path to God and enlightenment by actual experience of a love relationship with God. Christians warm to the Sufis' experience and remember that Christ warns about the dangers of putting holy writings in place of a life lived in union with God through him. 'You diligently study the Scriptures because you think that by them you possess eternal life. Yet you do not come to me to have life.'[2] Through a mixture of teaching and lifestyle the Sufis renounced the world and pleasures. They were the missionary arm of Islam spreading the faith in a charismatic manner through personal testimony, dance and song, and led others into a personal experience with God. They distanced themselves from ecclesiastical politics and were recognised for their deep spiritual life, their reflection on the quality of the moral life, voluntary poverty and a delicate conscience to avoid sins.[3]

When Sufis meet together in worship they sing their love songs to God through religious poetry put to music, rhythmic chant and prayer and sometimes dance until they enter a heightened spiritual state of rapture. Francis lived in this mystical spirit in accordance with Christ's commands: 'Remain in my love. If you obey my commands you will remain in my love, just as I have obeyed my Father's commands and remain in his love. I have told you this so that my joy may be in you and that your joy may be complete.'[4] Francis so lived in union with the Spirit that he would suddenly be overcome with the presence of God, even as he walked along the street, and be lost in joyful ecstasy. Bonaventure relates when Francis would not let any call of the spirit go unanswered: 'when he experienced it, he made the most of it and enjoyed the consolation afforded him in this way for as long as God permitted it. If he were on a journey, he would stop and let his companions go on, while he drank in the joy of this new inspiration; he refused to offer God's grace an ineffectual welcome. He was often taken right out of himself in a rapture of contemplation, so that he was lost in ecstasy and had no idea what was going on around him.'[5]

The Sufis follow a proscribed spiritual path through stages that includes repentance, renunciation of the world and self until only God remains, the remembrance of God (reciting the names or attributes of God), ecstasy in a spiritual union with God (which can include speaking in tongues), seeing God face to face, in union with him, when the person is lost in God. The end of the Sufi road is the escape from the world and self into a totally satisfying union with God. This language has brought them into persecution through the centuries through charges of pantheism. It is very difficult to interpret their poetry, which is deliberately written in veiled terms, as a mystery that must be unravelled by the initiated. In order to understand, or more correctly to enter into the mystery, the Sufi learner is put under the tutelage of a master, or sheikh, who acts as a spiritual advisor. It is easy for Christians to read our experience of Christ into Sufi writings. The question is still being asked: 'Is Christ the end of the road for every Sufi or are we reading too much of ourselves into their experience?' I think we have not yet understood the mystic facet of Christ, especially as he is portrayed in the Gospel of John. It could yield a startling and enriching study when compared to the experience of the Sufi masters. We know we have not experienced the depths of a satisfying and joyful union with God where we see him face to face and experience what Christ promised, 'On that day you will realise that I am in my Father, that you are in me, and I am in you.'[6] This resonates with the expressions of the Sufis through the ages.

Rabia Al Adawiyya

Rabia Al Adawiyya (713–801) was born in Basra, Iraq and sold as a slave. Through her faithful life and religious testimony she converted her master and he freed her. She retired to live in a rush hut and spent her days in poverty and prayer and her companion recorded her utterances when she was lost in ecstasy in worship. Her life's credo was to love God to the exclusion of every creature. Love God for himself and not for any hope of reward either on earth or in heaven. God should not be loved out of fear. She said, 'If I worship you for fear of hell, burn me in hell.' She worshipped God simply because he was worthy of worship and for his beauty and she longed to die in order to meet God. She once sat indoors on a lovely spring day to teach that external magnificence is only a reflection of God's inner kindness and generosity.[7] The Sufis have no gender discrimination, recognising many women as spiritual leaders. Sufi men are discipled by women as well as men. Francis shared the mystics' recognition of the equality of women and submitted to their spiritual leading in a mutual spiritual reciprocity – he recognised Clare as God's mouthpiece in his decision to remain in the world and not become a hermit.

Ibn Al Arabi

Called the 'Greatest Master', Muhyi Al Din Ibn Al Arabi died thirteen years before Francis was born. He was one of the greatest and most controversial figures in Muslim history and like all the mystics he remains an enigma. He disturbed the Muslims in their beliefs. Many hated him, calling him a blasphemer, and many loved him claiming he had true knowledge of God. His statements, along with those of other mystics, can be interpreted as pantheism, or seen as the search for a relationship with God ending in unity with God. As with all the Islamic mystics, he was very open to Christ and identified himself equally with Muslims and Christians. He spoke of Christ as the Word, the Spirit and servant of God, and God's tongue. 'In my youth I denied *the others*' belief and made them my enemy, now my religion is the religion of love. My heart is open for a pasture for animals and a monastery for monks.' Is this pantheism or an understanding of God's presence in all his creation in a similar manner as Francis understood it and found God in animals and all kinds of people?

Ibn Al Arabi speaks of the loving giving of God in 'The Ring Settings of Wisdom' – his beautiful description of the great urge within the divine for the reality of his being, which is love, to be poured out into existence. The divine longing to be known is love, and he describes the release of this longing as a breathing that expresses and relieves the longing. This creative exhalation of the 'Breath of the Merciful', *Al Rahmaan*, takes us to the birth image through the root of the word from which also comes womb. For Ibn Al Arabi love and mercy are not just an attitude, but the very principle by which all things were created and exist and by which all things in the divine mind are released into actuality, as objects of the divine witness and perception. This concept of creation and birth is closely tied into the very nature of God the merciful.[8] Dr Mohammed Shahroor describes the same meanings. 'The word *merciful* comes from *rahm* and it means, gentle, compassionate and merciful, and family relationships. The Quran added to the word another meaning, *to give birth*. From this came the word for God, *The Merciful*. Of course we know that God does not himself give birth physically, but he brings into existence things that were not by his powerful word.'[9] So Ibn Arabi's picture of God is the creator with the compassion of a mother for the child in her womb.

Ibn Arabi's major themes were the perfect man and the

polished mirror that reflect God. He equates the perfect man with Christ and Muhammed. Christians can easily read Ibn Arabi's *Perfect Man* and see Christ.

> He is the living being, without beginning, without end.
> He is the word, discriminating and integrating.
> He is to the world the ringstone of the ring
> The plane of inscription
> The sign by which the king deals his coffer
> He is called vice-regent then
> Since the transcendent guards him through his creation
> So he made him his vice-regent charged with the safeguarding of his property
> And the world is preserved as long as the complete human being remains in it.
> Don't you see that if he were no more . . .
> The entire order would vanish into the afterworld
> Where he would be the eternal seal on the treasure chest
> That is the afterworld.[10]

Arabi talks of the perfect man who perfectly combines heaven and earth within himself, who is at once the eye by which the divine subject sees himself and the perfectly polished mirror that perfectly reflects the divine light.[11]

Christians believe, as the Gospel states, that, 'Christ is the expressed image of the invisible God. For God was pleased to have all his fullness dwell in him.'[12] Christ mirrors God to us. Jesus Christ is at once the perfect man: 'Son of Adam' born of a woman, and the perfect 'Son of God': his origin is from God and has no human father. Our Lord Jesus Christ is the Word of God, the living utterance of God, God's complete expression. We are not able to separate the word (the expression of the thought) from the thought. God is One: his thought and his word, his power and his spirit.

Ibn Arabi was born in Andalous (Muslim Spain) and studied the Sufi writings from an early age – two of his Sufi tutors were elderly women[13] – and he became so well known as a youth that Ibn Rushd (Averroes) requested to meet him. He wandered through many countries and died in Syria. His ideas were a challenge to orthodoxy and he was charged with nonconformity by an inquisition in Syria. His influence even spread to the intellectuals of Europe, especially in England and France. Several centres still exist today in Spain and Europe, keeping his influence alive where he still exerts a great influence over Western intellectuals.

Ibn Arabi was with us on the night I described under the stars in Tunisia with the crowds lost in poetry. A collective cry went up during one of his poems where Christ and Muhammed are cited in the same stanza. He wrote one of the most profound descriptions of the effect of meeting Christ I have ever heard: 'The person who catches the disease of Christ can never be cured.'

Jalal Al Din Al Rumi

Rumi was born in Afghanistan on 30 September 1207, five months before Francis heard the call to his ministry in the St Mary of the Angels chapel. His family fled the Mogul army and settled in Konya, Turkey, giving him his surname by which he became known. Rumi means 'from Roman Anatolia'. He is also known as 'moulana' (master) and is very popular in Iran. He died in 1273. Rumi gave an esoteric interpretation to the Quran; 'There is no God but God' became 'There is no reality but God. There is only God.' His beliefs could be summed up by one statement: 'The remembering that everything is God.' In the poem of this title he writes:

A person blended into God does not disappear. He, or she,
is just completely soaked in God's qualities.
Do you need a quote from the Quran?
'All shall be brought into our Presence'
Join those travellers . . .[14]

To the Sufi what matters is your personal experience of God, not your religion. Rumi wrote: 'The love religion has no code or doctrine, only God.'[15] Francis echoed the mystics' love code in his great emphasis on having no strategy to reach the world except through love. Francis did not get this idea from Sufis, but from the New Testament: 'Keep yourselves in the love of God';[16] 'Abide in my love.'[17] It is no accident that the apostle John, who is described as the disciple whom Jesus loved most, wrote a whole book describing how to love each other and the world.[18]

Rumi also reinterpreted the ritual Muslim ablutions before prayer:

> The proper prayer is: 'Lord wash me. My hand has washed this part of me, but my hand can't wash my spirit. I can wash this skin, but you must wash me.'[19]

Jesus taught that ceremonial washing was only symbolic of the cleansing needed from God: 'Nothing outside a man can make him unclean by going into him. What comes out of a man is what makes him unclean. For from within, out of men's hearts comes the evil that makes him unclean.'[20] Jesus taught that he had authority from God to wash a person's sins away. 'You have been washed, cleaned up, in the name of the Lord Jesus Christ and by the Spirit of our God.'[21]

Rumi, like all the Sufis, spoke highly of Jesus and he also spoke on the same themes as Francis.

> Stay bewildered in God
>   and only that.
> Those of you who are scattered,
>   simplify your worrying lives. There is *one*
>   righteousness.
> Be generous to what nurtures the spirit.
> Too often
>   we put saddlebags on Jesus and let the donkey run loose
>   in the pasture.[22]

Francis insisted his friars live in abject poverty and refused to even own a rude hut. He believed this simplicity nurtured the spirit.

Rumi said, 'Someone once asked a great sheikh what Sufism was. He answered, "The feeling of joy when sudden disappointment comes".'[23]

Francis' description of perfect joy was to arrive at a Franciscan monastery and be verbally abused and rejected and refused entry. Perfect joy is to willingly endure all hardships, insults and humiliations for the love of Christ. James the brother of Christ wrote, 'Consider it pure joy whenever you face trials of many kinds.'[24]

Rumi said, 'If you want to wear a robe of spiritual sovereignty, let your eyes weep with the wanting.'[25]

Francis said, 'I weep for the passion of my Lord Jesus Christ, and I should not be ashamed to go weeping through the whole world for his sake.'

Rumi said that 'to remember who one was before the advent of grace is to know one's lord.'[26] Francis offered his life as a gift to God out of gratitude for God's grace in his life. St Paul said, 'I do not deserve to be called an apostle because I persecuted the church. By the grace of God I am what I am.'[27]

Rumi kept many Sufi forty-day periods of seclusion, and meditation and fasting – sometimes three in a row. Francis practised the same ascetic lifestyle, wrecking his body until he was nothing but a skeleton. We note the Sufis practised the same forty-day fast time-periods as the Church.

Rumi said, 'When you feel gloomed over, it is your failure to praise.'[28] Francis said, 'Let the friars be aware of being sad and gloomy, like hypocrites; but let them show themselves joyful in the Lord, gay and pleasant.' St Paul said, 'Be joyful always, pray constantly, give thanks in all circumstances, for this is God's will for you in Christ Jesus.'[29]

Rumi was walking in the market place and heard a beautiful music in the rhythm of the goldsmith's hammering. The story goes that he began turning in harmony with it, an ecstatic dance of surrender and union with the turning universe and yet a great centred discipline. Thus began the dance of the whirling dervishes. Francis heard this dance of creation and had it in his blood. He even broke into an excited dance as he got carried away with his message when he preached to the Pope. On one occasion Francis sought God's guidance for the right path to take while on a journey – by whirling on the one spot. He had a companion monk whirl around in one spot and then stop. The direction the monk faced when he stopped was the 'right path'.[30] Was this the influence of the Sufis (whirling and seeking the right path under God's guidance), or being simple and childlike?

Francis liked to describe Christians as Christ's friends. Rumi always spoke of God as the friend. Both Rumi and Francis searched for God, and found him, in all creation – the ocean in the drop.

Rumi said, 'One day I was going along looking to see in people the shining of the Friend, so I would recognise the ocean in a drop.'[31] 'Christ is the population of the world.'[32]

Francis said, 'When you see a poor person, you must consider the one in whose name he comes, namely Christ, who took upon himself our poverty and weakness. The poverty and sickness of this man are therefore a mirror in which we ought to contemplate lovingly the poverty and weakness which our Lord Jesus Christ suffered in his body to save the human race.' Had Francis heard of Ibn Arabi's mirror? Mother Theresa lived by this philosophy and taught that the poor person who comes to you is Christ in disguise.

Rumi said, 'When you make peace with your father, he will look peaceful and friendly. The whole world is a form for truth. Make peace with the universe. Take joy in it. Resurrection will be now . . . a new beauty. This abundant, pouring noise of many springs in your ears, the tree limbs will move like people dancing, who suddenly know what the mystical life is. The Friend will become bread and springwater for you, a lamb and a helper. Union with that one is grace.'[33]

The descriptions in this exhortation overflow with familiar Christian symbolism straight from the Bible. Christians have always found Christ the friend, the bread, the living water, the lamb of God, the helper through the presence of the Spirit of God, joy, truth, resurrection, peace and beauty! And the rushing water is symbolic of the Spirit as God pours life into us resulting in such great joy and peace there is no release except in the dance. All this happens when we make peace with our Father.

Francis took joy in the universe, made peace with its creator and overflowed with joy.

Highest, all-powerful, good Lord
Yours is the praise, the glory, the honour,
And every blessing,
They belong to You alone,
and no one is worthy to speak your name.
So Praised be You, My Lord with all your creatures,
especially Sir Brother sun . . . and he heralds You, his Most high Lord.
Praised be You, my Lord, through Sister moon and stars . . .
through Brother wind . . .
through Sister Water . . .
Yes and praise to You, my Lord, through Brother Fire . . .
Praise be You, my Lord, through our Sister mother Earth[34] who nourishes us and teaches us . . .

Rumi wrote poems extolling the Sun of Tabriz which was symbolic for his soul mate and Sufi master, who in turn was symbolic of the friend, God.

Rumi said, '(the prophet) Mohammed says, "Love of one's country is a part of the faith." But don't take that literally! Your *real* country is where you are heading, not where you are.'[35] Francis insisted his Order be wandering mendicants in this world. They were in search of their real homeland . . . 'and were longing for a heavenly homeland founded and built by God. Our citizenship is in heaven.'[36]

'Rumi said in the midst of the Crusades, "I go into the Muslim mosque and the Jewish synagogue and the Christian church and I see one altar." This is a radical idea now, but Rumi held the conviction in the thirteenth century with such deep gentleness that its truth was recognised.'[37] Scholars today are still rereading Francis' life in order to understand how deeply Francis believed this.

There are other sayings and poems of Rumi that I have not included. Rumi and Francis both used earthly and earthy examples to describe spiritual truth. Francis did some shocking things and Rumi does not hesitate to use any thing or human experience as a door to spiritual understanding and some of his images are more shocking than Francis' actions.

Al Hallaj

Hussein Ibn Mansour Hallaj (died 922CE) is recognised as one of the most Christ-loving of all mystics and their greatest martyr. He is accepted as the pinnacle of the Sufis. He practised a severe asceticism, eating little and spending most of his time in prayer. He held secret meetings at his house and was known for performing miracles. The systematic survey of Hallaj's course of life and attitudes shows that he was governed by the powerful archetype of Jesus Christ – an in depth comparison of the two figures would be a revealing moment in the history of Islamic mysticism.

There were many spiritual events in the life of Hallaj that seem consciously or unconsciously to draw and build on Christ's life events: the wanderings, journeys, sermons, encounters, and death. His overt and provokingly daring statements gripped people's minds and were passed on throughout centuries. One of these statements was identification with Christ:[38] 'Go! Warn my friends that I sailed the seas and my ship broke. On the supreme example of the Cross I intend to die. For I seek neither the Batha (Mecca) nor the Medina.'

He taught that Sufism was the internal truth of all true religion. Because he emphasised the importance of Jesus as a Sufi teacher, he was accused of being a secret Christian. His very famous statement 'Ana al Haqq' struck Muslims as an expression of his belief in the Incarnation. Ana means 'I', while 'al Haqq' means 'truth', but 'al Haqq' is also one of the ninety-nine supreme names of God. He was condemned for blasphemy for believing God can enter human life. He taught that God can be in humans and humans can be united with God through the mystic path by yearning and submission to God.

The attitude of Hallaj during his own execution, which turned into a crucifixion more brutal than Christ's,[39] is patterned after Christ and reproduces in an amazing way the agony of Jesus Christ on the Cross. When he was tortured he never protested, but cried out 'by killing me you give me new life'.[40] He was dismembered and crucified. This was his last public prayer while he could still speak, 'O Lord, make me grateful for the blessing which I have been given in being allowed to know what others do not know. Divine mysteries which are unlawful for others have thus become lawful to me. Forgive and have mercy upon these Thy servants assembled here for the purpose of killing me; for, had Thou revealed to them what Thou hast revealed to me, they would not act thus.'[41]

The mystics all longed for death, especially martyrdom, in order to experience the ultimate unity with God, their greatest love. The Muslim mystics speak a language that Christians can understand: the quest for a personal relationship with God, the quest to fully discover the love of God and lose oneself in worship of God until worshipper and the object of worship are lost in unity and the sea of love. Their expressions of this experience are similar to Christ's words: 'Father, just as you are in me and I am in you, may they also be in us . . . I in them and you in me. May they be brought to complete unity to let the world know that you sent me and have loved them even as you have loved me . . . though the world does not know you, I know you. I have made you known to them, and will continue to make you known in order that the love you have for me may be in them and that I myself may be in them.'[42] The mystics' contemplation of the divine presence in all creation crosses all religious boundaries. Christians join in this hymn of praise in the words of the New Testament, 'In Him we live and move and have our being'.[43] St Paul felt no hindrances in quoting from a pagan poem.

Many Iranians in the West have recently influenced the New Age movement through preaching the unity of religions by using Rumi, Hallaj and others. However, we do not have to unite and obliterate differences in order to celebrate truth wherever it is found and be tolerant of other people's beliefs. Through St Paul, God says 'Keep your eyes open, hold tight to your convictions, give it all you've got, be resolute, and love without stopping.'[44]

Fakhr Al Din Al Farisi

There is another mystic who – although little is mentioned about in the history books – is a major player in the plot. God prepared the road to Sultan Kaamil through the mystics, and records testify that Fakhr Al Din Al Farisi was attached to Kaamil's court and was present during Francis' discussions with Kaamil. Fakhr Al Din was a distant disciple of Hallaj.[45]

The Sufis and Francis

The Sufis in Islam were a mirror of the Christian mystic monks. There has been a fascinating interplay between Christian mystics and Muslim Sufis over the centuries. A Sufi leader is called 'sheikh' – which means 'elder' or 'presbyter' in the Christian Church. Sufism developed along similar paths to Christian monasticism and becoming a monastic system with rules for novices and a spiritual director. It was similar to the Franciscans in that it was not a centralised institution, but a movement spread by wandering mendicant missionaries who set up house meetings wherever they went. God was working, preparing a meeting place for God-seekers in Islam as well as in Christianity. The mystics, in both religions, led people to an effervescent oasis in a desert of theological debate and a war of words and swords, where the thirsty came together in search of living water.

Christianity and Islam both influenced one another through the meeting of the mystics. 'Brother Anselm was a Majorcan mystic of the dark ages – and saint to the Christians. But this was very far from being all. Among the Muslim Spaniards he was the sanctified Sufi Abdullah Al Tarjuman.'[46] He passed on Sufi teachings in his works. Raymon Lull, mentioned previously, was also a Franciscan. He was martyred in North Africa. According to Lull's own writings, Lull was an adapter of Sufi books and exercises.[47] Roger Bacon was one of the earliest and most farseeing of scientists. He believed that the world was round and predicted airplanes and cars. After studying at the universities of Oxford and Paris, Bacon became a Franciscan friar and taught at Oxford. He also wrote on the Sufis and was familiar with their works.[48] Albert Magnus who had studied in Arab schools, inspired St Thomas Aquinas. Numerous popes were graduates of Arab schools including Gerbert and Silvester II.

Miguel Asin Palacios, a devout Christian and renowned Spanish Arabist, discovered the influence of the school of Sufi philosophers and what they had given to the world. They provided the substance of the allegories of Dante, the teachings of the school known as the Augustinian scholastics, and the wisdom of the founders of modern Western philosophy – Duns Scotus and Roger Bacon from Britain, Raymon Lull of Majorca, St John of the Cross. Solomon ben Gabroil[49] – a Jewish philosopher of Malaga in Arabic Spain in the eleventh century – based his 'Fount of Life' on Massarah's works of Greco-Muslim philosophy and restored them to Europe. The *'Fount of Life'*, translated into Latin in 1150 as 'Fons vitæ', inspired the Franciscan school.[50] Christian mystics, and scientists including Bacon, were accused of occultism and persecuted, as were their Muslim counterparts in the East. In the same manner that the Sufis challenged the dogmatism in Islam, they challenged the dogmatism in the Church.

'At the deepest levels there is a mutual communication with the mystics of the Christian west. Christian contemplatives used Sufi books, Sufi methods and Sufi terminology. Sufism, it is now declared, is able to produce true mystical experience because Sufis revere Jesus. Further, Sufism was profoundly influenced in its early days by Christianity. The implication is that Sufic ideas are not to be rejected. If St John of the Cross and Lull could use them, there must be some good in them.'[51]

Christians are drawn to the Sufis because the Sufis are drawn to Christ. 'The mystics remained true to the Koranic vision of the unity of all rightly guided religion. Jesus, for example, was revered by many sufis as the prophet of the interior life. Some even amended the Shahadah, the profession of faith, to say; "There is no God but Allah and Jesus is his messenger", which was technically correct but intentionally provocative.'[52]

Sultan Kaamil loved the Sufi love songs to God – poems that expressed the deep personal experience with God. It was an experience he sought to deepen. Kaamil loved the Sufis and when Francis walked into his court, wearing a tattered woollen robe, preaching God's love and peace, renunciation of the world and the sublime death of martyrdom for the love of God, Kaamil, saw a Christian Sufi. He recognised Francis' message for it was a path he was travelling.

Recent studies are contemplating the influence of the Muslim mystics on Francis. The image of a barefoot Sufi in a plain woollen robe with a begging bowl is often found in depictions of the Middle East. It is also an accurate picture of Francis going barefoot from house to house for his evening meal in his brown woollen robe. Francis has been claimed as a secret Sufi who was introduced to the Order through the troubadour songs. His desire to reach the Middle East and his warm reception by the Sultan is also explained because he was Sufi. 'Francis spoke Provençal, the language used by the troubadours. The troubadours are recognised relics of Muslim musicians and poets. Francis' own poetry so strongly resembles in places that of the love poet Rumi that one is tempted to look for any report which might connect Francis with the Sufi Order of the Whirling Dervishes.'[53]

Despite the similarities, I do not believe the material needs to suggest he was an Islamic mystic. There are many varieties of Sufism, and the ancient mystic teaching includes aspects which do not appear in Francis' teachings and life – such as Gnosticism's secret knowledge of God and attaining unity with God. Within organised religion there are those who are in love with God and hunger and thirst for a deeper relationship with God. These seekers recognise each other across religious boundaries. Francis does not use language that leaves us wondering how to interpret his *unity* with God and creation. He keeps a distance between the two, speaking of unity *with* creation and worship *of* God. He is not 'equally at home in' every religion, as the mystics claim to be. Christ is Francis' Lord of all. But Francis is totally respectful of the other's experience of God and at home *with* other religions. He rejoices in the light of God everywhere that he finds it. He practised what Rumi taught and looked for the ocean in every drop – he looked for God in every person.

Francis said he preached 'the true Gospel' to the Sultan. The records and witnesses of Francis' typical preaching give us the contents of his probable message to the Sultan. Francis practised evangelism without intolerance. Therefore Francis acts like his heavenly Father – without discrimination and having no strategy but love. What is this love? Love is the place of meeting. To love the other is to meet him. The first step in our redemption was when God came to meet us in his Son. At the place of meeting is the presence of the Holy Spirit. The dove descends and opens a new path to the heavens that leads us into the presence of God. Implicit in the place of meeting the other, is the willingness to receive from the other. Francis knew how to receive gifts from the poor and the so-called *enemy*. He allowed others to bless him – he found God in every person and received the blessings of God through every person's uniqueness. This was the basis of Francis' humility. Even God receives from us when we meet – he receives our praise and adoration and our love.

The following events in Francis' life and the fables about him have been symbolically interpreted to understand how he arrived at an evangelistic lifestyle of love.[54] When Francis took God as his father he thereby made all men his brothers – he conquered exclusivism. When he returned good for evil and converted the robbers by brotherly love – he conquered hatred and greed. In the story of the wolf of Gubbio (who devoured people), when Francis went out and entered into discussions with it leading it into peaceful relations with the city's inhabitants – he conquered fear of the other. 'He wanted to challenge another rampart dividing the two communities accusing each other of being the dominion of Satan. This parable pictures how Francis went out to Islam – which the Christians saw as a wild wolf – and tamed it leading them into peaceful coexistence.'[55]

Francis understood that every person in the world receives the call to enter into the mystery of unity with his or her creator. God does not discriminate and the call goes out freely across all barriers of race and creed. Francis not only heard the call, but wildly embraced it. To continue believing this, Francis had to find people of every race and creed who had answered the inner call to search for the true spiritual path, or risk losing his sense of joy and celebration of God in this world. He found birds and animals that responded to their creator's voice, now he had to find *infidels* who gave themselves to the light and love they experienced in God. He did.

There are those who believe the end of every Sufi's path is Christ. Others believe Christians read too much of our experience into the Sufis' sayings. Is Christ the mystery of the mystics, that even some of them have yet to discover? Is this the secret that Francis and Kaamil unveiled in the Sultan's tent?

Notes

1 Fitzgerald, L. & Casper, R. (1992) *Signs of Dialogue: Christian Encounter with Muslims*, Philippines: Silsilah Publishing.
2 John 5:39–40.
3 Fitzgerald, L. & Casper, R., op. cit., p. 201.
4 John 15:9ff.
5 Bonaventure's Major Life of Francis, Chaper 10, *Omnibus of Sources for the Life of St Francis*, p. 706.
6 John 14:20.
7 Barks, C. (1995) *The Essential Rumi*, San Francisco: HarperCollins, p. 284.
8 Austin, R. W. J. (1980) *Ibn Al'Arabi: The Bezels of Wisdom*, New Jersey: Paulist Press, p. 29.
9 Shahroor, M. (1990) *Al Kitab wa Al Quran*, Damascus: Maktabat Al Ahaali, p. 254.
10 Sells, M. A. (1994) *Mystical Languages of Unsaying*, Chicago and London: University of Chicago Press, p. 83.
11 Austin, op. cit., p. 35.
12 Colossians 1:15,18.
13 Shams of Marchena and Fatima of Cordova. Cf. Austin, op. cit., p. 3.
14 Barks, op. cit., p. 114.
15 Ibid., p. 167.
16 Jude 21.
17 John 15:9.
18 1 John.
19 Barks, op. cit., p. 195.
20 Mark 7:17 ff.
21 1 Corinthians 6:11.
22 Barks, op. cit., p. 256.
23 Ibid., p. 171.
24 James 1:2.
25 Barks, op. cit., p. 160.

26 Ibid., p. 287.
27 1 Corinthians 15:10ff.
28 Barks, op. cit., p. 228.
29 1 Thessalonians 5:16.
30 Barks, op. cit., p. 277. I have observed the dervish dance numerous times. It is best performed to a flute (symbolic Sufi instrument) and the dancer can whirl on the one spot for hours keeping rhythm, and then come to a complete stop without the effects of dizziness.
31 Barks, op. cit., p. 263.
32 Ibid., p. 204.
33 Ibid., p. 239 ff.
34 Ibn Arabi also spoke of God the Father and our Mother Earth and Nature.
35 Barks, op. cit., p. 194.
36 Hebrews 11:9,16; Philippians 3:20.
37 Barks, op. cit., p. 246.
38 Noreddine Zouitni, Hallaj and Christ, unpublished thesis.
39 He was condemned for 'witchcraft' in 913CE and imprisoned for eight years. After a seven-month trial he was executed on 23 March 922. He was scourged, cut to pieces, and crucified and his body was burnt.
40 Noreddine Zouitni.
41 Shah, I. (1964) *The Sufis*, New York: Doubleday, p. 425.
42 John 17:21–25.
43 Acts 17:28.
44 1 Corinthians 16:13 (*The Message* translation, Eugene H. Peterson, 1993, Colorado Springs: NavPress).
45 Jeusset, G. (1996) *Recontre Sur L'Autre Rive: Francois d'Assise et les Musulmans*, Paris: Editions Franciscaines.
46 Shah, op. cit., p. 272.
47 Ibid., p. 274.
48 Ibid., p. 270. Citing Bacon, Shah cites a Sufi book by Ibn Sabin who was in correspondence with Frederick II.
49 Shah, op. cit., p. 275.

50 Hitti, P. (1974) *History of the Arabs*, New York: St Martin's Press, p. 580.
51 Shah, op. cit., p. 278.
52 Armstrong, K. (1993) *A History of God*, New York: Random House.
53 Shah, op. cit., p. 257.
54 Jeusset, op. cit.
55 Ibid.

Chapter Ten

CAPTURED BY ISLAM

Francis had an experience with Muslims that deeply affected his life and enriched his faith, and he brought back new innovations to worship – patterned on Muslim worship – that enrich liturgical worship for millions of Christians today.

Motive (niyya) is very important in Muslim prayers and worship. Before worship the worshipper must take a moment to consciously dedicate self and motive to God and not engage casually in acts of devotion. Francis insists upon a pure intention, one that is without ulterior motives. 'Implore my priests to be free from earthly affection when they say the Mass and offer single-mindedly and with reverence the true sacrifice, with a holy and pure intention . . . that their whole attention should be fixed on Him with a will to please the Most High alone. He told us to do this "in remembrance of Me", so the one who acts otherwise is a traitor.'[1] Francis prayed, 'Almighty eternal, Just and Merciful God, grant us in our misery that we may do for your sake alone what we know you want us to do, and always want what pleases you, so that cleansed and enlightened interiorly and fired with the ardour of the Holy Spirit we may be able to follow in the footsteps of your Son and so make our way to you by your grace alone.'[2]

The Muslim *muezzin* cries out five times a day from the

mosque, 'God is greater. Come to prayer.' Francis wrote to all the superiors in the Order: 'In the midst of all the people entrusted to you, give honour to the Lord. Each time have a public crier or through some other signal announce that everyone must render praise and thanksgiving to the Almighty Lord and God.'[3]

Francis utilised the ringing of bells as an equivalent to the Muslim call to prayer to be used as a signal to come to prayer and worship. 'Announce and preach to all the people ... tell them about the glory that is due to Him, so that at every hour when bells are rung, praise and honour may be offered to Almighty God by everyone all over the world.'[4]

He wanted to introduce and adapt the Islamic custom of the salaat (prayer) – ringing the *Angelus* had not yet been established – so he also addressed the secular rulers of the city-states attempting to attain it by two means. Firstly, the superiors and preachers should explain the meaning and purpose of this sign of prayer to the whole people. Secondly, those who bore responsibility in the secular sphere were to take up the Islamic custom and make it part of their system of laws. In both cases his aim was to reach all people. His idea was to establish all-embracing praise of God, which would unite Christians and Muslims in the same intention and worship 'all over the world'.

Francis was deeply impressed by the Muslims' reverence for God evidenced in their prostration and deep bowing during prayer. There are precedents for this through Scripture so it was not something new. When the Magi reached Christ they bowed down before him, Daniel prostrated himself in prayer, John fell flat on his face in the presence of the risen Christ and elders and angels in heaven fall down in worship, but it was not widely practised in the Western Church.

Francis wrote to his General Chapter: 'At the sound of His Name you should fall to the ground and adore Him with fear and reverence. Give hearing with all your ears and obey the Son of God. This is the very reason He has sent you all over the world, so that by word and deed you might bear witness to His message and convince everyone that there is no other Almighty God besides Him.'[5]

The statement 'there is no other Almighty God besides Him' is similar to the Muslim affirmation 'There is no God but God'. After a Muslim proclaims this he falls to the ground in worship.

Tradition has it that the Sultan wanted to load Francis with all sorts of presents, but in the end Francis only accepted one horn which – like the muezzin – was used to call the people to pray.[6]

Francis experienced a deepening respect for the writings of the Holy Scriptures and instructs Christians to observe an Eastern tradition deeply ingrained in Muslims. 'We are called to serve God in a special way . . . we must give proof of our creator by keeping the liturgical books and anything else which contains His holy words with great care. I urge all my friars and encourage them in Christ to show all possible respect for God's words wherever they may happen to find them in writing. If they are not kept properly or if they lie thrown about disrespectfully, they should pick them up and put them aside, paying honour to God who spoke them.'[7]

Muslims have a deep reverence for the actual writings of Scripture and treat them with honour. The Quran is kept in a special stand or on the most prominent place on the shelf. It is never placed carelessly on the floor, nor handled irreverently. Eastern Christians treat the Bible with the same reverence. Mrs Arafat is an Orthodox Christian and on one occasion during a conversation with her on a scriptural subject, I casually picked up the Bible and handed it to her with one hand. She held out both hands to receive it, raised it to her lips and kissed it before opening it. Her action was totally impulsive and unrelated to me, but it showed up my over-familiarity with the sacred and I felt convicted (I think quite rightly so). The Word of God should not be treated like any old book. Muslims treat the Quran with the same respect. Are these and other religious traditions just meaningless actions? Recently I was praying with a group of Christians who all live or work in Muslim countries. At the end of the prayer I noted that every Christian automatically finished the Amen with the proscribed Muslim ritual. They opened their hands palms up in the posture for prayer and then reverently wiped them over their faces (receiving the blessing), finishing with a deferential touch on the chest or heart. This tradition carries such a powerful symbolism that those Christians, who were all from non-liturgical churches, practised it even when there were no Muslims present. It seemed too irreverent to simply walk out of God's presence. Just like Francis they found some practices in Islam enriched their faith so they brought them back into Christian worship.

Muslims also treat bread with great respect. Bread is a sign of God's grace, the gift of life. Bread is never thrown out. Stale bread is given to animals or left on the gatepost, or tops of walls for the poor to collect. Any bread found fallen on the ground is treated how Francis saw it treated and told his followers to treat it: 'picked up and put in a suitable place'. Francis had a Catholic reverence for the presence of Christ in the Communion bread and took Jesus' words literally, 'I am the bread of life who gives my flesh for the world.' The Muslims' respect for bread would touch him deeply.

In all his sermons Francis began with the blessing, 'God give you peace'. The people were completely astonished by this greeting for they had never heard any other cleric greet them that way. Some challenged it in an angry way: 'What is the meaning of this kind of greeting?' Francis told his people, 'Let them talk, they do not have a sense of the things of God. Don't be ashamed, because nobles and princes of this world will show respect to you because of this greeting.'[8] Is Francis stating what happened when he used this greeting in the Muslim world and was honoured by the Sultan? Francis also introduced incense into the worship of the Roman Catholic Church. At the beginning of the day Muslims burn incense in places of business, in homes, and at shrines in conjunction with prayers – it is symbolic of blessing and cleansing and Francis would have observed this practice. The Eastern Orthodox Church also used incense and Francis would have seen their worship. Some scholars believe that incense was originally introduced to Islam from the Eastern Church.

Francis was never reconciled to the Crusades, but never spoke against the Church. He sent his own knights of his Order out into the world waging a crusade of prayer, powerlessness through poverty, peace and reconciliation. He lodged his protest of the Crusades by refusing to send his Brothers to minister to the Crusaders. When seven fanatic Brothers in the Order wanted to go to Marrakech, Morocco, Francis was opposed. They were not going in the Franciscan spirit but saw Islam as a diabolical religion and went to attack it. They went to the market places and preached against Islam and Mohammed. The Moroccan Sultan made a number of attempts to save their lives but their fanaticism finally forced his hand and they attained their goal of martyrdom. Francis refused to have the accounts of their exploits read in his presence. He alluded to praise of himself in the records as a reason, but the short shrift he made of the whole affair suggests his displeasure in it. Years later a Franciscan cardinal canonised the martyrs as saints. They became heroes because they went to battle. Francis was opposed to the battle mentality and to his Brothers who engaged Muslims as enemies, and he was opposed to service that was not given with the motive of love alone, but in the hopes of success.

Francis understood that conversion and any visible results is God's work, not ours. At one stage Francis became extremely discouraged when some of his Order were giving a bad example. He asked God to take the whole thing back as it wasn't going how he planned! He complained to God, 'Lord I give you back the family you gave me.' But the Lord refused to take it back and answered him, 'Tell me, who converts men? Who gives them the strength to persevere? Is it not I? Don't be saddened about this. Do what you have to do and do it well. Apply yourself to the work, for I have planted the Order.'

The Franciscans today apply this to their mission to Muslim lands. 'Muslims were his brothers who must be shown the true path to salvation that only Jesus Christ can give. It seems that his failure (in seeing Muslim conversions) was to be the characteristic mark of Francis' missionary programme, for he did not seek visible results, but wanted to bear witness to Christ and make a commitment of his life. A new attitude developed in Francis and he told his brothers how they should deal with Muslims. They should testify to their faith by a simple peaceable presence and an attitude of service.'[9] 'In his contacts with Muslims, Francis became aware that they were not the "cruel beasts" they were supposed to be in the eyes of Christians. He saw their high moral standards and admired, above all, their profound veneration and submission to God. For Francis, this was a sign of the presence of God and of His divine action. That no Muslims were ready to be converted indicated to Francis that the time had not yet come. For Francis, the will of God was not expressed in an unconditional obligation to preach the Gospel, but in awaiting the right moment, which God Himself would designate. He clearly understood that Muslims had to be accepted as they were, for thus had they been created by God . . . His disciple will have to be patient, then, ready to serve in humbleness of spirit, the spirit of "minoritas" and submission. The Friars minor were generally well accepted and kindly received by the Muslim when they came thus. However, when they arrived in the haughty spirit of the Crusaders, denouncing Mohammed, then they were persecuted and killed, sometimes under torture (as in the case of the brothers in Marrakech) . . . For Francis the witness of life is the first method of evangelisation. The attempt to live among Muslims in such a way that the Good News will be proclaimed in our lives should provoke the questions, Why are they like that? Why are they concerned about us?'[10]

'I can't figure you out. Why are you going to so much trouble to help us? What's your hidden agenda?' our Muslim friend asked guardedly. Mazhar replied, 'If I see a chance to do good and I don't help it's a sin. The opposite of love is indifference.' If we have an agenda – other than living out our faith – it is simply to have the opportunity to be asked to explain the reason for hope that is in us.

In another country the relaxed dinner party was flowing around loved Arabic music, jokes and delicious food with a few religious topics tossed in by either the Muslims or Christians present. Suddenly one of the Muslim men animatedly took centre stage declaring, 'The difference between Islam and Christianity is that Christians love *the other*. To love an enemy. That's unique to Christianity. Christians follow the example of Christ who loved the world enough to die for all humanity.' His statement impacted me deeply, firstly that the witness of sacrificial love bears fruit and secondly with a sadness for our general failure to live up to this, particularly among Muslims.

Francis told his Brothers to wait to declare the Gospel until God opened the way. Thus sharing our faith is simply the evidence of our conversion. Francis' advice is a corrective to the approach of the brothers who went to Marrakech. Their preaching to the Muslims was really a means to an end. The Gospel did not own them, it served them. I hesitate to assess the actions of people who were so passionate about their faith that they were martyred, but it seems that they did not view their mission to Muslim lands as a ministry of service. They were not serving Muslims, but expecting Muslims to serve them in attaining their goals. If Christians serve God by battling others for the sake of a reward, we thus become spiritual mercenaries. God wants ministers of his peace – not mercenaries. Francis taught by preaching and example to serve God through sacrificially serving others for no reward, except to be obedient to Christ and remain in Christ's love. In other words, we live this way because we are converted, not because we plan to convert others. The New

Testament tells us 'love from the center of who you are . . . be good friends who love deeply.'[11]

Franciscans today understand that their ministry in Muslim lands calls for 'abandoning the spirit of superiority which often leads to place our Christian culture above theirs. Christ humbled himself to serve. This will also favour our being true Brothers and Sisters to Muslims – demonstrated through our love for them, our participation in sorrow and joy with them in the events of life, and in being sensitive to whatever hurts them. It also helps us break down our ghettos and to co-operate with Muslims in common projects rather than fostering our own.'[12] Francis understood that he was supposed to concentrate faithfully on doing the task God entrusted to him and leave the results to God. If we heard of someone being captured by Islam the usual interpretation would be a negative one. Francis was captured by Muslims when he first arrived in the battle ground in Egypt and then captured by Islam when he formed personal relationships with Muslims. His capture has enriched the faith of millions of Christians.

Notes

1 Writings: Letter to a General Chapter, Assisi, Ms 338, *Omnibus of Sources for the Life of St Francis.*
2 Ibid. p. 108.
3 Ibid. p. 115–116.
4 Ibid. p. 113.
5 *Omnibus*, p. 104.
6 All points in this chapter on how Islam influenced Francis are taken from a Friar's paper: 'Franciscan Mission among the Muslims' Assisi, Italy 1982, On the Occasion of the 8th Centenary of Francis' Birth. Lesson 20, Correspondence Course on Franciscan Missionary Charism (CCFMC Office, Asia.) Published by Missionzentrale der Francisker, Bonn, Germany.

7 *Omnibus*, p. 107.

8 Legend of Perugia, *Omnibus*, p. 1043.

9 Rule 1221 and 1221.12.

10 Assisi Paper.

11 Romans 12:10 (*The Message* translation, Eugene H. Peterson, 1993, Colorado Springs: NavPress).

12 Assisi Paper.

Chapter Eleven

THE PLACE OF MEETING

'Blessed be the womb that carried you.' My brother-in-law Ali
beamed at me raising his open hands extended in a blessing. His
seventy-four years gave him a large girth but no wrinkled skin on
his round chalky pale face. The crystal blue eyes fixed on me
reminded me of my mother's eyes, inherited from grandfather
Bill. Ali's bald head was covered with the typical Arab head-dress
– with a black cord holding it in place (today's was white – at
other times it was the equally characteristic red and white check).
His long traditional brown robe was a wool blend against the
winter cold of inland Syria. Actually, I never address Ali by his
first name. Kinship terms are usually used in the Middle East, so
I address him as 'Father of Talal', the name of his eldest son. He
always addresses me as 'Mother of Faris', and he now finished
his blessing with this addition. I would be surprised if he easily
remembers my first name. It is never used in the family as they
address me by the particular kinship term by which they are
related to me. For most of the family I am 'my uncle's wife' (the
term specifies paternal or maternal uncle); for the rest of the
family I am 'Mother of Faris'.

Ali and I were sitting on the floor on opposite sides of the
narrow living room, reclining on bright cushions propped against
the walls. He sat cross-legged with his brown robe tucked over his

bare feet. It is impolite to confront people with the soles of your feet, whether barefooted or wearing shoes. We always sit bare-footed – shoes are left at the door of the house and house slippers are removed at the door to each room so that floor coverings are kept clean. An old bedsheet was an integral part of the living room furnishings. It lay on the floor cushions in readiness to cover any female bare legs in danger of being exposed. It was now in use over my lap allowing me to stretch my legs out comfortably underneath its shelter. The rest of the floor was covered with a bright blue Eastern rug. A pot-bellied paraffin stove comman-deered the centre of the room between us. Its tin chimney clung to the roof from where it snaked along the walls to the air vent. An enormous chandelier vied for centre stage with the stove. Family photographs looked down on us from their resting places, hung traditionally high near the ceiling. Typical of most country homes the room was sparsely furnished. The only piece of furni-ture it boasted was an ancient glass-fronted buffet displaying bric-a-brac, a framed verse from the Quran, and a large picture of the holy family in Bethlehem. Behind Ali on the wall hung the prized family treasure: the family tree in a gold embossed frame declaring the Mallouhis' descent from the prophet Mohammed. When Ali's wife first showed me the tree she impressed upon me, 'This is a true genealogy researched by a reputable firm. It's not bought with a price like so many others. With this firm the policy is "No descent: No tree".' I had responded by looking suitably impressed. Who am I to question family lore? They are proud of their Muslim heritage. Mazhar's great-uncle, Haj Anis Mallouhi, was a religious leader (Cadi Isharia') in Syria. On the other hand another uncle translated all of Chairman Mao's works into Arabic. The one family has turned out protagonists for Islam, Christianity and Communism.

My eyes scanned around the room and locked back on Ali trying to read him as he waited for my answer. His expression told me he considered this was normal conversation. Yet he had just brought my mother's womb into a room where even bare legs were not acceptable! Then I realised it was one of those many polite pleasantries requiring a prescribed answer. Plastering my face with a serene smile, my mind frantically dived into dark crevices searching for the response. I definitely had not learnt this greeting in Syrian nor in any of the other Arabic colloquial dialects I have attempted to learn: Egyptian, Moroccan, Tunisian, and Jordanian. Maybe literary Arabic held the key? The search didn't yield any results. Feeling like Alice's frozen Cheshire cat I had to quickly say something suitable before I looked imbecile. Didn't a woman cry out something like this to Jesus? That didn't seem appropriate either. It was actually something about nursing breasts and I didn't want any more anatomy in the room with us. Another second and it would be too late and he would give up expecting a response, so I blurted out somewhat incoherently 'You and I both'. He nodded, and settled back puffing on his water pipe. Tranquillity settled on the room with only the sound of the water gurgling in the glass-bowl base of the pipe as he drew in the aromatic apple smoke through the long red, velvet-covered tube.

Approximately 200 hundred of my in-laws live in this Syrian country town. Our family and the entire town of 30,000 people are all Muslims. My husband is the only known person to have become a Christian. It was a very individualistic decision, running counter to a community where the smallest social unit is not the individual person, but the extended family. In this community, people who want to be alone are suspected of being mentally ill. So I was never left alone. No matter what I wanted to do, there would be someone who would drop what they were doing in order to accompany me. I was never alone in the street – a family member was always with me showing me the town and introducing me to relatives and filling me in with inside information. While buying medicine I discovered the chemist was a relative. The hairdresser was a relative, the street-stall vendor, the obstetric gynaecologist, the skin specialist, the sheep trader, the policeman. As we passed through the town, I was proudly introduced to people as one of the family members. When walking in the street I was brought face to face with the wider dilemma of my identity. I was one of the persons belonging to that small town. I had a rightful place in the community and the townspeople had a place to slot me: I belonged to the Mallouhi clan. But there is a sense in which I don't belong. I am not only different because I am a Westerner. I am a non-Muslim member of a totally Muslim town. I was reminded of this when I walked the whole town and there was not a single church. This was unusual, because I have always lived in large Muslim cities and there were churches for expatriates or for Christian minorities. Mazhar and I were two Christians, and that didn't constitute a minority worth building a church for! I was reminded of it when we were standing at a taxi stop and an old acquaintance of Mazhar's, whom he had not seen for thirty years, recognised him and came over to greet us. After the pleasantries he enquired, 'So are you still following Christ?' Naturally he would remember. It was the talk of the town and is still intriguing.

Whether I sat in the living room between the holy family and the Quran, or walked in the streets with many mosques but no church, I reflected on the problem of how to bridge the gap between our communities. Sometimes the comments from both Muslims and Christians about the 'other side' made the gap seem like a bottomless abyss.

Muslims' reasons for rejecting Christianity usually swing around to perceiving Christianity as part of the colonialist endeavour and perceiving Christ as a Westerner with no relationship to Eastern culture. If Christ were walking the streets of his birthplace on the West Bank of Palestine today, I believe he would be mind-boggled by this perception of him. Who is this Christ and what sort of Christianity is this that no longer has anything to say to Eastern Muslims? Francis was able to bridge this gap and extricate Christ from the trappings of the medieval Western Church and take to Muslims a Christ who would woo the Sultan.

At the beginning of this century, Christians' sincere desires to live unspotted by the world's systems – believed to be under the dominion of Satan, and thus in opposition to God – resulted in a distrust of human culture and fear of contamination by it. In the West this was evidenced in the popular movement of separation from secular society. When cultures were not of the Judeo-Christian tradition this distrust flowered into abhorrence and antagonism. The thinking went something like this: if these people did not believe in Christ, then it wasn't just their religion that had no light, but their whole culture belonged to the realm of Satan. Therefore in those cultures, in order to follow Christ, a person had to reject his religious beliefs, his culture, his family and anything else connected to his or her past life.

When Mazhar responded to Christ's call in the 1950s he was told he needed to leave his old sinful life behind. This was explained in detail – he needed to change his name; stop drinking in coffee shops; refuse to join his family's religious celebrations; stay away from mosques; stay away from Muslims; stop fasting; pray with a different posture, and eat pork to prove he was converted. It wasn't surprising that his family angrily opposed his conversion and he soon no longer had any relationships with his old friends whom he had rejected. He experienced a terrible identity crisis and total dislocation from his culture, family and friends. This person who Jesus found in order to give an abundant life was on the road to auto-destruction. In spite of this he was still not totally accepted by the Christian community. The New Testament states clearly that 'the kingdom of God is not a matter of food and drink, but righteousness and joy in the Holy Spirit'.[1] Moreover it also tells us to stay put in the communities where Christ finds us. God's advice (through St Paul) to the Corinthian Christians who lived in an idol worshipping, immoral community was not to totally separate from it but, even in that severe situation, to stay where they were and live in a new way.[2]

At the start of the twenty-first century we are somewhat aware of our cultural gridlocks which confine and cloud the Gospel.

We have removed some of them, but without doubt we are still blind to many. The challenge to understand the supra-cultural message of Christ and live it remains a wide road ahead of us no matter where we live, East or West.

As we share our faith with others it is vitally important to understand that our religious traditions are not the Gospel and may actually have little relationship to the Gospel message and even be obscuring it. Following Christ does not mean joining the *Christian* culture that has grown up over the centuries. It does not require leaving one's family and people. To follow Christ does not require one to take a new *Christian* name, or to wear a different style of clothing. Nor does it require using the symbol of the cross, nor worshipping on a certain day, nor a certain style of worship – like praying sitting with hands steepled (similar to Hindus) in a church building. It does not require adopting new wedding, birth or death traditions. Nor does it require eating different foods like pork, or drinking alcohol, or using pictures of Christ, or celebrating certain holidays. It does not mean using different everyday words and greetings. It does not mean ceasing to fast and pray. None of these cultural expressions are essential to following Christ. The only reason we may need to change any of these practices – in any culture of the world – is if there is a direct link with sin or Satan. Then there is a need to beware of confusing culture and religion.

So what does it mean to believe in and follow Christ? The one thing following Christ requires is to believe his words about himself – that he is the Word of God bringing us back into unbroken communication with God. His own path led to self-sacrifice for us all, and so to be his disciple involves first and fore-most self-denial on a daily basis. It is easy to perform religious duties and still be ourselves, but God asks much more. We have to die to self in order to walk in holiness; to follow God's command, 'Walk with me and be perfect.' It means to enter into a relationship with the living Christ, to learn from him and obey his commands for living a life pleasing to God. It means acceptance of his other followers as family members. This following is voluntary. Christ does not force anyone to come after him, but calls men and women and leaves them to decide.

This is the kind of Jesus that Francis took to the Muslims. Francis was able to redefine the contemporary meaning of *Christian* to not mean *enemy* and the Sultan understood. Francis stripped Christ of his foreign occidental trappings – which placed him in the enemy camp – and introduced the Sultan to a Christ who was born, lived and died among the men and women of Palestine. This Christ understands and loves Muslims and died for them. This is the Jesus who Mazhar met and why he calls himself a Muslim follower of Jesus – not a Christian.

The distance between the two religious communities can seem huge – like opening a map of an enormous desert with Christians at one edge and Muslims at the other. How can we cross the desert between us? The journey looks so arduous that the temptation is to give up the idea. But all long journeys are begun with just one small step in the right direction. By the time we finish a journey of many small steps – where we meet the other and interact together in small oasis experiences – we will probably have a better idea of what to do when we eventually reach the other side. The journey may look scary, but one small step is easy. The following stories are from people who took that small step and found themselves near the other end of that enormous desert.

Les is an economic development practitioner working in Indonesia, where the following story took place.

His name was Mubarak and he ran a small all-purpose neighbourhood kiosk which shared a wall on the right side with the home my wife and I rented at the time. Although an Indonesian, Mubarak traced his lineage back to an Arab clan with which he and his family were still quite close and to whom he was quite loyal. Since a good number of this branch of his family resided in Saudi Arabia, during the Gulf War, Mubarak presented loyalty and allegiance to Saddam Hussein as more or less a family and Muslim article of faith. This was accompanied by a very verbal and publicly displayed berating and demonising of all that was Western, most especially directed toward George Bush and the American political system. It was quite ironic that it would be us – Americans – who moved next door and became his nearest neighbours. When the Gulf War broke out, our relationship felt the impact, but not necessarily in ways one might expect.

One of the factors which had bearing upon our friendship long before the war broke out was the fact that my American patriotism was never the sort one frequently encounters in the States – and this became all the more so upon my conversion to Jesus almost twenty years ago. Thus, upon initially meeting Mubarak in 1989 – and coming face to face with his stereotypes as to who I had to be – he wasted no time in establishing conceptual identity-religion-based boundaries which he took to be strictly required between us. However, over the course of the next two years, as I had occasion to drop by his kiosk almost daily, Mubarak began to discover that many of his stereotypes were ill-suited to who my wife and I really were. As an example, he was quite surprised when it came up in conversation that while I lived back in the States, I had often written to my congressional representatives protesting what seemed to me relatively unconditional US backing and funding of the state of Israel, in spite of that country's generally heinous treatment of the Palestinian community residing within their borders (let alone touching upon the whole issue of borders itself!). Mubarak was even more surprised to hear that at home I had become a rather close friend with Alex Awad – the brother of Mubarak Awad who was at the time a leader in the Palestinian non-violent resistance movement. Thus, we had many views concerning the US in common – many more than he had anticipated at the outset. Especially as it became apparent that the US and its international constituency were going to face off with Iraq and Saddam Hussein (although the relative esteem in which we held Saddam remained an issue over which we differed), we grew to respect and appreciate each other more and more. I believe he began to see that I did not view the conflict in such simplistic oppositions as 'evil versus good' (as George Bush was wont to ever-so-publicly frame the issue).

That was the background for how the day of 17 January 1991 unfolded for me – the date in which the US and its allies launched their midnight flurry of sorties upon Baghdad. I vividly remember walking back from my morning lecture that day (I was at the time studying the Indonesian language at a local university), taking my time meandering down our small, narrow street, greeting all of the people lining the sides of the alleyway, persons I knew who happened to be about their usual morning busyness, tending to their affairs and family. Almost in passing, one of them mentioned that 'your country' had launched its anticipated assault upon Iraq just a couple hours previously (since the middle of the night in Baghdad is the middle of the morning in Java). I stopped dead in my tracks. What would this mean for me – a known American citizen – in this small, predominantly Muslim neighbourhood? Closer to the bone, what would it mean for my relationship to Mubarak? The two issues were not unrelated since, being of Arabic extraction, Mubarak was held in high esteem in the local mosque and therefore in the neighbourhood as a whole.

I decided to find out straight away. I briskly walked the remaining 100 metres or so to Mubarak's small kiosk – with the plan of broaching the issue under the pretence of needing another tin of sweetened, condensed milk. As I approached, one by one Mubarak's customers sensed my coming and looked up at me. I could almost feel each additional set of eyes upon me – more palpably still, it wasn't difficult for me to read their minds – 'What is Mubarak going to say?' 'What is the American going to say?' 'What will each of them do?' 'Will they fight here and now?' 'Should we run or should we stay?' 'Will we have a small gulf war here in front of this small store?' People seemed to stop dead in their tracks and all exchange ground to a halt.

However, as Mubarak finally looked up at me – for a brief moment with a quite sombre look – he broke into a huge smile. He said 'Did you hear the news?' I answered that I had. 'It doesn't need to affect us though, does it?' he said in the presence of everyone. 'No, it doesn't, Mubarak. You know where I stand,' I replied.

It was as if the entire place had just been covered with a thick blanket of noxious, choking smoke and yet someone had graciously thrown a bucket of water over the whole area, clearing the air and allowing all to breath again. I walked up to Mubarak and we shook hands. I believe at that moment in that minuscule hamlet in West Java, a tiny glimpse of God's goodness and reconciliation broke through the ever-present shroud of stereotyping, prejudice, and pigeonholing that often accompanies Muslim-Christian relations. Mubarak and I continued to be friends and we continued to debate the issues, especially as the War carried on. Many there who saw probably puzzled at the fact that, true to Mubarak's words, 'it didn't need to affect us'.

When my wife and I moved away from that neighbourhood Mubarak tenderly handed me a letter (one which I was admonished in typical Asian fashion not to open until later) which urged me to continue my good quest for Allah and his truth. He stated that we would remain neighbours and friends even though distance separated us. But more importantly, in it he called us fellow seekers of Allah. I believe that our mutual response to the events in Baghdad on 17 January 1991 had something to do with that statement. I hope it somehow, miraculously, leads to so much more. I also wish Mubarak God's blessing in his faith journey and my prayer, of course, is that he would find God in the person of Jesus.

In Colorado, in the same city where Muslims are antagonised by the Prayer Center, a different type of Christian witness took place. Stephen and Joan heard about a Muslim community from the Arabian Gulf connected with a local mosque and decided with their church to reach out to them. The Muslims were invited to host a dinner for both communities in Stephen's home. The Muslims cooked the food and taught the Christians how to observe the correct customs. They were shown how to remove their shoes, outside the room, and ate in the Gulfi fashion – seated in a circle on the floor with cloths spread over the rugs and eating from communal plates. During the meal each group asked questions about the other's religion and culture. The Christians asked the Muslims some hard questions like 'Why do you make your women veil and stay inside the house?' The women replied that they were not forced to do either. Veiling was a modesty custom which some preferred and took great pride in, while others simply complied. The men pointed out that in some Gulf countries women not only are a significant part of the work force but also hold government portfolios. The men admitted that they preferred their wives to stay at home for the family's sake and also because they liked to protect them because they were precious.

Afterwards the Christians glowed as they recounted anecdotes that led them into a new world of Muslim awareness, so different to their previously-held ideas. The Muslims were deeply touched and profusely thanked their hosts repeatedly, 'This is the first time anyone in America has shown a genuine interest in us and our religion in all the years we have been here. We cannot thank you enough or tell you how deeply we appreciate this night.' They left with a new appreciation for Christians.

Lois is a doctor working with her husband with an international medical agency in Central Asia. Lois needed a language helper and – after knocking on doors in her neighbourhood – met Mallika, an eighteen-year-old Muslim girl who invited her to meet her father, Ahmad, an English professor and local television personality. Lois found the family very welcoming and the mother friendly, but discovered on the first visit that Ahmad loved the British and passionately disliked Americans. Lois is American. The father agreed to be her tutor and taught her culture and language. Lois helped the family with medical problems, once answering a call from Ahmad's wife for help in the middle of the night. Lois consciously avoided fulfilling Ahmad's stereotype of 'brash Americans'. When Lois' father visited her she introduced him to Ahmad and this helped break some of the ice in their relationship. During a four-year friendship between the families, Ahmad and Lois never discussed religion. Then Ahmad had a heart attack and was hospitalised and he asked for Lois and her husband to stay with him in the ward. Lois sensed he now accepted them as friends and recognised that they had no strings attached to their relationship. She felt a compulsion and liberty to share with him the story of Christ and Nicodemus. In response he told them how afraid he was and they had a heart to heart talk. Six months later Ahmad's mother died and Lois and her husband went to offer condolences to the family. Lois said, 'I was sitting with all the women and he came into the women's part of the house and wept on my shoulder. I knew now after eight years he had accepted me as a daughter. God broke down his prejudice when he saw my respect for him and my compassion for his mother.' Ahmad also discovered Lois as an individual and stopped judging her according to his preconceived images.

At a Christian conference in Germany the discussion turned to what was perceived as the Islamic encroachment on their society. There are an estimated two and a half million Muslims in Germany – mainly Turks – and Christians at the conference saw Islam as a threat to Christianity. Some believed foreigners are dangerous because they have too many children and will become a majority; others believed Muslims had designs for taking over Germany. Delegates expressed alarm over the rising number of mosques being built and saw moves to be allowed to broadcast the prayer-call as sign of the implementation of this plan. One delegate told how the call to prayer sounded so evil and it affected him in a negative way. He 'got goosebumps'. There seemed to be a general consensus of his feelings. A minister who had lived in the Arab world stood, 'I do not share this experience at all. I think the call to prayer is melodious and beautiful and it's a reminder to me to keep focused on God all through the day's events. I miss it since I returned to Europe. If we have church bells ringing every hour why shouldn't the Muslims have the call to prayer? This is a democratic country.' She was definitely the odd one out and no one made any comment. She felt that the attitudes expressed during the meetings not only verged on the hysterical, but that much misinformation about the numbers of Muslims in Germany and their activities was accepted as truth. The Christians felt under threat from Islam and fear distorted reality. The minister, in attempting to break down this intolerance, played the Muslim call to prayer to a class of Christian teens preparing for Confirmation. They ridiculed it claiming, 'We can pray whenever we want to.' The minister asked how often they prayed and they admitted 'Never'. This minister is searching for ways to live together in harmony with the Muslim community and purchases the communion bread from a Muslim Turk.

We met a Turkish Muslim family in a country town in Germany, which could not praise the local Christian community enough for the practical help they received from them when they immigrated. The Christians helped with no expectation of the family forming any link with the church, but this demonstration of Christ's compassion for a stranger in need caused the Muslims to question why the Christians cared.

In 1997 the Central Mosque in Woking, Sussex, was fire-bombed. This was the first mosque built in Britain and the event was sadly symbolic of the tension between the Muslim and majority community. The Anglican Bishop went to Friday prayers and spoke of his sadness at this act of vandalism in a house of prayer and assured the Muslim congregation that Christians wanted to be their friends. The local Catholic Church sent money to help with repairs.

Sally Sutcliffe[3] was driving past a mosque in Stoke-on-Trent and noticed some strange graffiti on the mosque wall: 'Jesus Crist is Lord'. 'I felt deeply ashamed that anyone purporting to be lifting up the name of Jesus had done so in such an offensive way and also annoyed that they couldn't spell Christ! It left me feeling baffled. That Jesus Christ is Lord is of course a fundamental truth that we dearly want to share with our Muslim friends, but this must be the least appropriate way of doing it. Not only does any type of graffiti hammer home the message that Muslims are disliked by the majority population in Britain, but this particular message must confirm the myth that Christians are on a modern-day crusade against Muslims.' Sally and her husband wrote a letter to the mosque leaders apologising that they had been targeted for this type of vandalism and disassociated themselves from the attack. A week later one of the elders rang them up. He was deeply moved by their letter and had it read out in the leaders' meeting and conveyed the Muslim community's gratitude for their solidarity. He invited them home and Sally 'had a wonderful chat with his wife and daughter about all things spiritual'.

In an inner city area in Britain some Muslims came to ask the local Christian minister, 'please tell the Christians not to vandalise our mosque'. The mosque had been the target of long-term vandalism and was eventually burnt down. The vicar explained that those responsible were not Christians and that his church had also had problems with crime and vandalism. He got to know the imam and other mosque leaders. This contact led to a series of meetings where Christians visited the mosque and had a cup of tea together and had question and discussion sessions and vice versa at the church. This continued for two or three years with two or three meetings a year. It evolved into a men's group which played cricket together. Before this happened, a small group of Christians had begun meeting to pray for their Muslim neighbours, to study how to relate better and had begun visiting Muslim families.

Mazhar and I were invited to speak to a church near Stockholm about Islam after tensions with the Muslim community became local front-page news. The Muslims were strategically planning to gain a majority voice in the municipality – giving rise to fears of a take-over. The church was labelled intolerant after the pastor made some comments to the press and the communities polarised with the possibility of dialogue unlikely. Ignorance and fear were the key ingredients. The Christians were fearful of the Muslims' motives. The Muslims really wanted equal opportunity, but their expressions of desire for Islamic leadership of the Swedish municipality undermined their cause. Our visit was mainly to restore bridges of dialogue from the Christian side by demolishing the fear-inducing stereotypes of Muslims. We also held a public meeting in a community centre and some Muslims attended and were able to voice their concerns and desires in face to face communication with the Christians.

On another occasion we spent three weeks in Sweden visiting churches from north to south, teaching about Islam and helping Christians relate to Muslims and share their faith with them. We were amazed at the concern in these Christian communities for how to relate to their new Muslim neighbours, who were mainly refugees. These Christians gave up their Saturday afternoon leisure time to learn about Islam and find ways to serve the Muslim community in their midst.

Marian and Ralph took a holiday in Turkey.

While swimming in the sacred Pool at Hieropolis a wonderful Turkish woman advised us that we should go to Yalvac (ancient Antioch of Pisidia) as Paul, the apostle, had gone up there probably for his health. When we walked to the bus, the driver came toward us to take our luggage, but then walked right by us – we did not resemble folks who usually take his bus. When we convinced him we really did want to go there, he and his helper took care of us. It was rainy, and a five-hour trip. When we arrived we were the only people left on the bus and he looked at us to see where we were going. In my best Turkish I said 'otel'. He picked up our two small duffle bags and walked into a building camouflaged in a wall. At a narrow entrance a clerk sitting at a small desk pressed underneath a flight of stairs informed him that it was 'yoki', which we had already learned, meant 'no way'. We returned to the bus and the driver's assistant gesticulated and said 'maison'. We knew enough French to know we were heading for a house – and expected a guesthouse. The driver took us to his mother's home. He called out and three children, fifteen, fourteen and ten years of age came running to the bus. They took our bags and led us through one of the doorways in the solid block-long wooden wall along the road. Inside we ascended a flight of stairs and at the top we entered a room with some low furniture around the sides. The whole room and furniture was covered in layered Turkish carpets.

There had been no communication by voice, as we knew no Turkish and they knew no English, but smiles and joy were without end. After we sat down with these four plus his wife, his mother, his sister and her two children who were all living in the complex, we discovered that we could do a minimum amount of communicating with our phrase book and theirs. We laughed, talked about how old everyone was and the bus driver told his family the story of our arrival.

I have since heard that a Muslim family would look at visitors as gifts from God and that is how we were treated. Eventually, after lots of smiles and explaining where we planned to go next, the bus driver said we couldn't get there from here! Then his face lit up and he gave us the correct bus information to do so and motioned for us to sit down on the floor. We were all in a circle on the rich carpets when out came a huge tray full of the evening meal. There were chickens, some kind of rice soup, salad greens handed from one to another like a sheaf of hay, lots of great bread – and for dessert, they went out and picked some very delicious apples. We ate from common serving dishes with a big spoon. A special treat was a glass of Ayran for each of us. They did not have any – it was only for the guests.

Eventually, it was time for us to think of sleeping. The bus driver, his wife and three children stood up, picked up our luggage, motioned for us to come with them and we were back out on the street again by the bus. We all got in the bus and the driver took the bus several blocks and then parked again. This time we were at their own home where they laid down the back of a sofa and made a bed for two with the most beautiful hand embroidered sheets and pillow cases and sateen quilt. The bathroom was the usual hole in the ground with a hose for cleaning. We were soon asleep. When we awakened in the morning, all had left the house except the mother who had a fabulous breakfast which she brought in to us and then sat and joined us in eating.

After breakfast, we walked to Antioch of Pisidia. When we got back to the house, the children were home from school and a neighbour lady had come in to 'view' us. We looked at all the beautiful handiwork the family made and they gave us some doilies. Then we grabbed a taxi to the bus station outside of town. We have wonderful memories of our Turkish Muslim family and are hoping to have them visit us in America one day. Meanwhile we keep in mail contact with the help of friends in both countries who translate notes for both families and we regularly pray for them.

'In May 1996, the GIA, a radical Islamic group in Algeria, kid-napped seven Trappist monks in the Atlas Mountains threatening to hold them hostage until the French government released several Algerians from prison. When France refused, the fanatics slit the monks' throats. All France was horrified, and every Catholic church in France – 40,000 of them – rang its bells at the same time in the monks' memory. But what was most remarkable about the tragedy was something that foreshadowed it two years earlier. The prior of the monastery, Christian de Cherge, had a premonition that he would soon die a violent death, and wrote a letter forgiv-ing his future assassins. He sealed the letter and left it with his mother in France. Discovered after his murder, it read in part:

If it should happen that one day I become a victim of the terrorism that now seems to encompass all the foreigners living in Algeria, I would like my community, my church, my family, to remember that my life was *given* to God and to Algeria; and that they accept that the sole Master of all life was not a stranger to this brutal departure. I would like, when the times comes, to have a space of clearness that would allow me to beg forgiveness of God and my fellow human beings, and at the same time to forgive with all my heart the one who will strike me down. I could not desire such a death – how could I rejoice if the Algerian people I love were indiscriminately accused of my murder? My death, obviously, will appear to confirm those who hastily judged me naïve, or idealistic: 'Let him tell us now what he thinks of it!' But they should know that my deepest longing will be finally set free. If God wills, I will immerse my gaze in the Father's, to see with Him his children of Islam as he sees them, filled with the gift of the Spirit . . . For this life lost, totally mine and totally theirs – I give thanks to God. In this 'thank you' which is said in everything in my life from now on, I certainly include you, friends of yesterday and today, and you, O my Muslims friends of Algeria, a hundredfold as promised! And you also, my last minute-friend who will not have known what you are doing. Yes, for you, too, I say thank you and *Adieu* and commend you to the God in whose face I see yours. And may we find each other, if it please God, the Father of us both. Amen. *Insha' Allah!*'[4]

After the massacre of the monks in Algeria an Arab journal (Al Quds Al Arabi) ran the following testimony. The journalist, a Muslim Palestinian, went to a monastery in Sweden which was housing Muslim refugees from war. He told the nun that he was a Christian from Bethlehem – expecting to receive a warmer welcome, but was surprised at her answer, 'We are all children of God.' Ramadan was expected to be announced and the nun stayed up all night in contact with Muslim leadership in order to prepare a pre-dawn breakfast if the Fast began. The paper ran the story (before the prior's letter was published) as a statement of repentance from the world's Muslim community, comparing it with the brutal treatment the monks received in Algeria. It commended the Christians for their indiscriminate love, while recognising they were following in the steps of Christ.

The family of Lebanese refugees slowly picked their way down the ramp from the cargo ship and spilled onto the wharf in Alexandria, Egypt – shell-shocked, lost and bewildered. We asked where they were headed and offered to help with directions. They needed to get to the American Embassy in Cairo in the hopes of obtaining a visa to join a family member in America. They were seven adults of an extended family and had limited resources for a hotel. The remainders of their worldly possessions were scattered on the road at their feet – as many suitcases as they could carry and two sacks of apples. Mazhar and I exchanged glances and knew we had made the same decision. We gave them the address of our home in Cairo and the key to the door telling them we would finish our holiday in Alexandria and join them after one week. I was very pregnant, but when we returned home my body wasn't the only thing that bulged – our little two-bedroom apartment seemed to have persons sleeping in every corner to accommodate nine people. We then found out their names and heard their story. They stayed one week while they tried to get papers to America. The women taught me to cook some of their dishes and we ate all their apples – which were unavailable in Egypt at the time. We exploited that great Arab custom of whiling away the evening together with music, jokes and laughter – and horribly sad war stories. When they discovered they were in a Christian home a shocked silence fell, then tears as they readjusted their experiences at the hands of Christians. They explained that Christians had bombed their Shiite village in southern Lebanon. We tried to explain that real followers of Christ do not bomb and kill. They could not obtain visas to the USA and they returned to war in Lebanon, with fewer resources than when they left. We had a letter from them, but after that the *Christians* bombed their area again.

Muslim extremists attacked national Christians in a town in southern Egypt, burning, looting and killing. The Christian family hid behind barred doors, praying for deliverance but preparing to meet the Lord. When the rampage was over and they survived, they discovered Muslim neighbours had guarded their front door, risking their lives for their friends.

Jim Fleming is a Catholic priest ministering in multi-cultural Birmingham. 'It is important to remember that no matter where we go or who we meet God is alive and present in that person and place. He has been there before we ever came. People gladly share what they believe in and it calls for a listening attitude on our part. This is our gift to others as we open our hearts to them by our sense of wonder as we learn of the new and unfamiliar in what others share with us about their faith. I am convinced that what we all believe in can be challenged and deepened by participating in the *God experience* of other religions.' Jim and the others in his Order are regularly invited to speak to Muslims at the local mosque.

Jack's experience with a Muslim happened in Australia. 'We first met this man from a different country at a meeting where he was sitting on his own. When we spoke with him we found he had recently arrived in Australia and at subsequent meetings we discovered he was from an Islamic background. We knew being in a strange country he would need a network of friends to help him through the many decisions that would be forced upon him and we reached out to him with the promise of sincere friendship. We never once thought of him as a Muslim. He was simply the person God put in our path and he needed our friendship. On reflection I guess we shared what we had. As a disciple of Christ, God is asking us "What resources do you have as a person?" This is the meaning of the story when God asked Moses what he had in his hand. God wanted to show Moses that the authority and power belonged to him and that Moses was asked to surrender his resources to God. Our new friend needed to be able to speak the language of his new homeland. Our resources fit his need – we had a home and a family where he could practice this language in an environment of love and co-operation. We felt called to make a commitment of time and ourselves and to place no expectation on him in any way. When our friend needed accommodation, the family of Christ offered to help and provided him with the help he needed. These opportunities to bring Christ to our friend were both practical and visible and had no strings attached. As our friendship grew the family of Christ supported him using their resources. Our friend became part of our family in the deepest sense. When his Muslim relatives flew over to visit him they were very appreciative for our friendship and even attended church with us. We – Muslims and Christians and those who love Christ – had a wonderful experience together.'

The twentieth century gave birth to a new Francis in Muslim-Christian relations, but he is not widely known. We noted Louis Massignon in a previous chapter but he deserves special attention. Massignon was recognised in the academic world as a scholar with unusual gifts. He was also assistant political officer attached to the Mission of the historic Georges Picot, High French Commissioner for the occupied territories in Palestine and Syria. He visited Algeria in 1904 and caught a life-long interest in the Arab world. On a later visit to Iraq he became seriously ill and a Muslim family in Baghdad cared for him. His spiritual crisis took place after he was arrested in Iraq, accused of spying and sentenced to death. He tried to commit suicide, lost consciousness and was suddenly awakened to a spiritual experience that changed the course of his life by meeting a *Stranger*. 'The Stranger who had held him in his hands on the day of his anger, would henceforth be the pole of his life, to be sought and loved, not by an act of pure will, but by a total surrender: by purification from sin, and then renunciation of the joys of the world in which he hoped to attain to that reality which had revealed itself, gratuitously, in a moment of vision.'[5]

For Massignon the Arab world meant sacred hospitality, deep friendships and spiritual life. It was during his experiences with Muslims in the Arab world that he found faith in Christ. His conversion had taken place in the Arab East, the first prayer he was able to say was in Arabic, and an Arab family of Baghdad had shown him kindness and hospitality in his hour of need.[6] Throughout his life he continued to strive for a deeper spiritual experience and deeper relationships with Muslims.

Charles de Foucald (another fascinating character who left the culture and wealth of France to establish a Franciscan Order in the Algerian desert) invited Massignon to join him as a monk in the desert. Massignon struggled to find his calling, and ended choosing to continue to serve God in the academic world and marriage. Massignon's choice 'sprang from a sense of some debt which he owed to Arabs and Muslims. His academic life was dedicated to God and the Muslim world and the path of uniting the two was his study of Hallaj. Massignon believed in the efficacy of the prayers of saints and the possibility of substitution, of one person accepting a debt to God which others owe. The bearers of this work are those who move towards the final goal of life, union with God in love, and who take on themselves the sufferings and imperfections of others, the sinners, the ignorant, the poor and the oppressed. He claimed he learned this from the writer J. K. Huysmans who he met in adolescence. Huysmans on his deathbed offered his sufferings for Massignon's conversion. Passionately desiring to belong to the chain of witnesses and substitutes, not without a longing for martyrdom in the desert, like that of Charles de Foucald, the meaning of life had come to be one of prayer and intercession by which he might give back to Muslims something of what he thought he had received from them. In the world of Islam he had known the oneness and greatness of God: the prayers of Christians might give them what Islam could not give, the Incarnation and the cross.'[7]

It is interesting to note that Islam had the same effect on Francis and Massignon. After Francis returned from the Muslim world he celebrated and concentrated on those aspects of Christianity that are unique to it – the Incarnation (he instituted the nativity crib) and the Cross (he received the stigmata).

Massignon founded a community of prayer and later in life was ordained a priest in the Greek Catholic Church (which allows married priests). This was kept a secret as long as he lived. It was the basis for his service to the Muslim community in France where he lived *among* them in the Franciscan manner: 'visiting prisoners, teaching Algerian immigrants, assisting students, practising non-violent protest against the excesses of French colonial rule.'[8] The Muslims' hopes and pains were his and he demonstrated with them against France's occupation of Algeria and was imprisoned.

The efficacy of the intercession of saints was a mutual Catholic-Sufi belief and Massignon had no difficulty seeing the sufferings of Hallaj in this vein. He is largely responsible for changing the attitude of the Catholic Church to Islam. A Muslim writer explains how Massignon influenced the Vatican. 'Massignon believed Hallaj should be declared a Christian saint and have a saint day named after him. He believed the roots of Islam went back to Abraham's secret prayer at Beer Sheba[9], "Oh that Ishmael may live in your presence!" and God's reply, "As for Ishmael I have heard you, behold, I will bless him and make him fruitful and multiply him exceedingly; he shall be the father of twelve princes, and I will make him a great nation." Building on the story in the Torah and the Gospel that the Arab came from

Ishmael the son of Abraham and Hagar, he wrote, "The Arab race started with Hagar's tears. The first recorded tears in the Bible." Christians and Jews see themselves as the descendants of Isaac and the chosen of God and Muslims rejected in the rejection of Ishmael. Massignon warned that the Muslim religion, coming after Moses and Jesus, was a warning from God for the judgement of God coming and the answer to the secret prayer of Abraham. Islam came as the conscience for Judaism and Christianity, like the warning of John the Baptist to the Jews for rejecting Christ who came to them. Massignon warned Christians of their duty to enlighten all humanity, because they are chosen by God to be his messengers. There is no doubt that God heard Abraham's prayer and blessed Ishmael. Genesis 2:20 states "And God was with the boy as he grew up."[10]

The intolerance in Francis' century forced him into silence on how his experiences with Islam impacted him and his faith. The comparative acceptance of other cultures and religions in our century gave Massignon a platform to speak openly and build bridges. Did Francis dream of the bridges Massignon built? I believe Francis would have rejoiced to see Massignon's day. And did the Muslim mystic who enticed Massignon into the depths of Christ rejoice to see Christ's day?

There are a number of elements in the preceding stories of Christians' positive relationships with Muslims which embody Francis' approach to the Muslim world. The heart of Francis' attitude is the understanding that God does not discriminate. When we realise that God does not love the handful of Christians in a Muslim city any more than he loves the six million Muslims in Casablanca – or any other person in the world – we have finally discovered what God went to great pains to teach Jonah so long ago. When this truth really becomes a part of our personal faith it will change the way we interact with the world. God has no favourites. God so loved the *world* that he gave His only Son.

Francis did not engage in the battle or the debate. One of the ways we erect barriers against others is that we judge people according to their theological statements, rather than recognising their search for God. Henri Nouwen said, 'We find the God we want to give in the people to whom we want to give Him.' Most of us want to win the argument – and thus lose the person. This is winning the battle – and thus losing the war. In both instances we lose our testimony. It is easy to talk of spiritual victories, yet live as practising atheists; to talk of the Prince of peace, yet practise war.

Francis went to the Sultan simply because God sent him with a message, not because he wanted to do something successful for God with Muslims. He did not see Muslims as a frightening cultural block, but simply persons for whom Christ died. The moment we categorise people we become in danger of being manipulative. Our focus is Christ – not evangelism, not success, not the battle. Francis was Christ to the people he went to. If God's spirit indwells Christians then we will touch others with this treasure. The living of the message where Christ is received through a shared life is evangelism. There is no adequate formula or strategy with which to share Christ. How can a living relationship be reduced to a formula? Strategies belong to the battlefield. Francis disengaged from the battle and made himself vulnerable. His example calls us to get out of the battlefield and get into living out the life of Christ. Living the message means we must be willing to pay the price – no matter where we live and who our neighbour is. There may be a price to pay – Francis was beaten up before he reached the Sultan. Are we prepared for the possible unpleasantness of a decision to wholly follow Christ wherever he leads us? It will probably take us against the grain of our contemporaries and into the battle against the real enemy, that is self. Francis' life and message is the alternative way in the midst of the current battle-mentality against Islam. His simplicity challenges our dependence on methods and strategies; his indiscriminate care for people exposes our intolerance and indifference, and his crazy obedience to the Gospel confronts our excuses.

Francis' adventure with Islam is a call to lay down arms and take up an active life waging peace and love. When Muslims are sceptical of our creed, confused by our message and wounded in our warfare, the most credible witness left is our lives. The arguments and the battle are centuries old. Muslims need to see Jesus and the only way most of them will see him is in us. Muslims are still waiting for Christians who will cross the battle lines to meet them in the spirit of Jesus. And what about those Muslims who see us as the enemy? There is only one biblical way to deal with enemies – out-love their enmity, just like Francis and the one he served.

So there is no end, only the possibility of a new era, for the celebration of our faith never ends. It must be lived, so let us, you and I, go out to the other, and love and serve the Lord.

THE BEGINNING

Notes

1 Romans 14:17.
2 1 Corinthians 7:20–24.
3 Author of *Aisha My Sister*.
4 Arnold, C. (1998) *Seeking Peace*, Philadelphia and East Sussex: The Plough Publishing House, p. 106.
5 Hourani, A. (1992) *Islam in European Thought*, New York and Melbourne: Cambridge University Press, p. 123.
6 Ibid., p. 124.
7 Ibid., p. 127.
8 Ibid.
9 Genesis 17:18–20.
10 *Al Ijtihaad*, Issue 31–32 (1996), Beirut: Al Falah Publishers, p. 172.

BIBLIOGRAPHY

Abu ElAssal, R. (1999) *Caught in Between,* London: SPCK.

Abdullah, A. (1997) *Methodologies in Missionary Work to Muslim Countries*, Nida'ul Islam September–October 1997. Australia: *www.islam.org.au*

Accad, F. (1997) *Building Bridges*, Colorado: Used by permission of NavPress Publishing. All rights reserved.

Al Jabarti's Chronicle: Napoleon in Egypt, translated by M. Weiner, Princeton University Press 1993.

Ali, A. Y. (1989) *The Meaning of the Holy Quran,* Maryland: Amana Corporation.

Al Masri, S. (1989) *Khalf Al Hijab,* Cairo: Sinai Publishing House.

Al-Quds Al-Arabi, 15 December, 1992, p. 4 London.

Armstrong, K. (1993) *A History of God*, New York: Random House.

Arnold, Christoph (1998) *Seeking Peace,* Philadelphia and East Sussex: The Plough Publishing House.

Attiyah, E. (1972) *Al Arab*, Beirut (There is an English Edition by Penguin Press, THE ARABS).

Austin, R. W. J. (1980) *Ibn Al' Arabi: The Bezels of Wisdom,* New Jersey: Paulist Press.

Barks, C. (1995) *The Essential Rumi,* San Francisco: Harper

Collins, Originally Published by Threshold Books.

De Beer, F. (1977) *Francois que disait-on de toi?* Paris: Editions Franciscaines.

Blincoe, B. (1998) *The Blincoe Report*, November 1998, Mesa, Arizona.

Boff, L. (1984) *St. Francis: A Model for Human Liberation,* Quezon City, Brazil: Claretian Publications.

Boullata, K. (1990) *Faithful Witnesses: Palestinian Children Recreate their World,* Kuwait Society for the Advancement of Arab Children, Kuwait: Olive Branch Press, USA.

Braibanti, R. J. D. (1995) *The Nature and Structure of the Islamic World,* Chicago: International Strategy and Policy Institute.

Chapman, C. (1998) *Islam and the West,* Cumbria, UK: Paternoster Press.

Chapman, C. (1998) *The Faith to Faith Newsletter*, 1 November 1998. Trinity College, Bristol.

Chesterton, G. K. (1996) *St Francis of Assisi*, London: Hodder & Stoughton.

Christianity Today, 5 February 1990, p. 57.

Close, R. *The Only Effective Defense Against Terrorism is to Rebuild America's Reputation for Fairness*, Issue October/November 1998.

Cornerstone, Issue 10 (Christmas), 1997, Jerusalem: Sabeel Liberation Theology Center.

Cragg, K., interview in *The Christian Century* Chicago, 17 February 1999, p. 183.

Doyle, E. (1980) *St. Francis and the Song of Brotherhood*, New York: Seabury Press.

Dalrymple, W. (1999) *From the Holy Mountain: A Journey among the Christians of the Middle East,* New York. Henry Holt & Company.

Durkeim (1998) *Introduction to Culture and Control: Boundaries and Identities*, Study Guide, Deakin University, Melbourne.

Engelbert, O. (1965) *St Francis of Assisi*, Quincy, Illinois: Franciscan Press.

Farmaian, S. F. (1992) *Daughter of Persia*, New York: Crown Publishers.

Fitzgerald, L. & Caspar, R. (1992) *Signs Of Dialogue: Christian Encounter with Muslims*, Philippines: Silsilah Publishing.

Franciscan Mission Among the Muslims, Occasion of the 8th Centenary of Francis' Birth, A Friar Paper, Assisi, Italy, 1982.

Graham, C. (1987) *The Origins of Australia's virulent anti-Arabism. Australia's War image of the Arabs*, Free Palestine, 43 Jan–Feb 1987.

Hamra, V. (1997) *Einsichten Und Erfahrungen Zum Thema, 'Islam', Studien-Ergebnisse, September–November 1997*, Berlin. (Unpublished paper used with permission.)

Hanania, R. (1996) *I'm Glad I Look Like A Terrorist*, Illinois: Urban Strategies Group Publishing. *www.hanania.com*

Hilliard, A. & Bailey, B. J. (1999) *Living Stones Pilgrimage*, Indiana and London: Notre Dame Press.

Hitti, P. (1974) *History of the Arabs*, New York: St. Martin's Press.

Hourani, A. (1992) *Islam in European Thought*, New York and Melbourne. Reproduced with the permission of Cambridge University Press.

Houseman, L. (1935) *The Little Plays of St Francis*, London: Sidgwick & Jackson Ltd.

Ibn Munqidh, U. (1987) *Memoirs of An Arab-Syrian Gentleman and Warrior in the Period of the Crusades*. Translated by Phillip Hitti, London: I.B. Tauris & Co. Ltd.

Jabbour, N. (1993) *The Rumbling Volcano*, Pasadena, CA: Mandate Press.

Jeusset, G. (1996) *Recontre Sur L'Autre Rive: Francois d'Assise et les Musulmans*, Paris. 1996 Les Editions Franciscaines.

Jourevski, A. (1996) *Islam wa Messihiyya*, Kuwait: Dar Al Maarifa 1996.

Jourevski, A. (1996) *Almumahidaat al fikriyya lilhiwaar Al Messihiyyia wa Al Islam*, Al Ijtihaad Issue 31, 32, Spring 1996 Beirut: Al Falah.

Jusoor, (1996) *Anti-Arab discrimination and racism during 1995*, Issue 7/9 1996, Maryland: Kitab Inc.

Kabbani, R. (1989) *Letter to Christendom*, Camden, UK: Virago Press.

Küng, H. (1994) *Great Christian Thinkers*, London: SCM Press.

Latourette, K. S. (1975) *A History of Christianity*, Vol I, New York: Harper & Row.

Levine S. (1989) *Beirut Diary*, Illinois: Intervarsity Press.

Lewis, B. (1966) *The Arabs in History*, New York: Harper & Row.

Maalouf, A. (1984) *The Crusades through Arab Eyes*, New York: Schocken Books Inc. Random House.

Mallouhi, C. & Gustafson, R. (1998) *Little Batustan of Bethlehem*, Issue 9/10 (*The Open Veins of Jerusalem*), *Jusoor*, Maryland: Al Kitab Inc.

Massignon, L. (1994) *Hallaj: Mystic and Martyr*, New Jersey: Princeton University Press.

Noonan, H. & Gasnick, R. (1987) *Francis of Assisi: The Song Goes On*, Los Angeles: Franciscan Communications.

Oldenbourg, Z. (1996) *The Crusades*, New York and Toronto: Random House; Orion Books, London; Editions Gallimard, Paris.

Omnibus of Sources for the Life of St. Francis of Assisi, edited by Habig, M. (1973) Quincy, Illinois: Franciscan Press.

Palestine Report, Vol. 4, No 34, Feb 13 1998, Jerusalem.

Passait, J. (1996) *Al Messihiyyah wa Al Islam*, Al Ijtihaad Issue Spring 31, 32 Beirut: Al Falah.

Plough Reader, *The Spoils of War*, Spring 2000, East Sussex: Plough Publishing House.

Said, E. W. (1981) *Covering Islam*, New York: Random House. Copyright 1981 by Edward W. Said. Reprinted by permission Pantheon Books, a division of Random House Inc.

Seigel, E. & Ahmed, N. (1999) *Shared Memories* 16 September 1999 and other American-Arab Anti-Discrimination Committee files. Used by permission. www.adc.org.

Sells, M. A. (1994) *Mystical Languages of Unsaying*, Chicago and London: University of Chicago Press.

Shah, I. (1964) *The Sufis,* New York: Doubleday.

Shahroor, M. (1990) *Al Kitab wa Al Quran,* Damascus: Maktabat Al Ahaali.

Smith, Mary Lou (1998) *Perspective on Peace*, Middle East Council of Churches, October 1998.

Talbi, M. & Bin Othman, H. (1992) *Ayaal Allah,* Tunis: Dar Siras Al Nashr.

The Washington Report on Middle East Affairs, Washington, D.C. www.washington-report.org

Curtis, R. H. *Osama Bin Laden Repeating George Habash's Deadly Errors*, Issue Oct/Nov 1998.

Fuller, G. *Words to Remember*, Issue Oct/Nov 1998.

Gordon, N. *Jerusalem's Silent Conquest: by Denying Palestinians Equal Rights Israelis Expedite Palestinian Expulsion*, Issue March 1999.

Meehan, M. *With World Attention on Iraq, Israel Seized Opportunity to Demolish Record Number of Palestinian Homes*, Issue April 1998.

Meehan, M. *Israeli High Court Postpones Decision on East Jerusalem Residency as ID Card Confiscation Continues*, Issue June 1999.

Meehan, M. *Eviction of Silwan Family Sets the Scene for Accelerated Ethnic Cleansing of Jerusalem*, Issue Jan 1999.

Sosebee, S. J. *'Compromise' at Ras-Al Amoud Results in more Israeli 'Facts on the Ground' in heart of Arab East Jerusalem.* Issue December 1997.

Sosebee, S. J. *Israel Plans to Drive Palestinians From Homeland through Harassment, Permit Denials, Demolitions.* Issue December 1997.

Zogby, J. J. *Arab Americans Must Condemn All Purveyors of Hatred* Issue Oct/Nov 1998.